At the
Confluence *of* Change
a History of Tonto National Monument

At the
Confluence of Change
a History of Tonto National Monument

Nancy L. Dallett

Western National Parks Association
Tucson, Arizona

At the Confluence of Change: A History of Tonto National Monument
Nancy L. Dallett

Western National Parks Association
Tucson, Arizona

Copyright © 2008 by Nancy L. Dallett
Published by Western National Parks Association
The net proceeds from WNPA publications support educational and
research programs in the national parks.
To receive a free catalogue, featuring hundreds of publications, email:
info@wnpa.org or visit our online store at www.wnpa.org.

Written by Nancy L. Dallett
Edited by Melissa Urreiztieta
Designed by Simpson & Convent
Cover photograph: *Lower Cliff Dwelling* by Adriel Heisey
Printed by Friesens
Printed in Canada

contents

illustrations

acknowledgments

Special thanks to:

Bob Spude, National Park Service
Noel Stowe, Arizona State University
Duane Hubbard, Tonto National Monument
Bradley Traver, Tonto National Monument

Thanks to the following people for their help in archival research:

Greg Davis of Superstition Mountain Historical Society
Catherine May and Shelley Dudley of the Salt River Project Research Archive
Khaleel Saba of the Western Archaeological Conservation Center
Scott Anderson of the Sharlot Hall Museum
Lisa Gazelter of National Archives, Laguna Niguel
Karina Robinson for conducting research in National Archives, Washington, D.C.

Thanks to the following people for interviews:

BOB ARMSTRONG, Tonto National Forest Roosevelt
GARY CANTLEY, Bureau of Indian Affairs
CHRIS DOWNUM, Northern Arizona University
MIKE JACOBS, Arizona State Museum
TRINKLE JONES, Colorado Plateau Cooperative Ecosystem Studies Unit
TOM LINCOLN, Bureau of Reclamation
MARTIN MCALLISTER, Tonto National Forest

TODD METZGER, Flagstaff Area National Monuments
GLEN RICE, Arizona State University
ARLEYN SIMON, Archeological Research Institute archeologist
JOHN WELCH, Bureau of Indian Affairs
SCOTT WOOD, Tonto National Forest

Thanks to the following former Tonto National Monument employee for interviews:

KAREN ARMSTRONG, archeologist 1970-1972
LEE BAIZA, superintendent 1992-2003
SHIRLEY HOH, natural resource manager 2004-2005
RON ICE, archeologist 1967-1969
CAROL KRUSE, superintendent 1987-1991
HANK JONES, park ranger 1962-1965
JAN RYAN, park ranger 1993-1999
JIM TROUTWINE, superintendent 1983-1986
JAMES VALDER, superintendent 1975-1979
BOB VIKLUND, seasonal ranger 1950-1952
PHILIP YOUNG, park technician 1977-1981

introduction

Even now, after a century of study, we don't know enough. We want to know much more about who they were and why they chose the shelter of caves 1,200 and 1,600 feet above the Salt River. Did these people we call the Salado seek protection from the environment? From other people? Perhaps from both? We do know that they constructed dwellings in the caves, cultivated corn in the valleys, produced polychrome pottery, created cotton and agave textiles, and enjoyed relatively good health.

We know this much because they left marks in the towering sandstone cliffs that survive today as the cliff dwellings in Tonto National Monument. Visitors by the millions have come during the past one hundred years of federal management to gaze at these marks and to try to visualize the long-ago people who made them. It's a challenging task because so much has been eroded by time and misfortune. Also difficult to grasp is the drama that has played out behind the scenes at Tonto, as generations of dedicated men and women worked against considerable odds to identify, analyze, preserve, and maintain these archeological treasures of the American Southwest.

In the total life of the cliff dwellings, one hundred years is quite short. Yet over the past century, both federal agencies involved (the U.S. Forest Service, 1907–1933, and the National Park Service, 1934–present) and visitors have left their own marks, literally and metaphorically, on the monument. This book is the story of those marks. It is the life story of a small, isolated national monument that survived and thrived while repeatedly affected by changes in values, knowledge, preservation techniques, bureaucratic alignments, and accessibility, all of which had significant consequences for what the monument is now and what its future will be.

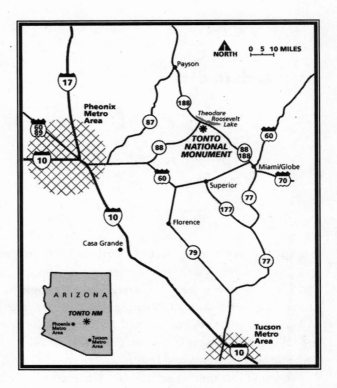

Figure 1: Site location map from Tonto National Monument General Master Plan, 2003

Chapter 1 offers an overview of three national movements in the first decade of the twentieth century that had a profound impact on the Tonto Basin: reclamation, conservation, and preservation. The U.S. Reclamation Service plugged the confluence of the Salt River and Tonto Creek with a dam, and the U.S. Forest Service set aside 2.9 million surrounding acres as a national forest to protect the watershed. The 1906 American Antiquities Act gave the president the power to declare historic landmarks, historic and prehistoric structures, and other objects of historic or scientific interest. In 1907 President Theodore Roosevelt designated the Tonto cliff dwellings as a national monument.

The cliff dwellings serve as an excellent vantage point from which to see the influence of these three national movements. They are also witness to a great archeological loss, for shortly after legal protection was granted for the cliff dwellings, perched high above the river bottom, hundreds of related sites located in the river bottom were flooded and lost to future generations. Chapter 1 is the story of these gains and losses.

Chapter 2 goes back in time and examines the features that attracted people to the Tonto Basin for thousands of years. It offers a brief examination of land tenure from Paleo-Indians through early twentieth-century miners, ranchers, and dam builders. It addresses the perennial questions of who got there when, what resources they used, and what legacy they left before the cliff dwellings were set aside as a national monument.

Chapter 3 opens with the designation of the Tonto cliff dwellings as a national monument under the U.S. Department of Agriculture, Forest Service. It examines the Forest Service's lack of resources for patrolling and preserving the cliff dwellings, as well as the subsequent arrangement made with the Southern Pacific Railroad to provide a custodian, onsite housing for the custodian, roads, trails, parking facilities, and fences. While it is not possible to know exactly when during the Forest Service's administration (1907–1933) vandalism and structural deterioration occurred, comparative photographs show the cliff dwellings suffered damage, and written accounts testify to the degradation of the monument as a result of cattle grazing on the Tonto National Forest during that period.

Chapter 4 examines the first two decades of National Park Service administration, including the first stabilization and excavation projects at the monument, efforts to restrict grazing, and construction of roads to the monument and trails to the cliff dwellings. It also reveals the desperate condition of parking, sanitation, and other public and staff facilities at the monument and how, ironically, negative publicity and a fire helped secure emergency funding to bring the infrastructure up to acceptable levels.

Chapter 5 looks at how Mission 66, a National Park Service project of immense proportions that infused millions of dollars into parks and monuments, enabled Tonto to begin to live up to its potential as a national monument. This chapter in Tonto's history culminates with the opening of exhibits and facilities in a new visitor center in 1965.

Chapter 6 describes the changes in environmental consciousness during the 1960s and 1970s and notes two important milestones: the *natural* milestone of gaining physical control of the monument's land by eliminating grazing and installing a boundary fence, and the *cultural* milestone of completing a "100 percent archeological survey," which documented sixty-five archeological sites on the monument.

Chapter 7 reprises the themes introduced in chapter 1, revisiting the influences of reclamation, conservation, and preservation, this time at work in the Tonto Basin in the first decade of the twenty-first century. It shows how values changed from the time of initial designation of the monument—when there was no process in place to analyze the archeological resources that were flooded by construction of the Roosevelt Dam and creation of the lake—to eighty years later when a full analysis of potential loss to archeological resources was required before the dam height was raised. It begins with an analysis of how major changes to the nearby dam, roads, and recreational facilities on Roosevelt Lake provided both opportunities and challenges to Tonto National Monument, and concludes with the staff's creation of a vision for the monument in the twenty-first century, which is now beginning to be implemented.

Throughout its one hundred-year administrative history, Tonto has been profoundly affected by the national movements in reclamation, conservation, and preservation. It has been equally impacted by changing relationships among the federal bureaucracies that implement these movements. The Bureau of Reclamation, the Forest Service, and the National Park Service operate on different philosophies concerning conservation, access, and preservation. Each developed a cadre of professional staff, followed mutually exclusive management theories, and wrestled with each other as they defined their roles and authority to manage land. One hundred years of this history still influence their relationships, and current employees will be well served to be aware of it as they work on new cooperative ventures.

This account reveals one hundred years of shifting voices and values: how federal agencies codified archeological ruins at the turn of the twentieth century, how mid-century excavations resulted in losses (even gauged by archeological standards of the time), how opportunities to collaborate were lost, and how voices of environmentalists and Native Americans began to join the dialogue and today exert immense influence on land management, preservation, and repatriation.

Just as important, the history chronicles a continuum of care by dedicated staff. Their one hundred-year history is punctuated by many decisions—some positive, some negative. But this study reaches beyond the comfortable judgments of hindsight to explore the forces at play and, when possible, the personalities and motivations that coped with those forces and led to change. As Tonto National Monument staff makes twenty-first-century choices, they similarly will affect the legacy they will leave to the future. How much preservation is too much? How much accessibility is too much? These and other basic questions remain open, as perhaps they must always be. This account is offered in the spirit of using history to pinpoint events, trace trends, and learn from the triumphs and missteps of the past. Its goal is to help guide the equally momentous present and future choices that will be made at Tonto National Monument, as today's and tomorrow's staff and visitors leave their own marks on the land.

At the
Confluence of Change
a History of Tonto National Monument

chapter one

RECLAMATION, CONSERVATION, AND PRESERVATION: THREE CURRENTS CONVERGE

An old sandal. Fragments of baskets. Centuries-old rope, twine, corncobs. It was May 24, 1883, when pioneering naturalist Adolph Bandelier sifted through ruins in the remote Tonto Basin of central Arizona Territory. In his journal, Bandelier noted,

> The height of the cave is about 20 to 25 feet. Into it the house had been built. It is a perfect pueblo house, but small. The walls are of large stones, broken to suit, and laid in clay mixed with gravel, which gives it the appearance of concrete . . . Many of the roofs are perfect. They are of vigas, above them are either splinters or round sticks of ocotillo, above it reeds, and then two-and-a-half inches of mud. The floors, as far as visible, are black. There is some pottery about, handsomely painted . . .[1]

These were not extraordinary discoveries for this seasoned explorer of the American West. But Bandelier's careful account of an obscure canyon ruin began a chain of events that had profound consequences for water, land, and archeological remains of previous civilizations. A site that had been abandoned and ignored for centuries became Tonto National Monument, as it was swept up in the confluence of three powerful national movements in American history: reclamation, conservation, and antiquities preservation.

In 1905, a quarter-century after Bandelier's visit, the U.S. Department of the Interior Reclamation Service began constructing the Salt River Project Dam, and the U.S. Department

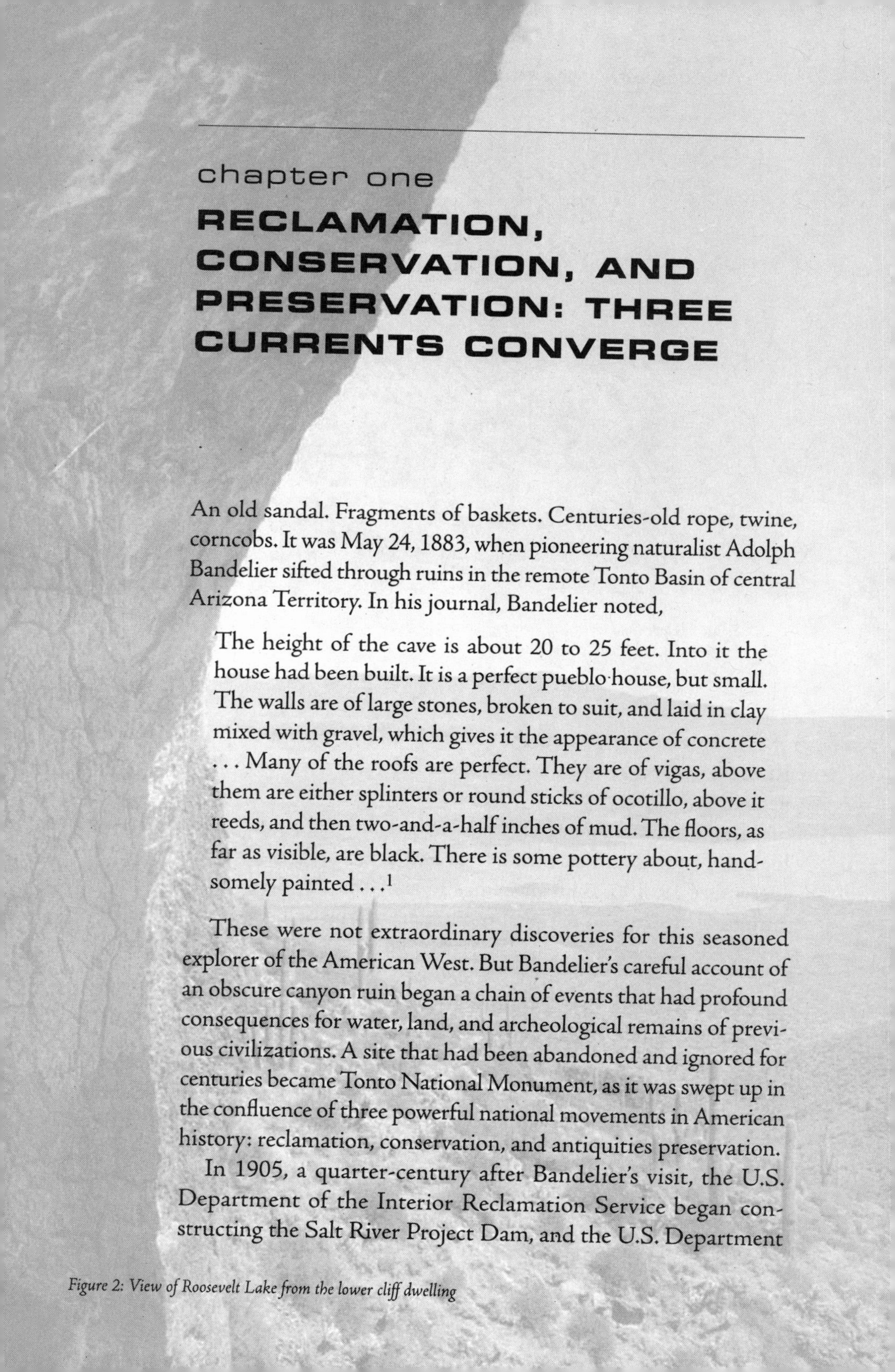

Figure 2: View of Roosevelt Lake from the lower cliff dwelling

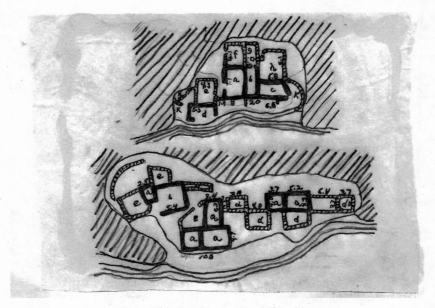

Figure 3: Upper and lower cliff dwelling illustration by Adolf Bandelier, 1883

of Agriculture designated the Tonto National Forest to protect the Salt River watershed. As we shall see, these federal actions were deeply interconnected.

The Antiquities Act of 1906 established national public policy for archeological, historic, and scientific sites and structures. Shortly thereafter, on December 19, 1907, cliff dwellings in the Tonto Basin were designated as antiquities worthy of national monument status by presidential proclamation.[2]

RECLAMATION: THE MOVEMENT TO MAKE USEFUL THE STREAMS AND RIVERS OF THE ARID WEST

The 1905–1911 construction of a dam at the confluence of Tonto Creek and the Salt River in the Tonto Basin, a mere 5 miles from the cliff dwellings, became one of America's first national reclamation projects and a model for many to follow. From colonial times, the dominant cultural tradition had been to look upon the landmass of the North American continent and its resources as a limitless cornucopia. It was seen as an inexhaustible trove of natural wealth that would support an unending number of uses—its forests would provide timber for anything that could be built, as its wildlife and fertile land would support as many people as could ever live here. There were dissenters, and some argued for the need to protect and conserve resources. For example, seventeenth-century British colonists protected timber resources and passed ordinances to control their cutting and sale. Aware of shortages back home, they saw it necessary to conserve timber in their new home. In fact, American conservation history is rife with examples of voices raised to protect water sources and quality, efforts to conserve range conditions, and the struggle to maintain public lands.[3]

From colonial times on, debates raged about how best to balance the use and protection of natural resources. The last third of the nineteenth century, a period of rapid deterioration of natural resources we now call "the great barbecue" because of the speed and scale of environmental destruction, led to a widespread awareness of the need for conservation legislation. In the latter part of the nineteenth century and early part of the twentieth, Congress passed arid land reclamation, forest protection, and antiquities protection legislation, which had an immediate and dramatic impact on the Tonto Basin: the construction of the Roosevelt Dam, the designation of the Tonto National Forest, and the establishment of Tonto National Monument.

Rapid urbanization in major eastern cities also suggested to reformers that the country was losing its prized Jeffersonian agrarian values. One solution was to encourage people to move out of the cities and migrate West. In addition, the Progressive Movement was born based on the belief that social problems could be engineered away as effectively as technical ones were being tamed by rapidly advancing technology. The Progressive Movement united conservationists, progressives, and social and civil engineers, all supported by the new scientific disciplines of hydrology, agronomy, and forestry. These new professionals were able to frame debates about resource protection, the role of the federal government in creating the best social and industrial conditions for the largest number of people, and the need for large-scale engineering projects to extend the ideal of self-sufficiency and the family farm into new areas of the country.

Into this context of the fear of rapid urbanization and overcrowded cities, the desire to spread out the population, and the need to make the West's arid lands productive came Civil War hero, botanist, zoologist, and geologist John Wesley Powell. In 1878 Powell reported to the U.S. secretary of the interior that many farms west of the 100th meridian could, indeed, be productive. To reach its potential, he added, this land required an efficient, predictable, well-

Figure 4: Major John Wesley Powell, age 40, 1874. Courtesy of Grand Canyon National Park, 13868.

managed watering system. There was widespread agreement on the need, but disagreement on the question of who best could and should construct that system. Could farmers construct it? Corporations? Or was it the role of the federal government? Debates raged for more than twenty years on whether—as Powell believed—autonomous irrigation and grazing districts should be created that conformed to natural watersheds, or whether the federal government should finance and control irrigation in the West. Powell proposed that an irrigation survey be conducted of western lands and streams, and that the resulting irrigation networks be built and controlled on a local basis. At the same time, several insufficiently engineered, privately financed dams failed, resulting in deaths and property damage. Because of these disasters and a variety of political, scientific, and personal rivalries, the argument swung in favor of federal responsibility for "reclaiming" the arid lands of the West and "making deserts bloom" by ensuring adequate engineering technology for massive water storage and distribution systems.[4]

President Theodore Roosevelt, who entered office in 1901, embodied the spirit of the turn-of-the-century conservation movement, the Progressives, and the belief in technical solutions. He considered it well within the role of national policy to aid in irrigation as a part of the need to encourage the best social and industrial conditions in the West. On June 17, 1902, he signed the Francis Newland National Reclamation Act, legislation that for the first time authorized federal dollars for dam construction "to make useful the streams and rivers of the arid West by the federal government building engineering works for water storage."[5]

Many projects competed to be the first in line for federal funds. One of the first large-scale reclamation projects was one designed to store waters at the confluence of the Salt River and Tonto Creek. It was known at the time as Tonto Dam.

The Tonto Basin in central Arizona was considered an ideal site for a federally financed dam to provide irrigation for the Salt River Valley downstream. Although the Salt River Valley received less than 7½ inches of rainfall a year, which technically defined it as a desert, the rich alluvial soil promised high productivity if enough water could be brought from the mountains northeast of the valley.

The future of central Arizona was directly linked to the ability to provide reliable water. This had been so since the founding of Phoenix, when the remains of centuries-old Hohokam canals were discovered and reused to transport and store water from the Salt River. From their town's earliest days as a supply point for the mining camps and for forts constructed to wage the Indian Wars, Phoenix residents became increasingly aware of the need to maintain and enlarge the capability of the canal system, both to withstand flooding and to further population growth and cultivation of the land. While the ancient Hohokam provided central Arizona's first irrigation system, nineteenth-century settlers and farmers were quick to realize the limitations of the system and the need to expand it. For approximately twenty years, they cleared and reused the ancient waterways; but by 1885 they cut the new Arizona Canal across the valley, and the people of Phoenix became convinced of the need for a larger storage reservoir in the mountains rising to the northeast.

They weren't alone. As early as 1889 others had envisioned a dam at the confluence of Tonto Creek and the Salt River. In 1893 Wells Hendershot of the New York–based Hudson Reservoir and Canal Company filed a claim in anticipation of being able to store water behind a dam to irrigate land in the Salt River Valley below. At that time, the Hudson Company projected it would be a $3 million project, that the masonry dam would be 225 feet high, and that the reservoir would extend for thirty square miles.[6] Despite some enthusiasm, there was a general lack of confidence

Figure 5: Water flowing through a prehistoric canal near Phoenix, Photograph by Walter Lubken 1907. Courtesy of the Salt River Project, CI–12.

that a private company could raise the funds needed for so large and remote a project.

At the same time, support was growing on the national level for federal policy to address the need for large-scale irrigation projects. The National Irrigation Congress, which began meeting annually in 1891, addressed the economics, politics, and management of large-scale irrigation projects; in 1896 Phoenix formally joined the conversation by hosting the fifth congress.

Federal reports on issues such as dam siting, soil conditions, and potential for crop productivity in the Salt River Valley were rich with the promise of fertility and productivity. One such account was written by Edward Bender in January 1898 for the Special General Land Office. Bender referred to the Salt River Valley as

> one of the largest bodies of agricultural lands between the states of California and Kansas. It is walled in by mountains and watered by a stream which has its source in one of the loftiest ranges and is fed by the melting snows and by a hundred tributaries. Near the river is found a dark alluvial mold, with a depth of from 6 to 15 feet, adapted to cereals

and grasses; back from this is a belt of rich loam of remarkable fertility and near the foothills the surface is of a light and porous nature, suited to the culture of fruit. Of fruit, the yield is almost unprecedented, from the fig tree being gathered two and even three crops a year, while few portions of this coast are better adapted to the cultivation of grapes, the product of which reached six or seven tons to the acre.[7]

Site surveying and technical data gathered in 1897 and again in 1900 on the proposed site for the Salt River dam confirmed the Hudson Company's selection of the Tonto site as the most advantageous. By 1901 Arthur Powell Davis's report to the U.S. Geological Survey concluded,

The gorge on the Salt River is an especially favorable site for a masonry dam, and the most permanent, conservative, and secure form of high dam that is known to engineering science can be constructed. The formation is sedimentary, with the strata inclined at an angle of about 30 degrees to the horizontal, dipping toward the reservoir, a most favorable condition for retaining stored waters and for the stability of the dam.[8]

Figure 6: Site selected for the Salt River Dam, 1904. Courtesy of the Salt River Project Research Archives, R– 014.

Frederick Newell, the hydrographer in charge for the U.S. Geological Survey Division of Hydrography in Washington, D.C., described the importance of the project as follows:

> The Work is of great value, not only to the Salt River Valley, but to other portions of the arid region where water storage will in the future be undertaken, as the careful work of Mr. Davis has demonstrated the feasibility of utilizing natural resources, particularly in the making of cement and turning to advantage previously unsuspected means for conserving water. Throughout Arizona and the entire Southwest the development of agriculture, and to a less extent of mining and other industries, rests upon water conservation, since in these vast areas the streams are for the most part of small volume and are subject to occasional destructive floods. The impounding of these is one of the most important fundamental steps to be taken toward the utilization of the vast area of vacant public land.[9]

Arizonans were also organizing themselves. The formation of the Salt River Valley Water Users Association (SRVWUA) in 1903 provided a structure for valley farmers and others to formally compete for federal dollars for a storage reservoir. The SRVWUA water storage committee's goal was to position the Salt River Valley's request for a federal project in the most favorable light. It needed to convince the federal government that the Salt River dam project met two major criteria for federal dam-building funds: that it was in a place where an unparalleled public interest could be served by a dam, and that there was a large measure of cooperation among the people and their legislatures. The lobbying efforts of the SRVWUA were successful, and in 1903 the Department of the Interior announced four inaugural projects for the U.S. Reclamation Service, including the Tonto Dam. In 1904 the Hudson Company conveyed to the U.S. government all right, title, and interest in the dam site. The newly formed U.S. Reclamation Service began building roads to the dam site, and the people of Arizona had high hopes for the future.[10]

A May 31, 1905 article in the *Arizona Republican* characterized the dam's significance as biblical, and provided details of its construction and a glimpse of its potential for the future of the valley. Titled "How Living Waters Have Been Brought Unto the Thirsty Land," the article began with a prologue from 2 Kings 3:16, "Thus saith the Lord: Make this valley full of ditches," and read as follows:

Figure 7: Construction of the diversion dam on the Salt River. Courtesy of the Salt River Project Research Archives, R–058.

Whenever success has been achieved in large measure comes a fitting time to tell how it all happened. To the people of the Salt River valley now is assured a measure of success beyond the liveliest dreams of a half decade ago. A quarter of a million acres of the most fertile land on earth are to have an abundance of water for the irrigation of crops that will never fail, with annual abundance of fruits of the soil bringing to the community riches continuing and enduring. No more will there be drought nor paralyzing doubt of the future but, with the husbandman will abide plenty and prosperity and growth will come unto the cities. [11]

The drama of dam construction was chronicled in the local, regional, national, and international press. Civil engineering journals regularly covered the progress of design and construction, and experts in large public works planning from all over the world visited the site to consult with the engineers. Historian and poet Sharlot Hall wrote a 27-page article for *Out West* magazine.[12] The U.S. Department of the Interior Reclamation Service hired photographer Walter Lubken to document the 1905–1911 dam construction projects and their impact on the surrounding areas. Lubken provided a complete record of the road construction, the town of Roosevelt, the camps, the laborers, and the surrounding area. He also provided one of the earliest photographs of the Tonto cliff dwellings.

CONSERVATION: THE FOREST RESERVE MOVEMENT

While the construction of Roosevelt Dam was monumental in scale and significance, an additional and related effort was launched to ensure continued protection of the Salt River watershed. Hand-in-hand with the attempt to secure land and funding for dam construction came the effort to secure land and authority for dam and watershed protection. To do so, all of the land in the Salt River and Tonto Creek watersheds needed to be designated a national forest reserve. Watershed protection—not timber production—would be the justification for the creation in 1905 of a largely treeless Tonto National Forest.[13]

The nineteenth century brought a growing awareness of and concern about the process of desertification, and the young disciplines of hydrology and forestry began to promote conditions that helped to temper fluctuations between drought and flood, especially in the West. While John Wesley Powell and others argued that trees should be cleared because they prevented rainfall from reaching the soil, opponents argued that forests served as great conservators of water and soil, and that without them conditions would inevitably decline. With this link between forests and water supply established, new agencies of the federal government began to impose regulations.

Environmental historian Paul Hirt summed up five main reasons why Americans were concerned with the loss of forest lands in the mid to late-nineteenth century: (1) the concentration of landownership in the hands of powerful corporations; (2) the depletion of natural resources; (3) the damaging effects of exploitive logging, mining, grazing, and agriculture on soil and water; (4) rural instability caused by migratory industries that would exploit a resource and then move on; and (5) waste and inefficiency in natural resource use. Many groups—including scientists, intellectuals, politicians, sportsmen, garden clubs, women's clubs, and chambers of commerce—agitated for governmental reform. As many as two hundred bills related to forests were presented to Congress between the 1870s and 1890s.[14] The American Forestry Association lobbied for a system to preserve and administer reserves. In 1891 Congress settled the debate by taking up an authorization from President Benjamin Harrison to establish forest reserves. The National Forest Reserve Act made it possible to withdraw land from the public domain for timber and watershed protection. It was far from universally popular. Western states

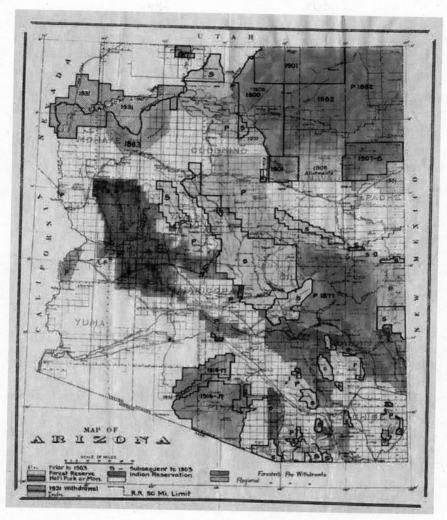

Figure 8: Map of Arizona, 1955. Courtesy of the Sharlot Hall Museum, Map 203.

and territories, in general, resented the creation of reserves, as it constrained their rights for timbering, mining, grazing, and any other forms of use and extraction. Despite their resistance, Congress withdrew 21 million acres from private ownership by 1897 and designated them as national reserves.

The link between arid land reclamation and forest reserves is well symbolized by the National Irrigation Association's 1900 meeting slogan, "Save the Forests and Store the Floods." The two conservation movements—for arid land reclamation and for forest reserves—found it expedient to work together.

Leaders of the reclamation movement saw the preservation of forests as essential to a dependable water supply of good quality, and framed an image of forests acting as nature's storage reservoirs. By 1903 the official publication of the American Forestry Association and the National Irrigation Association was titled *Forestry and Irrigation*. Both organizations supported the creation of federal bureaus staffed by professionally trained foresters, agronomists, and hydrologists to "harness" water and timber for rational and effective uses.

It was not immediately clear which federal agency would be responsible for the reserves, the Department of the Interior or the Department of Agriculture. Responsibility for different aspects of the forest reserves was divided between the two. In 1891 the Department of the Interior was charged with administering the reserves, and in 1897 it was charged with patrolling, enforcing laws, and other routine matters. During the same period, the Department of Agriculture Division of Forestry was responsible for examining, studying, and making technical decisions. If the Department of Agriculture wanted to address a problem, it could do so only if requested by the Department of the Interior. Forestry Division studies documented the effects of depleted forage, erosion, and the replacement of grasses with shrubs and trees.

Longtime ranchers recognized the effects of unregulated grazing, especially given the droughts of 1892 and 1893, but they did not accept the imposition of control and management by federal agencies without a fight. The only prior experience many stockmen had with federal restriction of grazing lands was when the various Indian reservations were withdrawn from availability for grazing, and it was assumed that the new forest reserves would also be placed off limits. The various publications for cattle and sheep ranchers, such as *Southwestern Stockman* and *Farmer and Feeder*, gave voice to ranchers' reluctance, wariness, and outright opposition. Ranchers lodged repeated protests against creating and enlarging reserves. In general, the amount and intensity of protest varied with the distance from organized range users and the amount of acreage involved.

Several forceful individuals shaped the original policies and politics of the forest reserves, especially President Roosevelt's agriculture secretary and close friend, Gifford Pinchot. Pinchot chafed under the constraint of sharing authority for the forests with the Department of the Interior. He lobbied for the Department of Agriculture to have full authority over the forests, and he prevailed when President Roosevelt transferred 65 million acres to the Division of Forestry in the Department of Agriculture on February 1, 1905. Two years later, the Division of Forestry was renamed the United States

Forest Service, with Pinchot as chief forester, and the reserves were renamed national forests.

The Water-Conserving Power of the Tonto National Reserve

Fifteen forest reserves across the nation, comprising 13 million acres, were already established by the time of Arizona's first reserve, the Grand Canyon Forest Reserve, which was designated in 1893 to protect timber around the Grand Canyon.[15]

In 1898, Edward Bender documented the watersheds of the Salt and Verde rivers and recommended reserving land to protect them. Three reserves followed: the Black Mesa, the Prescott, and the San Francisco reserves. When the San Francisco Reserve was set aside on January 12, 1901, the *Arizona Republican* called it a "blessing on the Salt River Valley" and wrote,

> The value of this action to the people of the Salt River Valley cannot be overestimated. It not only will bring great benefit to their water system but will give a great impetus to the water storage movement and will encourage the establishment of industries in the valley that rely upon an adequate water supply for success.[16]

The *Arizona Republican*, at that time controlled by Dwight Heard, who supported Roosevelt for president, ran articles extolling the virtues of forests and explaining how they were related to successful ventures in the valley. On February 22, 1901, for example, an article referred to the forest as the "greatest safeguard" against loss of water, and quoted Vice President–elect Roosevelt as saying

> The reservoirs cannot last if they fill full of silt, and the only way to prevent this filling with silt is to preserve the forests themselves. The forest is a great sponge for absorbing and distilling water. It is the great preventer of erosion, and erosion is always the danger point in any irrigation system.[17]

In subsequent articles, Roosevelt explained the need for expert and responsible management of the forest reserves as going hand-in-hand with the need for expert and responsible engineers to construct the great irrigation systems. A Rio Verde Forest Reserve was proposed and, in 1901, Interior Secretary Ethan Hitchcock required the Division of Forestry and the General Land Office to study the area before withdrawals would be recommended. The proposed Rio Verde Forest Reserve was divided into two sections for study:

the western 1.75 million acres were assigned to S. J. Holsinger and the eastern half million acres were assigned to A. E. Cohoon.

Cohoon's study summarized the protective value of the proposed Rio Verde Forest Reserve as follows:

> Some of the main reasons why these mountains should be put into forest reserve are: On account of the protective value which they will be to Tonto Basin Reservoir (if protected) in preventing silt and debris from entering through the numberous [sic] tributaries to the Salt River drainage basin; because the whole area is a rough, mountainous country covered with timber and brush, which is valuable for holding and preventing its rapid run-off in early spring; to regulate grazing so as to prevent the watersheds from being overpastured and destroyed by fire; because of a large agricultural and mining population in Salt River Valley dependent upon water for irrigation, mining and domestic purposes; because the mountains are better adapted for growing forests and for cattle raising than for other purposes, and if not properly protected will eventually become less valuable for either; and lastly, that practically all the residents as well as many others on the Salt River and elsewhere are in favor of its creation. Therefore, it is respectfully recommended that the reserve be created and made a part of Black Mesa Forest Reserve.[18]

The collective studies by Holsinger, Cohoon, and Bender led to the recommendation to create a 1,121,280-acre Tonto Forest Reserve, rather than to enlarge the Black Mesa Forest Reserve as earlier recommended. Cohoon and Holsinger's joint report of 1905 claimed,

> The creation of this reserve is highly important, both for the protection of the timber for future use and for the protection of the headwaters of the many important tributaries of the Salt River which have their sources in and drain through the region under consideration. The U.S. Reclamation Service most emphatically avers that upon its establishment largely depends the success of the Tonto Dam project. The local sentiment is practically unanimous in favor of its creation.[19]

President Theodore Roosevelt created the 1,115,200-acre Tonto Forest Reserve by proclamation on October 3, 1905. In large measure, it was intended to serve as a sponge for the Salt River and Tonto Creek watershed and to ensure the success of the new dam by preventing silting behind it. Within a short time, the Salt River Valley Water Users Association began arguing for the need for additional lands to be included in the Tonto Forest Reserve. In 1907, Joseph H. Kibbey, the territorial governor, reported to the secretary of the interior that

> possibly in no other section of the United States is there so keen an appreciation of the value of forests as in Arizona, nor is it possible for the National Administration to meet anywhere more loyal support than is accorded in this Territory to the policy of protecting the forest domain. Our people have learned through years of observation what it means to have natural growth removed from the soil. They have seen overstocking of the ranges and forests followed by denudation . . . and the loss of nature's system for holding water in the soil. They have seen cattle trails become water courses for the run-off of floods, the gashes thus made in the soil becoming deep ravines . . . that quickly drain districts of rainfall. Such developments are of moment in a country in which water is of precious value for irrigation and for stock on the ranges, and very naturally the people of Arizona have been led to study with care the questions of conserving the waters and saving the forests. In each instance the action of the President in creating National Forests in this Territory, in late years at least, has met with the heartiest local approval.[20]

Under the guidance of the director of the Reclamation Service, Frederick Newell, and in response to requests by the top engineer for the dam, Louis Hill, the boundaries among the Crook, Black Mesa, and Rio Verde forests were redrawn and land in the Superstition Mountains and the Queen Creek drainage basin were added to the Tonto. This resulted in a presidential proclamation on January 13, 1908, that doubled the size of what was then called the Tonto National Forest to 2,449,280 acres. Further additions and adjustments were made in 1909 and 1910.

PRESERVATION: THE AMERICAN ANTIQUITIES MOVEMENT

As the dam was being built and the surrounding watershed protected, the Tonto cliff dwellings within the Tonto National Forest gradually gained the attention and prominence to be designated a national monument. There is an irony in all this concern for water, because it was in fact the dryness of the Southwest that had protected the area's prehistoric sites, dwellings, and material culture for hundreds of years. But by 1900 it was obvious that curious and acquisitive visitors had vandalized and removed many artifacts from southwestern ruins, including Tonto. It was also clear that it would henceforth take more than favorable climatic conditions to continue to protect the sites.

According to Ronald Lee's history of the Antiquities Act, written for the National Park Service, a series of developments over five decades in both public and professional understanding of the value of antiquities led to passage of the Antiquities Act in 1906. During those fifty years, the nation's archeological, historic, and scientific sites and structures were being both prized and looted, and the disciplines of anthropology and archeology were maturing to a point where there was conflict about who should serve as the "experts" to investigate, excavate, and house the recovered artifacts.[21]

Lee notes five milestones that set the stage for formally surveying the country's archeological sites: (1) establishment of the Bureau of Ethnography and the appointment of John Wesley Powell as its first director; (2) the election of an anthropologist, Lewis Henry Morgan, as president of the American Association for the Advancement of Science, signifying the emerging recognition of the field of anthropology; (3) the affiliation of practitioners in anthropology, ethnography, and geology into the Anthropological Society of Washington, reflecting the increasing numbers of people interested in these emerging fields in the nation's capital; (4) the establishment of the Archaeological Institute of America to promote archeological research, in part to study indigenous life in the Americas; and (5) the publication of Frederick W. Putnam's seminal work on archeology and ethnography, which was a culmination of his research on the ruined pueblos of Arizona and New Mexico and the Indians of southern California. These five events collectively revealed the need to research the ruins of the American Southwest and set the stage for the formal investigation and documentation that followed.[22]

In 1880 the Archaeological Institute of America engaged Aldolph F. Bandelier, a student of Morgan's, to conduct research on the pueblos and ruins of New Mexico. Bandelier later surveyed throughout New Mexico, Arizona, and Mexico. His publication, *Final Report of Investigations among the Indians of the Southwestern United States, Carried On Mainly in the Years from 1880–1885*, published in two parts in 1890 and 1892, documented many of the ruins throughout the country that eventually became designated as national monuments, including the cliff dwellings at Tonto. Bandelier's investigations focused attention on the amount of destruction treasure hunters caused, which fueled debates about the need for restricting access and passing preservation measures. Further publications by Bandelier, Jesse Walter Fewkes, Victor Mindeleff, and others added to the scholarly inquiry and built up documentation in the fields of archeology, ethnography, geology, and anthropology.[23]

At the same time as these disciplines became more academically rigorous and institutionalized, the public also gained more exposure to prehistoric ruins and contemporary cultures in the American Southwest. International expositions, in Madrid in 1892 and in Chicago in 1893, displayed collections of southwestern artifacts to large audiences and created a national interest in archeology and anthropology. Publications such as *The Land of the Cliff Dwellers* by Frederick Chapin and others by Charles Lummis fed these new appetites. The infamous pothunting and vandalism at Pecos, New Mexico, drew attention to vandalism and the consequences of unrestricted access.[24]

In the isolated Tonto Basin of central Arizona, the locals considered the ruins part of their shared cultural assets and thought nothing of removing artifacts from their prehistoric settings. Native Americans and Anglo-Americans felt a variety of attachments and sentiments about ownership and display of antiquities. Some of this disparity was dependent upon the relationship they claimed to either the original inhabitants of the ruins, or to subsequent generations who "settled" the land.

One of the consequences of having professional archeologists survey sites was the questions the process created about who would control the sites and the artifacts. Would it be individuals, organizations, institutions? And to what extent would they be in public or private control? The American Museum of Natural History in New York, the Field Museum in Chicago, the National Museum in Washington, and a myriad of university departments across the country that supported archeological investigations and excavations, including the University of Pennsylvania, University of California at Berkeley, and Harvard University, became the beneficiaries of the largest percentages of artifacts. Individual donors who sponsored expeditions were also informally rewarded with artifacts.

There was tension among professionally trained university-based archeologists, self-taught archeologists, and "pothunters" or "relic hunters." Regardless of the excavators' training, their intentions, the monetary rewards, and the final repositories chosen for the artifacts collected from archeological sites, a tremendous number of artifacts were made available to universities, museums, world expositions, and individuals.[25]

In 1882 Senator George F. Hoar of Massachusetts raised the issue of the deplorable conditions of the ruins of the territories of New Mexico and Arizona and the need for legislative protection of them. On May 8, 1882, he asked what role government should play in protecting against artifact plundering and grave robberies. He reported the following conditions and needs:

> That there are in the Territories of New Mexico and Arizona twenty-
> six towns of the Pueblos Indians, so called, in all containing about ten
> thousand inhabitants; that the number of their towns was once very
> much greater, that these remaining are the remnants of very ancient races
> in North America, whose origin and history lie yet unknown in their
> decayed and decaying antiquities; that many of their towns have been
> abandoned by the decay and extinction of their inhabitants; that many
> of their relics have already perished and so made the study of American
> ethnology vastly more difficult; that the question of the origin of those
> Pueblos and the age of their decayed cities, and the use of some of their
> buildings, now magnificent ruins, constitute one of the leading and most
> interesting problems of the antiquary and historian of the present age;
> that relic-hunters have carried away, and scattered wide through America
> and Europe the remains of these extinct towns; thus making their historic
> study still more difficult, and, in some particulars, nearly impossible.[26]

And he petitioned,

> Your memorialists therefore pray your honorable body that at least
> some of these extinct cities or pueblos, carefully selected, with the land
> reservations attached and dating mostly from the Spanish crown, of the
> year 1680, may be withheld from public sale and their antiquities and
> ruins be preserved, as they furnish invaluable data for the ethnologi-
> cal studies now engaging the attention of our most learned scientific,
> antiquarian, and historical students.[27]

There was general agreement on the significance of the archeological sites
and the need for their protection, but there was no consensus about the extent
to which the federal government should become involved. After seven years
of attempts to appropriate federal funding for archeological sites, Congress
appropriated funds to repair one archeological site. On June 22, 1892, the
prehistoric remains at Casa Grande, Arizona—which had suffered more
losses in the previous eleven years than in the prior three centuries—became
the first publicly protected prehistoric site in the United States.

A Need to Identify and Protect

A new sense of urgency about preservation prevailed at the turn of the century,
fueled by twin desires. One was to identify archeological sites so that they did
not pass from the public domain into private ownership. The other was to

protect the sites and their contents. Responding to the first need, the Bureau of American Ethnology began preparing an archeological map and accompanying information on the archeological sites of the entire country. As Edgar Hewett noted in his 1906 update on the creation of the maps and card catalogue,

> Activity in this branch has recently been especially stimulated in the pueblo region, which contains our most noteworthy antiquities, by the agitation in favor of a measure for the preservation of our national antiquities, which took final form in the law enacted at the last session of Congress; and, more especially, on account of the action of the executive departments of the Government having control of the public lands and reservations, in taking practical steps to utilize their agents and field forces in policing the ruins. With the view of facilitating this guardianship, card catalogues and maps showing all known ruins of the Southwest have been compiled by the Bureau and placed at the disposal of the departments; and a series of bulletins treating the antiquities of the various physiographic and ethnic areas of the Southwest, intended primarily for the use of the field men, is in preparation.[28]

Additional concerns about vandalism and the need for professionally led excavations, and agitation for effective legislation, eventually led to the passage of the Act for the Preservation of American Antiquities.[29] Edgar Hewett is generally credited with swinging sentiment toward federal legislation and drafting the specific legislative language that enabled its passage. His insistence on the precise wording in the act expanded the definition of what kinds of lands could be set aside from private ownership and use. Rather than the reserves being limited to archeological sites, land could also be reserved for its historic or scientific significance. If the land could be determined to be already in the public domain, of no economic value, remote, not productive agriculturally, nor part of the tourist industry, then it could be considered for inclusion in a national monument.[30]

In a 1906 article in the journal *American Anthropologist*, on activities directed toward the passage of protective legislation, titled "Preservation of American Antiquities: Progress During the Last Year; Needed Legislation," Hewett commented that during the previous fifteen months there had been rapid developments in preservation policy. He reported that approximately three-fourths of the remains of antiquity on lands in the public domain were under more or less efficient custodianship, and predicted that despoliation of ruins for commercial purposes would be stamped out. He reported that all ruins on the national forest reserves were under the care of forest rangers, that all unauthorized excavation and collecting was prohibited, that forest rangers had the power to arrest offenders, and that forest reserves were being created constantly in the Southwest, where antiquities were most numerous. In Arizona he listed the forest reserves where important archeological remains were located: the Grand Canyon, San Francisco Mountain, Black Mesa, Prescott, Pinal Mountains, Mt. Graham, Santa Catalina, Santa Rita, and Chiricahua forest reserves. On the issue of who should be granted the rights to excavate on forest reserves or Indian reservations, it was agreed that the Southwest Society of the Archaeological Institute of America would file a plan with the Bureau of American Ethnology designating the person in charge of fieldwork, that excavations would be conducted only for the advancement of archeology and not for commercial purposes, and that collections would be made only for permanent preservation in public museums. Hewett went on to argue that it was impossible to concentrate authority for all excavations in any one department and suggested that, if archeological work was proposed on forest reserves, permission must be granted by the secretary of agriculture; if on a military reservation, by the secretary of war; or if on an Indian reservation, by the secretary of the interior.

Hewett summarized how previous measures before Congress, new conditions, the spirit of the Archaeological Institute of America and the American Anthropological Association, and the wishes of various government departments were taken into account in developing proposed legislation. The national legislation called for fines, and possible imprisonment for destroying antiquities; it permitted the president to declare historic landmarks, historic and prehistoric structures, and other objects of historic or scientific interest by public proclamation; and it allowed the secretaries of the interior, agriculture, and war to permit examination, excavation, and collection on archeological sites.

Roosevelt signed the Antiquities Act into law on June 8, 1906. The rules and regulations were signed by the three departments Hewett proposed to be responsible for regulating excavation and collection on their respective lands—E. A. Hitchcock as secretary of the interior, James Wilson as secretary of agriculture, and William H. Taft as secretary of war.[31]

Preservation of the Tonto Cliff Dwellings as a National Monument

Theodore Roosevelt established Tonto National Monument on December 19, 1907. Proclamation No. 787-35 Stat. 2168 set aside 640 acres containing two prehistoric cliff dwellings under the Act for Preservation of American Antiquities Designation. Warning was given "to all unauthorized persons not to appropriate, excavate, injure, or destroy any of the prehistoric ruins or remains therefore declared to be a national monument, or to locate or settle upon any of the lands reserved and made a part of said monument by this Proclamation."[32]

The path to monument status could be said to have started with Bandelier's 1883 visit. The Archaeological Institute of America hired A. F. Bandelier to survey southwestern archeological sites, and he became the first archeologist to document the cliff dwellings we know today as Tonto National Monument. Bandelier's survey of southwestern archeological sites was essentially a fleshing-out of the journeys, work, and publications of Lewis Henry Morgan. Although Morgan did not visit central Arizona, his 1880 *Study of the Houses of American Aborigines* for the first Annual Report of the Archaeological Institute of America, and his urging for thorough scientific exploration and documentation of the ruins in New Mexico, Arizona, and the Yucatan, set the stage for Bandelier's work. With hindsight we can now see that Bandelier's work

> effectively operationalized Morgan's method. There first needed to be a survey of the living Pueblos, especially of house types, given Morgan's argument that they reflect social forms. Second, surveys and catalogs of published and archival resources were required, followed by assessments of their validity as historic documents. The earliest historic documents could also be used to define an "ethnographic present"—a description of a pueblo or tribe on a hypothetical "day before" the first contact between the Indians and the Spanish.[33]

In addition to studying how pueblos came to be how they are (drawing on Morgan's hypothesis that archeologists needed to understand the mode of life of living Indian tribes), Bandelier conducted his surveys by river drainage, drawing from John Wesley Powell's insistence that water was the controlling factor in the Southwest.

Bandelier's travels between 1880 and 1883 were designed to gather information about that region. He had been told about the many ruins and cliff houses in the Tonto Basin, and by January 1883, Bandelier began moving south through the Mogollon Mountains into Arizona. On May 16, 1883, Bandelier arrived in Globe, Arizona, and for the next several days recorded the ruin of Besh-Ba-Gowah, visited Wheatfields and recorded the "Los Trigos" platform mound site, recorded the ruin later known as Murphy Mesa, and arrived in Cave Canyon in the Tonto Basin on May 24, 1883. Bandelier noted the following in his journal:

> Left at 8 a.m., on horseback, for the cave dwellings. We rode down the river, past Archie McIntosh's house, and about four miles in all, and then turned sharply to the south. The caves are visible at a great distance. We entered a deep canyon where a spring rises. The canyon is narrow; it has no bottom, only a dry arroyo, which is the outlet of the spring. This arroyo is shrouded in verdure, mesquite, thorns of all kinds, large cottonwoods, and walnuts. It is a perfect thicket, and difficult to get through. The slopes rising to the canyon are covered with boulders, and unfit for cultivation.
>
> We first visited the lower cave. The slope is exceedingly steep, difficult, on account of the cactus and of the crumbling, slippery, shale cropping out. The height is almost vertical at places. The entire height to the cave is 68 of my heights, or 109 meters, equal to 363 feet. The cave is large, and the eastern declivity (it faces to the east) is often vertical. The height of the cave is about 20 to 25 feet. Into it the house had been built. It is a perfect pueblo house, but small. The walls are of large stones, broken to suit, and laid in clay mixed with gravel, which gives it the appearance of concrete. The proportion of stone to concrete is about equal. I found many metates about three of which were perfect. The manos are small, so as to work in the groove. Many of the roofs are perfect. They are of vigas, above them are either splinters or round sticks of ocotillo, above it reeds, and then two-and-a-half inches of mud. The floors, as far as visible, are black. There is some pottery about, handsomely painted, similar to that of the "Cerros" on the Rio Puerco, only much older.
>
> I found an old sandal, much fragmentary basketwork, rope, twine, and many corncobs. They are of the small variety, and I found one small piece of obsidian. No red-and-black pottery, but some faintly corrugated ware. The majority of the pottery, however, is dark red and very thick. The position of the pueblo is admirable for security and observation, but I cannot find any tillable lands short of two miles away. As to the timber, it is cedar, as to the small cross pieces, heavy pine in regard to the central posts and the beams. There are several center posts, and one of them is hacked off even. Others are slightly bifurcated.[34]

In the final report of his investigations, published in 1892, Bandelier characterized the size of the cliff dwellings as moderate, and the architecture as typical of compact pueblos and "just as much in place at the Chaca Canon, or on the Rio de las Animas as in the rocky recesses of the valley of the Salt River."[35] He described the roofs, ceilings, doorways, and hatchways as still mostly intact, although many had been burnt by the Apaches; and he reported that, owing to their being sheltered, many specimens remained intact, including sandals and cotton cloth. He surmised that since the pottery found in the caves was the same as that found in other ruins on the Salt River, the ancient inhabitants were of the same culture group, although not necessarily of the same tribe or linguistic stock. He evaluated the rock shelters as "still in an almost perfect state of preservation."[36]

During Bandelier's sojourn in Arizona, stories of his investigations and rumors of his death at the hands of Apaches circulated throughout the archeological world. One story went as follows:

At Fort Apache, Bandelier met Sergeant Will Barnes, the post telegraph operator. Barnes later reminisced that he and Bandelier were sitting one day in the telegraph room and the line was open. Messages began going back and forth between Whipple Barracks, at Prescott, and Fort Bowie, near the Mexican border. The message from Whipple Barracks said that Bandelier had been reported killed by Apaches, and the commandant at Bowie was ordered to verify his death and recover the body. With his enthusiastic approval, Barnes telegraphed Whipple Barracks, the Archaeological Institute in Boston, and Josephine in Highland that Bandelier was alive and well at Fort Apache. Bandelier wrote several letters humorously denying his demise; like Mark Twain and John Wesley Powell, he was able to say that reports of his death were greatly exaggerated. He ended his trip with visits to Casa Grande and other ruins in the Gila and Salt River drainage.[37]

Bandelier was aware of the limitations of both archeology and ethnology at the time. At the conclusion of his research, he readily admitted that the questions he could bring to his research were inadequate to draw conclusions about the prehistory of the Southwest. However, Bandelier was the first scholar who had the opportunity to conduct an archeological survey over a large area. He was intent on replacing romantic speculation with scientific truths. He undermined fanciful notions of the Aztec origins of the pueblo ruins and was the first to characterize the Salado traditions of the Tonto Basin. Bandelier included a composite of one hundred ground plans of dwellings as part of his final report of his investigations. His analysis and documentation served as the first professional voice for the significance of the Tonto cliff dwellings. Bandelier's research and writings had a powerful influence on the next generation of archeologists, especially Edgar Hewett, who reviewed prehistoric features on federal lands in Arizona, New Mexico, Colorado, and Utah and recommended specific sites for protection. Hewett's review endorsed Bandelier's analysis and included Tonto as worthy of designation as a national monument. Thus a national monument emerged from the confluence of two streams, of science and culture, and the timely blending of reclamation, conservation, and antiquities protection.

---

1. Lange, R.C. a. C. L. R., ed. (1970, 112).

2. See Appendix B for Tonto National Monument proclamations.

3. Runte (1991, 12). His chapter "The Origins of Conservation" is a good introduction to the fear of resource scarcity as the impetus for forest conservation. Recommended reading includes Roderick Nash's *Wilderness and the American Mind* (1982) for an introduction to changing ideas about wilderness and conservation, and Samuel P. Hays's *Conservation and the Gospel of Efficiency: The Progressive Conservation Movement 1890–1920* (1959) on conservation during the Progressive Era.

4. Karen Smith's *The Magnificent Experiment* (1986) is a good introduction to the national campaign for western irrigation requiring federal financing and especially its relevance to the Salt River Valley.

5. Smith (1982, 1).

6. Ibid. (1982, 21).

7. Bender (1898, n.p.).

8. Davis (1903, 35 and 50).

9. Letter from F. H. Newell, hydrographer in charge, to Department of the Interior, U.S. Geological Survey, Division of Hydrography, Washington, D.C., June 12, 1902, p. 7. Salt River Project Archive.

10. In addition to purchasing acreage for the reservoir site in the amount of $40,000 paid to the Hudson Reservoir and Canal Company., the government purchased 4,775 acres of land from individual homesteaders for a total price of $147,776. The following list of homesteaders who sold land to the government for the dam and reservoir is from the Arizona Historical Foundation's Richard Schauss collection, MSS-6 Box 1, Folder 9.

> "When Roosevelt Dam was constructed the government bought up 4,775 acres of homesteaded land for which it pai d $147,776.00. These were lands to be flooded by the reservoir. The differences paid per acre to the various owners were the subject of much cynical chit chat. Old time Gilenos still recall the "Politics." Below are listed the owners, acres and price. Wives names have been ommited [sic].

T.A. Pascoe	205.00 acres	$12,000
Andrew J. Henderson	80	3,500
Henry Armer	160	3,000

George A. Allen	160	800
J. Irvin Coleman	20	400
W.F. Cline	80	550
John H. Baker Sr.	160	3,000
George W.P. Hunt	275	6,525
J.E. Sturgeon	114.14	2,500
Mary A. Bacon Fuss	80	1,200
Joseph Thomas Flippen	140	1,050
Christian Botticher	80	2,500
Simon W. Kenton	80	3,500
John C. Wehrli	152.16	1,500
Charles T. Martin	152.16	500
Harry Zschoegner	80	2,500
John W. Nelson	80	600
John A. Smith	80	600
Herbert Hocker	16	1,300
Nicholas Hocker	160	4,000
Charles C. Griffen	120	6,000
Jacob S. Duey	80	2,200
William D. Fisher	80	1,050
Harry Zschoegner	40	500
Josephine C. Nelson	40	600
Jacob S. Duey	40	600
Joseph S. Mechem	40	400
J.E. Williams	160	1,200
George T. Peter	160	1,600
Chas. Debbs	380	4,700
Louise K. Bowman	80	2,000
Jane G. Dellinger	320	14,500
Thomas J. Cline	100	2,000
Elmer T. Boyd	80	1,000
SRV Water Users' A	120	2,000
John E. Campbell	40	600
William H. Miller	160	800

The government also paid $40,000 to the Hudson Reservoir & Canal Co. for the "reservoir site." No acreage listed.

11. Reidy (1905).

12. Hall (1905).

13. Marcus (1983) is a good introduction to the evolution of the Tonto National Forest.

14. Hirt (1994, xviii, 28–29).

15. In 1893, the Grand Canyon Forest Reserve set aside 1,851,520 acres; it was enlarged to 2,307,520 acres in 1905, then reduced to 2,257,920 acres in 1906. In 1898, the San Francisco Reserve set aside 975,630 acres; it was enlarged to 1,975,310 acres in 1905. The Black Mesa Reserve comprised 1,658,880 acres; it was enlarged to 2,030,240 acres in 1906 and to 2,572,249 acres in 1907. The establishment of Tonto National Forest set aside 1,115,200 acres in 1905; 1,288,320 acres were added in 1907 for a total of 2,403,520 acres.

By 1908 there were seventeen national forests in the territory, covering 13,163,710 acres. (See Lauver 1938, 42).

16. *Arizona Republican*, January 13, 1901.

17. *Arizona Republican*, February 22, 1901.

18. Cohoon (1904, 3).

19. Cohoon and Holsinger (1905, 3).

20. Kibbey (1907, 28).

21. Lee (1970).

22. Ibid.

23. Fowler (2000) is the best overview of various documentations of the Southwest—including topographical engineers; army observations; the Bureau of Ethnology; archeologists including the Mindeleff brothers, Fewkes, Bandelier, and others—and the development of archeology and ethnology in the West.

24. Elliott (1995) is a good introduction to public interest in the Southwest's prehistoric past. Snead (2001) is a good overview of the complex relationships between archeology and society and the politics and personalities that controlled fieldwork in southwestern archeology during the fifty years from 1875 to 1925.

25. For example, in 1906 the National Museum received accessions to its collections from a variety of sources, including gifts; loans; deposits; transfers; purchases; specimens made in laboratories; and by explorations made by the members of the staff, the Bureau of American Ethnology, and government surveys and expeditions. By June 30, 1906, it had 7,130 items in the physical anthropology division, 489,072 in the ethnology division, and 391,838 in the prehistoric archeology division.

26. Congressional Record, 47th Congress, 1st Session (1882, 3777).

27. Ibid.

28. Hewett (1906, 450).

29. Between 1900 and 1905, various congressmen introduced bills to protect American antiquities, to punish vandals, to survey sites, and to deny tourists the right to carry away materials that might be of scientific merit. Who should be allowed to excavate on sites and where the artifacts should be stored also become matters of heated debate. In general, it was agreed that only professional excavators should be allowed to excavate and that the Smithsonian was the proper repository. Edgar Hewett, appointed by the American Anthropological Society to promote legislation in favor of preservation, orchestrated the passage of the Antiquities Act.

30. Such land would have to be in the public domain because it was already part of a national forest or on a military reservation.

31. Lee (1970) provides complete documentation of the passage of the Antiquities Act as well as an analysis of its significance. On the occasion of the electronic version of Ronald F. Lee's history of the Antiquities Act being made available in 2001, the secretary of the department of the interior, Bruce Babbitt, provided an introduction and analyzed the 1906 Antiquities Act as having historical importance for natural resource conservation and for archeological and historic preservation in the United States because it established basic public policy with three aspects:

> First, it established that the archeological, historic, scenic, and scientific sites and structures are most valuable for the archeological, historical and scientific information they

contain, and for their commemorative, scenic, or inspirational associations, which makes them different from commercial resources that have primarily monetary value;

Second, the archeological sites and historic structures, and by extension, other kinds of cultural resources have a public value. That is, like clean water and air, the preservation of these kinds of resources contributes to the public good; and

Third, the investigation and removal of archeological resources must be conducted by appropriately qualified and trained experts using the best contemporary methods and techniques.

Lee characterized the passage of the Antiquities Act to be the work of:

A whole generation of dedicated effort by scholars, citizens, and members of Congress, which had begun in 1879 and culminated in 1906 ... This generation, through its explorations, publications, exhibits, and other activities, awakened the American people to a lasting consciousness of the value of American antiquities, prehistoric and historic. This public understanding, achieved only after persistent effort in the face of much ignorance, vandalism, and indifference, was a necessary foundation for many subsequent conservation achievements. (Quoted by Bruce Babbitt in paragraph10 of the introduction to Ronald Lee's *History of the Antiquities Act*, http://www.nps.gov/archeology/pubs/lee/Lee_BB.htm).

32. See appendix B for Presidential Proclamation No. 787–Dec. 19, 1907–35 Stat. 2168.

33. Fowler (2001, 177).

34. Lange and Riley (1970, 112–13).

35. Bandelier (1892, 425).

36. Ibid., 428.

37. Quoted in Fowler (2000, 175).

chapter two
ONE LAND, MANY PEOPLES

It seemed strange to be chatting and laughing so gaily in a house built unknown centuries ago by people unlike us in appearance but who had known joy and grief, pleasure and pain, same as our race of today knows them and who had laughed, cried, sung, danced, married and died, mourned or rejoiced their lives away in this once populous town or castle or whatever one would call it!

FROM THE DIARY OF ANGELINE
BROWN, 1880

Commanding landscapes, mild climate, arable soils, and abundant water and other resources—the features that made Tonto Basin attractive to federal stewards in the early twentieth century—were aped, in turn, by prehistoric Native Americans, and nineteenth-century miners, ranchers, and dam builders. Each, for better or worse, left a legacy. What follows is a brief overview of the geography of the Tonto region, followed by a look at how successive societies shaped the land, what choices they made, and the legacies they left.

The Tonto Basin lies in the transition zone in Arizona's central highlands, between the northern Colorado Plateau and the southern Basin and Range Province. The land consists of shifting environments and alternating mountains and valleys. The point where the Mazatzal Range gives way to the Tonto Basin is the geological boundary between the older and younger Precambrian

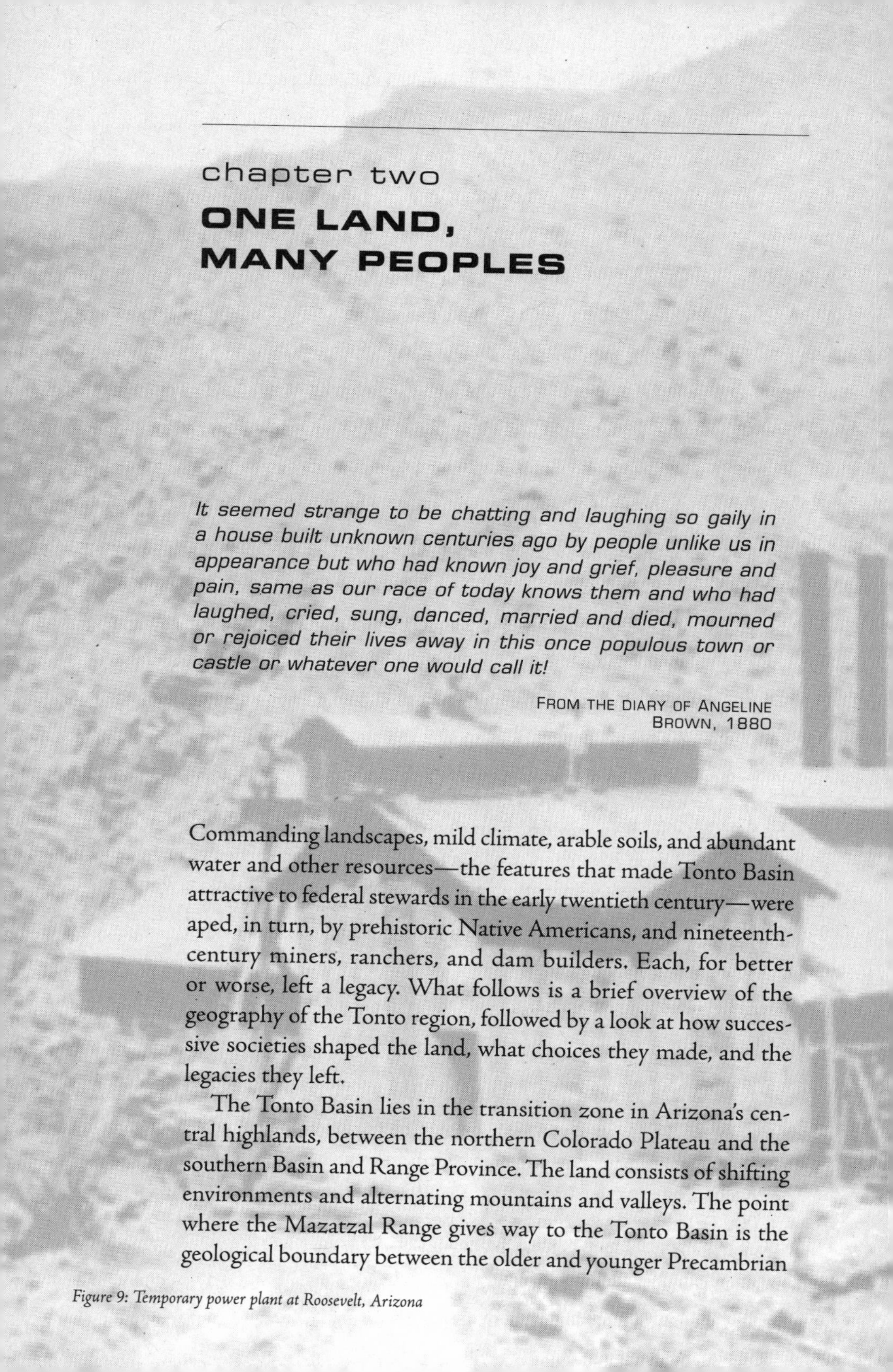

Figure 9: Temporary power plant at Roosevelt, Arizona

Figure 10: Four Peaks seen from the Tonto Basin. Courtesy Denver Public Library, Western History Collection, H. C. Tibbits, Z–5892.

rocks, so the very ground reflects a transition in epochs. The Salt River and Tonto Creek drain the Tonto Basin. While Tonto Creek is much smaller than the Salt, it provides a perennial supply to the basin. Between the Tonto Basin and the Mogollon Rim there are four biotic communities: the upper Sonoran oak woodland and chaparral, the upper Sonoran piñon-juniper woodland, the transitional ponderosa pine forest, and the Canadian fir forest. Erratic droughts and fire shaped the vegetation.[1]

PREHISTORIC PEOPLES ON TODAY'S TONTO NATIONAL FOREST

Approximately 8,000 to 10,000 years ago, people we now refer to as Paleo-Indians visited the area seasonally, hunting large animals such as camels, giant ground sloths, bison, and even woolly mammoths. They also gathered and processed seeds, nuts, and berries. Artifacts of Paleo-Indians are rare, but some have been found in the area around Payson.[2]

Archeologists refer to the next group of people to occupy the area, about 10,000 years ago, as Archaic period people. Over the long period from 8000z to AD 100, these people shifted to a more sedentary lifeway, planted corn, and

Figure 11: Artist's rendering of Griffin Wash Meddler Point archeological site

developed bow-and-arrow technology from earlier atlatl (spear-throwing) technology.

About 2,000 years ago, the people of the Southwest began using ceramics. Five cultural groups manufactured pottery and constructed substantial dwellings in sedentary villages between AD 300 and 1400, including those archeologists refer to today as the Hohokam, Mogollon, Sinagua, ancestral Puebloan (previously Anasazi), and Salado. These cultures all met in the area known as the Tonto Forest, a geographic transition zone between the upper plateau country and the Sonoran Desert, as well as a cultural transition zone—a place where these peoples exchanged goods, shared technologies, and participated in cycles of occupation and abandonment.

By 1,200 years ago, Hohokam from the Salt and Gila river valleys were irrigating food crops along Tonto Creek and the upper Salt River, growing corn, beans, squash, and cotton. They hunted deer, cottontail, and jackrabbit; gathered piñon pine, juniper, agave, walnut, and manzanita; and they traded—all of which constituted a remarkably vital subsistence strategy that enabled these cultures to persist in the region until 1450. These movements of people and goods extended across large areas: the remains of shells found at the cliff dwellings reflect a network of trade with people from the Gulf of California hundreds of miles away; fir and pine were brought in from at least 25 kilometers; and white ware pottery came from as far as 80 miles away.[3]

Tonto Basin is one of several areas in the Southwest associated with the Salado, a term that has generated archeological debate since the 1930s. The basin is located between the desert-dwelling Hohokam to the south and ancestral Puebloan groups of the mountain areas to the north and east. The geographic area contains a variety of architectural styles and material culture that represent both the Hohokam and ancestral Puebloan traditions.

Both architectural styles are sometimes found within single sites, suggesting a close mixing between the two groups. Recent research suggests that the intermixing of these two groups may have occurred from the late 1200s to the middle 1400s, when the Tonto Basin was depopulated. Site types in the Tonto Basin include cliff dwellings, fieldhouses, room blocks, compounds, and platform mounds. In addition, pottery—such as Roosevelt Red Ware, Salado Red, and Salado White-on-red—represent a key component of Salado material culture. These ceramics were found during excavations of the upper and lower cliff dwellings in Tonto National Monument.

Figure 12: Cliff polychrome bowl, circa 1400

SOUTHEASTERN YAVAPAI AND WESTERN APACHES IN THE TONTO

The Salado migration away from the Tonto National Forest area circa 1450 may have overlapped with the arrival in the area of the southeastern Yavapai and Western Apache. Five bands of Apaches entered the area, probably sometime after 1450: the Pinal, Aravaipa, Apache Peaks, Tonto, and San Carlos (today these groups comprise what is called the San Carlos Apache Tribe). The Tonto Apaches (who called themselves *Dilzhe e*), filtered into the Tonto Basin from the north and cultivated corn, beans, and squash. They used fire to create the best range conditions for hunting and gathering. They also became skilled horseman as early as 1600, which greatly increased their ability to trade and raid over long distances.

When restricted to the information found in the *written* record, it is obvious that the Yavapai and Tonto Apache managed to remain marginal to the colonial administrative and missionization system throughout the Spanish period. José Cortés, a lieutenant in the Spanish Royal Corps of Engineers in

Figure 13: An Apache wickiup on the shore of Roosevelt Lake. Courtesy Denver Public Library, Western History Collection, H. C. Tibbits, Z–5857.

1799, referred to the westernmost of the Apaches as the *Tonto* or *Coyoteros*, the "least known to the Spanish."[4] However, some Spanish military patrols came through the Tonto Basin, and it is suggested that Coronado's expedition from Mexico to Zuni passed through the area. Reports by the Spanish who ventured into the area refer to encounters with the Tonto, including one that resulted in the naming of the Tonto, referring to the "foolish" way they spoke the Apachean language.

Outsiders launched long-range trapping parties along southwestern rivers beginning in the 1820s, but records of these journeys are also sparse. James Ohio Pattie's accounts of traversing the area in 1826 were written long after the trips, and much was invented or exaggerated. But historians have pieced together parts of written and oral accounts to conclude that Pattie clashed with a band of Western Apache or southeastern Yavapai.[5] The U.S. military suffered from a lack of written information about the southwestern native populations when it established Fort Buchanan near what is today the Mexican border in 1857 to put an end to Pinal and Aravaipa Apache raids. The more northern Yavapai and Tonto Apache went unmolested until gold was discovered in their territory in 1863. As prospectors and ranchers came into closer contact with the Yavapai and Tonto Apache, the military carried out local versions of national policies—including extermination, subjugation, removal, and acculturation.

In January 1864, the Yavapai, led by Paramucka, clashed with civilian volunteers from Prescott commanded by King S. Woolsey. It is a matter of debate exactly where what is now called the Bloody Tanks conflict took place. Some claim it happened at the west end of what is now the town of Miami, while others say it took place in Fish Creek Canyon in the Superstition Mountains.[6] Around that time the military was constructing forts quickly, including Camp Grant in 1863, Fort Goodwin and Fort Verde in 1864, Fort McDowell in 1865, Camp Reno in 1867 (15 miles north of the Tonto cliff dwellings), and Camps Picketpost and Pinal in 1870. During the five years between 1865 and 1870, Chief Delshay of the Tonto band led the San Carlos Apache in several incidents, one of which led to the destruction of Camp Reno in 1869.

President Ulysses S. Grant created the White Mountain Apache Reservation in 1871, and between 1872 and 1874 General Crook waged a major military campaign to force the Tonto Apache onto the reservation. The heaviest fighting occurred in 1872–1873. Shortly thereafter, the White Mountain Apache Reservation was divided in two, Fort Apache and San Carlos. In 1875, 1,400 Tonto Apache at Camp Verde were force-marched to the San Carlos Reservation. They were completely removed from the Tonto Basin area by the summer of 1875. By the 1890s, small groups of Apache at San Carlos began to leave the reservation and took up life in their homelands in the Tonto Basin near Payson and Fort McDowell.[7]

There is little *written* documentation from the perspective of the Tonto Apache and Yavapai about their history in the Tonto Basin, and even less about their direct interaction with the cliff dwellings. One of the obstacles to inserting the Apache and Yavapai perspective into the history of the Tonto Basin is the inability of archeologists and historians to find clues in the landscape that reveal these stories. Apaches left little behind in the form of dwellings and pottery, the type of things that provide the bulk of evidence for archeologists and historians. The radical transformation of the Tonto Basin peoples and landscapes caused by federal reservations and land restrictions led to loss of traditional knowledge of and relationships with the land. The mature understanding the Apache people have of their landscape is expressed as *ch'igona' ai'nilis dashol'ees helz*, literally "don't let the sun step over you," which translates as "wisdom sits in places."[8] It is vital to understand how federal land-control policies affected traditional Apache practices. An ethnographic study should yield a new way of understanding how the Tonto Apache and Yavapai used the surrounding area; how they viewed and responded to the mountain peaks; the extent to which they fasted, prayed, meditated, and sought guidance in the peaks; the names they gave to places; and the clan traditions and ceremonial knowledge that may have included the area around the cliff dwellings.

It is doubtful that their use of the area created drastic environmental change in the Tonto Basin. Instead, the drastic environmental change came from nearby mining operations, and especially from grazing.[9]

MINING AND GRAZING COMMUNITIES IN THE TONTO BASIN

The roads required for the military campaigns of the 1870s made the area more accessible to prospectors who, beginning in 1875, were attracted to the claims in Superior, Globe, Clifton-Morenci, Richmond Basin, and McMillenville. The gold rush to Payson, which began in 1880, put even more people on the stage roads, especially the one that connected Payson and Globe and which ran past the ruins. Early mines have evocative names, such as the Ramboz, Rescue, and Bluebird in the Globe district; the Stonewall Jackson and the Nugget of McMillen in the Richmond Basin. These efforts to get at and profit from the mineralization of the basin brought more people into the area. The miners, in turn, required supplies and food, and ranchers, farmers, and merchants moved in to fill that need. Globe City (as Globe was known then) was founded in 1876, the *Arizona Daily Silver Belt* began publication in 1878, and Gila County was formed out of lands taken from Pinal and Maricopa counties in 1881 with Globe as the county seat. When the silver mines began to play out, world-class copper discoveries in Superior and Globe-Maimi created a second boom of intense mining activity. Between 1900 and 1910 some of the mines included the Miami Copper Company, the Inspiration Consolidated Copper Company, the Warrior Development Company, the Lost Gulch United Mines Company, and the Old Dominion Mining Company, Globe's greatest producer.[10] With the coming of the transcontinental railroad in 1869 and the Southern Pacific branch to Globe in 1898, the once-remote Tonto Basin was even more accessible.

However the enterprise that created the most change in the Tonto Basin environment was grazing, which was begun to fill the needs of soldiers at Fort McDowell and miners in the Globe-Miami district. In 1868, the army introduced domestic cattle to feed the troops. An officer at Fort McDowell noted the abundant water and grass in the Tonto Basin—the resources

Figure 14: Rounding up cattle in the Tonto Basin

required for large-scale grazing. The word spread, and soon hogs, sheep, and cattle began appearing at Tonto.[11]

David Harer and his son-in-law, Florence A. Packard, were some of the earliest hog farmers to supply the Globe-Miami mining district. Lewis Robinson began driving sheep into the Tonto Basin in an area now submerged under Roosevelt Lake. Christian Cline and his sons drove 1,600 cattle from near San Diego through Phoenix and up the old Reno Wagon Road to Tonto Creek. A sense of the numbers of ranchers present in the early 1880s is left to us from the requirement for ranchers to file their brands at the new county courthouse in Globe after Gila County was created on February 8, 1881. While many declined to file, forty-four cattle ranchers did so between 1881 and 1896.[12]

Additional information about ranching in the Tonto Basin comes from a senior forest ranger at the Tonto National Forest, Fred W. Croxen, who presented a paper at the Tonto Grazing Conference in Phoenix in November 1926 using information from his interview with the then-oldest cattleman in Tonto Basin. Croxen's report offers a portrait of the range conditions as encountered by some of the earliest ranchers in the 1870s.[13] Croxen's interviewees portray the Tonto Basin as a rancher's paradise. The natural resources were favorable, with good grasses and well-watered ranges. The built conditions were good thanks to the military, which needed usable roads and had enabled the live-stock industry to grow by removing the Apache from the area by the 1880s. Markets were plentiful, including Phoenix, Camp McDowell, and the mining camp of Silver King (near what is now Superior). While mountain lions were an obstacle to horse raising, the conditions for raising crops and other stock were favorable. Word of these enviable conditions spread, drawing settlers from California and Oregon, from the Mormon settlements in Utah, and from Texas and New Mexico. They came, naturally enough, equipped with experience in ranching under other conditions, and assumed the favorable conditions would persist; most had no experience with the precariousness of the desert.

Croxen cites Florence Packard, who spoke of ranges in the 1870s with "Blackfoot and Crowfoot Grama grass that touched one's stirrups when riding through it." Packard described Tonto Creek as, "timbered with the local creek bottom type of timber from bluff to bluff," and recalled, "the water seeped rather than flowed down through a series of sloughs and fish over a foot in length could be caught with little trouble." Croxen quotes Cliff C. Griffin as saying:

> The principal grass was Black Grama and a species of Sage. The Black Grama used to cover the slopes on each side of the river. In those days this came up in bunches, approximately five inches at the base, grew to a height of two to two and one-half feet with a sheaf-like spread of two to two and one-half feet. This was very nutritious, making the finest kind of feed for cattle ... and in the early days the settlers used to chop this grass for hay, using heavy hoes for chopping and with a hoe, rake and fork, he could fill a wagon in two hours with this grass.[14]

Cattle ranchers lived in homesteads scattered along the Tonto Creek. Their cattle ranged in open land, unfenced, and they worked together to round up the cattle, starting near the Tonto Box and proceeding down Tonto Creek to where it met the Salt River. There, each rancher would gather his steers from the collective herd and drive them to markets.[15]

These idyllic conditions didn't last long. Hog, sheep, and cattle ranching in the Tonto Basin had immediate negative impacts on the native vegetation that supported the animals. Livestock grazing and fire suppression com-bined to create changes that, in turn, decreased grasses suitable for stock and increased less suitable woody plants and shrubs. Droughts in the early 1880s periodically curtailed grazing, but the industry revived when rainfall increased.

The revival got a boost and expanded when the area became linked via the transcontinental rail routes. The wetter ranges and new transportation system enabled products to get to market more cheaply and quickly. These favorable conditions attracted yet more ranchers, and the size of the herds increased to reduce the costs of production. This industry expansion further depleted the grasses. Then the good times ended. A severe drought in 1892–1893 left the Tonto dry. Heavy rains followed, which washed away topsoil and created gullies. By 1895, the range was considered "at the ragged end of it all."[16]

In the late 1880s, range specialist J. J. Thornber succinctly described the effects of overstocking and the cycle that damaged increasingly large sections of the range:

> Under our arid conditions, this overstocking soon resulted in destructive overgrazing and tramping out of large areas of forage producing plants, often beyond recovery. With this completed, the herds were moved on to other less grazed districts to be denuded, in turn, of their plant growth. Naturally, such depletion of the plant covering was very much hastened by recurring droughty seasons or years, which matter became all the more serious with the gradual increase in stock over the country. After eating off closely and trampling out the plant covering in the neighborhood of watering places, the hungry animals were compelled to travel ever further for grass.[17]

A combination of overstocking and drought taxed the grasses, and by the late 1880s cattle and sheep ranchers, who had antagonistic relationships anyway, were blaming each other. Potter summed up the divisions among range users:

> Class was arrayed against class—the cowman against the sheepman, the big owner against the little one—and might ruled more often than right. Deadlines stretched their threatening lengths across the country, jealously guarded by armed men; battles were fought and lives sacrificed; untold thousands of animals were slaughtered in the fight for the range. Probably no class of men deplored this state of affairs more deeply than did the stockmen themselves, but they were victims of circumstance and governmental inaction with no course open to them other than the one they followed.[18]

Rapid growth of grazing in the Tonto Basin created seemingly irreparable environmental degradation, and spawned negative consequences for all involved.

Cattle and sheep ranchers may have been divided in their views of the relative merits of domestic grazing animals, but they were united in the conviction that posed an even greater risk to the range, namely the need for fire supression.[19]

FIRE ON THE RANGE

Fire, both natural and set, played a large role in shaping the vegetation of the Tonto Basin. The Mogollon Rim is the "virtual epicenter" of lightning-caused fires in North America. Dramatic summer thunderstorms sparked fires that shaped the ponderosa pine forests along the Mogollon Rim, which has the largest continuous stand of ponderosa pine in the world. From the scientific record, we know that fires kept the forest open; openness prevented fires from becoming excessively large; and grasses, tinder-dry in summer months, ensured regular fires.[20] In addition, Native Americans used fire to prepare the landscape for wildlife grazing and browsing. As the U.S. Forest Service tried to understand the impact of fires and grazing on the Tonto landscape, at least one ranger, S. J. Holsinger, argued that,

> The most potent and powerful weapon in the hands of these aborigines was the firebrand. It was alike used to capture the deer, the elk, and the antelope, and also to rout or vanquish the enemy. It cleared their mountain trail and destroyed the cover in which their quarry took refuge.

When Holsinger compared the practices and impacts of Native Americans versus white settlers, he characterized the white settlers as inferior, remarking,

> When the country was invaded and occupied by the white settler, though marked changes were inaugurated, the forest conditions were not improved. From a forest standpoint, a comparison drawn between the condition during Indian occupancy, with no domestic animals, and that with the civilized race, with its flocks and herds, would be decidedly to the credit of the former. Under the latter the destruction by fire was reduced; annual fires were replaced by accidental fires of less frequency, but more damaging. Wasteful methods of lumbering and the introduction of herds increased the sum total of forest devastation.[21]

Pinchot had an opportunity to witness the Apache burning grassland for deer hunting; it was understood that Native Americans' fires were set to create grasslands and good hunting.[22]

A. E. Cohoon, who wrote about Tonto Basin conditions when proposing additions to the Black Mesa Reserve in 1904, gave voice to local sentiment about the deleterious effects of fire, whether purposeful or accidental.

According to statements made by the old residents, fires have occurred in these mountains at intervals since the earliest invasion by the white men. Many accounts were heard of large fires which were raging when the country was first being settled. These fires of many years ago are supposed to have originated from the hands of Indians living in the adjacent White Mountain Indian Reservation, and others who go into the mountains during summer for their winter's supply of food. It is claimed by some that the Indians would set out fires during long seasons of drought as a means of inducing rain, while many such conflagrations were supposed to have been started by religious worshippers.

The most destructive fire of recent years happened in June 1900. This was a very large fire which could be seen for many miles and burned for about two weeks in the Sierra Anchas. It was reported that this fire was set in a very dry season by cowboys in order to drive a bunch of wild cattle out of thick brush and that the fire immediately got beyond their control and spread over a large area. At the time of the fire there was a high wind and only a few people were in the mountains. It did considerable damage to the forest, not only in destroying the valuable forest floor and undergrowth, but in killing large patches of reproduction of the most valuable species as well as the matured trees themselves.

Generally the settlers are rather careful with fires because they realize the destruction which would result to their range in case of a big fire. There seems to be a general sentiment among the residents against the spread of fires, and it is believed that they will readily give assistance in fighting as well as preventing them.[23]

In 1901, after a series of forest fires in the early summer, the relationship between grazing and fires was characterized as follows:

The loss by fire is infinitely greater than any grazing by cattle could cause, and the less grazing done, the more frequent will the forest fires become. The department may find this out some day, and then again it may not.[24]

Thus, while some rangers at the turn of the twentieth century understood fire as a tool for range management, ranchers feared its destructive aspects and eagerly cooperated to suppress it at all costs. Over the next sixty years, the Tonto Basin rangeland would be subjected to only accidental burnings; prescribed burning would not return until around 1960. It took until then to change policies and practices to allow burn and spray experiments to create open savannah-type grasslands and islands of cover for wildlife.

While the Apache's facility with horses may be well known, less famous is their experience with cattle raising. In 1883 the Fort Apache and San Carlos reservations received their first cattle from the federal government, though probably not of the best quality. By 1879 the Apache received 1,100 head and by 1921, 5,000 head. At the same time, the question of driveways through the Indian reservations for Anglo sheep and cattle ranchers became a heated topic. While the Apaches brought different sensibilities to cattle ranching and practiced it in nuanced ways that reflected their own understanding of and relationship with the land, their participation in grazing inevitably led to continued destruction of their environment.[25]

TWO PERSPECTIVES ON THE CLIFF DWELLINGS

It is difficult to know what the Tonto cliff dwellings and other archeological sites meant to the local people of central Arizona. To judge by the situation elsewhere in the Southwest, the dwellings were probably regarded by some as sacred and meaningful, by others as a curiosity that distinguished the area, and by still others as a place to augment personal collections on a first-come, first-serve basis. Two excerpts from writings about the cliff dwellings offer distinct perspectives. The first is a diary entry by a teacher about a class trip to the ruins in the 1880s that reveals her response to the cliff dwellings and their contents.

The diary entry is by Angeline Brown, a teacher in the Tonto Basin. On December 12, 1880, the 26-year-old teacher traveled with her six pupils to the cliff dwellings. The trip proved to be "far superior" to what she had anticipated and "worth the trouble." Her description is worth quoting at length, for it is the earliest written description of the cliff dwellings so far discovered:

> The dwelling is built of small rocks laid up in cement and is cemented inside and out and sets well back beneath an overhanging rock. This rock is I should think about 100 feet high and curves over something like this [referring to her drawing]. We found traces of 33 rooms and some 18 of them are in fair preservation. It has been seven or eight stories high or perhaps more I should think judging from the poles still clinging high up to the rock: There was originally no opening in the outer wall but

the dwellers in the house climbed up a ladder of some sort and went in at the second story, as the Zunis and kindred tribes do yet! One room is walled solidly up without any door opening into it—of course—one can enter it now from above for the ceiling is partly fallen in—another had had a door originally but for some reason the people living there decided to close that room also and so smoothly and well was the work done that not a trace of any doorway having ever been there can be seen from outside the room, but inside of it one can easily see the rocks filling in the doorway laid up in cement but not cemented over on this side. When the ceiling of this room was intact—after the door was walled up—it must have been nearly air tight and one wonders why it was done—it is located in a rather central situation in the second story. One can conjecture several reasons: it may have been to hide treasure, to hide a crime, to punish a criminal or for several other reasons. In one room in the first story a Mr. Danforth (I think is the name) two years ago this winter found the skeleton of an infant in the wall about four feet from the floor—or possibly a little less, I saw the place today. The child was wrapped in many folds of a silky looking cotton cloth—like some we found in the same room—with a kind of drawn work pattern in small diamonds and stars and had shredded bark in its mouth and ear holes, or rather leather like ears, for it was dried like a mummy, and sandals of yucca fiber on its feet made like a pair we dug from another part of the ruin only very much smaller. There were some turquoise and red pipe clay beads, clay doll and dog toys, and bone ornaments with it and a number of other trifles.

In several places are prints of fingers or of the hand—complete and perfect as the day ages ago when the hands were pressed into the plastic clay. There is much to be seen in the building that I've not time to speak of. One ought to stay a week to explore it if they hope to satisfy their curiosity.

It seemed strange to be chatting and laughing so gaily in a house built unknown centuries ago by people unlike us in appearance but who had known joy and grief, pleasure and pain, same as our race of today knows them and who had laughed, cried, sung, danced, married and died, mourned or rejoiced their lives away in this once populous town or castle or whatever one would call it! It made an "uncanny" feeling come over us as we rested till moonrise and talked of this long dead people and told the little we knew concerning them, but my children are a courageous crowd and tho' they ranged in age from 6 to 14 they never dreamed of being afraid. By and by the moon rose and softened the marks of time on the scarred, weather stained cliff dwellings till it was beautiful. Then, presently, we descended the mountain and getting into our saddles started home to Armer, reaching there about 9:30, tired but happy.[26]

It's unknown whether Angeline Brown or her students kept the pieces of cotton cloth and other artifacts they "found" in the cliff dwellings. What is known from her description is the condition of the dwellings in 1880, as her diary predates even Bandelier's description, hitherto thought to be the first. She indicates that the dwellings were in a precarious state, as her account notes that one of the children fell through a roof into a lower room piled high with cholla. Her diary entry reveals her sensitivity to the ruins, the care she took in recording its details, and the feelings she and her students shared as they contemplated their connection to long-ago residents. The reader gets a sense that Angeline Brown communicated to her students the qualities of this unique setting, connecting their story to the universality of human emotions in a very respectful way. Her diary gives a glimpse into the experiences people have at archeological ruins, connecting her to the past, and us to her.

Angeline Brown kept her diary for personal reasons, so it is unlikely that anyone beyond her acquaintance became aware of her experience of the cliff dwellings. The next to write about them was Bandelier, whose 1883 description was published in 1892 for the Archeological Institute of America (quoted in chapter 1, page 17.)

The second excerpt is from someone who became personally acquainted with the Tonto cliff dwellings at the turn of the century. James H. McClintock published newspapers in Phoenix, Prescott, Globe, Tempe, and Tucson, and served as editorial representative in Arizona for the *Los Angeles Times*. Enthusiastic about archeology and folklore, McClintock traveled and researched the territory. In an article in the *Arizona Graphic* on February 24, 1900, McClintock described the Tonto cliff dwellings as "an ancient Gibraltar," and gave the following description.

Near the headwaters of the Salt River of Arizona, in southern Tonto Basin, far up the steep western side of a deep gorge in a spur of the Superstition Range, is a group of cliff dwellings known to few save cowboys and prospectors, unmarked on any Smithsonian Institution map. The ruins may best be reached from Globe, thirty miles distant.

They lie a little north of east of Phoenix, seventy miles away, and about four miles from the Salt River, and its fringe of small irrigated farms. Locally the valley of the cliff dwellers is unnamed, save when referred to as "the big canyon back o'Pemberton's." There is little trouble in reaching the caves. Yet at the journey's end is a sharp climb up the cholla-strewn hillside, leaving the ponies in the shade of a solitary cottonwood in the creek bed far below.

There are two main "dwellings," either a very pueblo in size and fit in its day to house a regiment. They are about a half mile apart, wholly unattached, and separated by a deep side canyon.

The lower ruin is the smaller, but the better preserved of the two. The material used in its construction was a cement, made from the sedimentary or "hydraulic" lime of the region, moulded roughly into walls from eight to sixteen inches thick, each wall irregularly pierced with many small portholes or windows. In dimensions, the fortress well filled a shell-like open cave, 140 feet long, 40 feet in greatest depth and 30 feet in extreme height. Much of the exterior wall is gone, but enough is left to show that it was built upon the very edge of the cave ledge, above a sheer descent of twenty or more feet, now partially bridged with debris, but once unscalable. The face of the building was, undoubtedly, door-less, entrance being effected by ladders from the end of a narrow trail that yet is visible, worn deep by moccasined feet. But no ladders are necessary now. Past the little dooryard, where the feet of the ladder once rested, through a great gap that Time has made, access is easy into the innermost recesses of the ancient citadel, for within are many doorways though rarely over three feet in height. In three or four places the doorways were found closed by rough bricks of sun-dried clay, evidently of more modern emplacement.

The building is three-floored, even now. The ground floor, littered with the rubbish of centuries, is yet eight feet high. The second, evidently the main floor, had a twelve foot ceiling. From the roof floor, which I reached with little difficulty, I could touch the cave roof at front and rear. Here it was, without a doubt, that the primitive home guard peered over the low parapet that crowned the outer wall, and here, in comparative light, the baby Toltec of yore had his playground, after resting hours in the gloomy fortress depth below.[27]

McClintock's account also provides a sense of the vandalism that preceded his trip yet left still-plentiful evidence of pottery in the ruins.

The vandal has been before us in "the big canyon o' Pemberton's." Many of the rooms were roof-less, the cypress rafters burned away, blackened holes showing where once they had set in the walls. But the flames, through semi-carbonization, had to a measure assisted in the preservation of a part of the cave's contents. In the dry earth upon the floor we found half-burned corn cobs, mixed with broad bean pods and bits of fibre that showed that farthest back on the right, had plainly been the granary. In the next room were found several water tanks, excavated from the conglomerate rock of the hill.

Pottery there was, by the wagon load. Not a piece of it was whole. There were a half dozen corn mortars (metates) and a number of stone implements. The ornamentation of the pottery found compared more nearly than any I have ever seen from other cliff dwellings to the markings of the pottery of the valleys of the lower Salt and Gila, about Los Muertos, where Cushing dug, and at famous Casa Grande. There were the same terrace designs, jagged lightning flashes and twice-broken "life lines" (signifying nourishment) that distinguished the ware left by the plains dweller who built cities and dug great canals on the lower "deserts," and who is termed "Toltec" in the books of the ethnologist.[28]

McClintock took trips to the cliff dwellings to satisfy his interest in archeology. But he also traveled to the vicinity in an expedition sent out by Maricopa County to find potential reservoir sites for a dam.

DAM BUILDERS IN THE TONTO BASIN

While ranching caused long-term environmental change in the Tonto Basin during the last decades of the nineteenth century, construction of Roosevelt Dam, five miles from the cliff dwellings, caused an abrupt transformation in the first decade of the twentieth century.

During the dam's long construction period, from 1903 to 1911, several boomtowns sprang up to accommodate the laborers and engineers. Livingston was a tent-house community for Reclamation Service engineers and office personnel in 1903–1905. It arose 8 miles north of the dam site and close to one of the first construction projects, a dam that diverted water to a power canal to generate hydroelectric power during construction. The town of Roosevelt, three-quarters of a mile upstream from the dam, accommodated more than 2,000 people by 1907. Government Hill housed government employees; O'Rourke's Camp, on the north side of the river, accommodated laborers in tents and a boarding house. In 1908, the new Lake Roosevelt began to fill

Figure 15: The main street in Roosevelt, 1907

behind the rising dam, and the town of Roosevelt moved upriver. Once dam construction was completed, the workers left; M. C. Webb and his son, Cone, bought most of O'Rourke's Camp and created a resort called Hotel Point, featuring the Apache Hotel for tourists.[29]

Ironically, the massive dam project created a situation in the Tonto Basin that finally created some benefits for the Apache. The federal policies of extermination, removal, subjugation, and integration that reigned from 1860 to 1885 were radically challenged and revised in the face of severe labor shortages encountered during the federal government's efforts to begin construction. Louis Hill, the supervising engineer, was warned against hiring Apaches, but in desperation took a chance that they could contribute. The Apaches performed a variety of jobs, including quarrying rock, digging canals, erecting power lines, and working the cement mill. Their most prized skill was their ability to lay and fit rock without mortar, which was required for constructing road embankments through the rugged terrain of what became known as the Apache Trail. As many as 1,500 Apache laborers and their families left the

Figure 16: View of the Apache Lodge Hotel on the shore of Roosevelt Lake, 1916. Courtesy Denver Public Library, Western History Collection, H. C. Tibbits, Z–586.

San Carlos Reservation to live in camps near Roosevelt. This migration left a void at the San Carlos Reservation, previously home to 2,275 people in 1903, which had to be filled by Mexican laborers while the Apaches worked on the dam.[30] According to oral histories about the Apache work camps, Hill enabled them to live in their traditional ways, with their nuclear families and among extended family groups. He allowed them to share jobs and remain relatively free from intervention. The archeologists and historians who researched and documented this labor arrangement characterize the situation as follows:

> In the midst of one of the most elaborate engineering projects of the time, the Apaches, paradoxically, seem to have been temporarily sheltered from the bureaucratic attacks of the Office of Indian Affairs and the

onrushing twentieth century. For a short time, the Apaches were allowed to live more as Apache than they could have on a reservation.[31]

The extent to which the Apaches used the cliff dwellings for any purpose is not clear, but they referred to them as "The Rock House Packed Together."[32]

One curious—even bizarre—note concerning the impact of dam construction on the cliff dwellings was found on a card dated September 10, 1954, in a file of information about Tonto National Monument history found in the basement of the monument in 2005. While the information is not verified, it is worth citing what Aaron J. Cosner, a tour leader at Tonto, wrote at the time:

> Thaddeus T. Frazier of Roosevelt stated that about the year 1910 an engineer employed on Roosevelt Dam used dynamite to blow out the front walls of both upper and lower ruins.
>
> Mr. Frazier further stated that the artifacts he secured at that time were only in his possession for a short while. As a government employee [sic] he was forced to surrender them to the Smithsonian Institution where they now presumably are.
>
> This information was given to Tour Leader Aaron J. Cosner, who at once advised Mr. Dale King of the matter. There is some hope of the eventual return of these artifacts to Tonto N.M.[33]

Of course, the principal impact on the cliff dwellings was from the creation of the lake that backed up behind the new dam. It is an unsettling irony that, at the same time that the cliff dwellings were declared worthy of national monument status, hundreds of archeological sites in the river bottom below were inundated by the rising water, forever burying the broader historical basis for understanding the celebrated dwellings perched above.

---

1. Sowards (1997, 10–16).
2. Wood, McAllister, and Sullivan (1990, 16).
3. Soward (1997), chapter 1. See Redman (1993) for Shoofly Village archeology and its relationship to Tonto Basin.
4. John (1989, 50). Elizabeth A. H. John's *Storms Brewed in Other Men's Worlds: the Confrontation of Indians, Spanish, and French in the Southwest 1540-1795* is a good source of information on this general subject.
5. Kroeber (1964, 124 and 135).
6. Miles and Mechula (1997, 14).
7. Wood (1990, 35).

8. Basso (1996, 5) and Coder et al. (n.d.)

9. Basso (1971) and (1983) are good sources of information on the Western Apache. Miles and Mechula (1997) offer the story from the San Carlos Apache perspective.

10. Gila Centennials Inc. (1976) is a good source of information on the shift from silver to copper mining in the Globe area.

11. Barbour (1999, 8 and 9).

12. LeCount (2003, 13–14).

13. Croxen (1926) Croxen was district ranger of the Mazatzal District at Tonto Basin and the Payson District from 1910 through 1930.

14. Ibid.

15. LeCount (2003), p. 13

16. Lauver (1938, 27–28). Lauver cites the figures for cattle on Arizona ranges as 30,000 in 1879, 142,000 in 1880, and 502,000 in 1886. She also discusses the impact of holding some range in reserve for drought years and how this was detrimental to all conditions as a result of the 1892–1893 droughts (p. 145).

17. Cited in Antle (1992).

18. Cited in Rowley (1985, 16).

19. Lauver (1938, 150–153).

20. Sowards (1997, 14–27). For literature on the wet-dry cycle in the American Southwest see Pyne (1982).

21. Holsinger (1902, 24).

22. Ibid. (1902, 25).

23. Cohoon (1904, 15–16).

24. Lauver (1938, 151).

25. Iverson (1994) provides the story of "when Indians became cowboys."

26. Brown (1880, n.p.).

27. McClintock (1900, n.p.).

28. Ibid. McClintock published a similar description of the cliff dwellings in 1916 in volume 1 of his three on Arizona, (see McClintock 1916, pp. 14–15).

29. Rogge et al. (1995, 31–46).

30. Ibid., pp. 143, 136.

31. Ibid., pp. 147–48.

32. Ibid., p. 162.

33. Old accession cards and some survey notes, TNM file box.

chapter three

THE EARLY YEARS OF TONTO NATIONAL MONUMENT: THE FOREST SERVICE ERA 1907-1933

The early days of Tonto cliff dwellings' official existence were marked by ambitious, even noble, intentions—and distinctly limited resources. When, on December 19, 1907, Theodore Roosevelt proclaimed the Tonto cliff dwellings "of great ethnologic, scientific and educational interest," he added that "the public interests would best be promoted by reserving these relics of a vanished people as a National Monument with as much land as may be necessary for the proper protection thereof."[1] Roosevelt backed that sentiment with a warning. Unauthorized persons were advised not to "appropriate, excavate, injure or destroy any of the prehistoric ruins or remains thereof declared to be a National Monument, or to locate or settle upon any of the lands reserved and made a part of said monument by this Proclamation."[2] This was the official fanfare afforded the nation's seventh national monument, after Devils Tower, Wyoming; El Morro, New Mexico; Montezuma Castle, Arizona; Petrified Forest, Arizona; Chaco Canyon, New Mexico; and Gila Cliff Dwellings, New Mexico.

Such a stern presidential proclamation might suggest that the newly created U.S. Department of Agriculture, Bureau of Forestry would be equipped for and charged with documenting the ethnologic and educational import of the cliff dwellings, and with setting the boundaries of the new Tonto National Monument with signage, fencing, and patrols. But this was not to be. As noted in chapter 1, Edgar Hewett expressed optimism in 1906 about safeguards protecting antiquities and claimed that the ruins were under the efficient custodianship of forest rangers with the

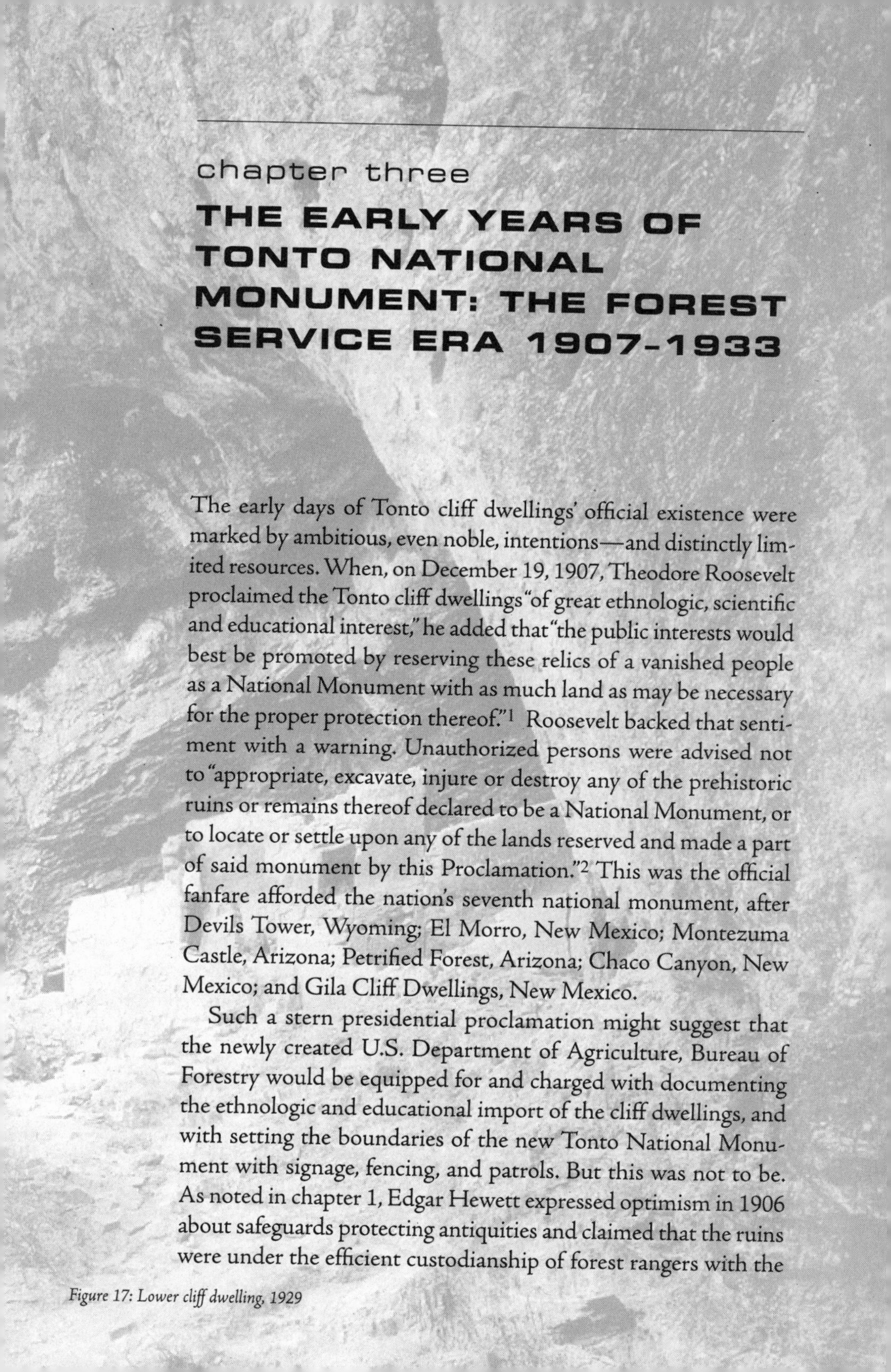

Figure 17: Lower cliff dwelling, 1929

power to arrest offenders. Hewett also assured his readers that excavations would be conducted only for the advancement of archeology and not for commercial purposes, and that collection of artifacts would be permitted only for permanent preservation in public museums. Unfortunately, no funds for staff or equipment accompanied the designation of the Tonto cliff dwellings as a national monument. Forest Service rangers were not trained to study or understand the cliff dwellings, nor equipped to protect them. In fact, their territories were vast; it would have been impossible to attend to the needs of visitors to the national monument or to protect the cliff dwellings. The rhetoric soared far above the reality.

The reality was that the Forest Service rangers were unable to adequately patrol and protect the cultural resources on Forest Service lands. Instead, other and more powerful interests determined how the watershed, the forest, and the monument within the forest were used and protected. For example, the Southern Pacific Railroad wanted to expand services and facilities for tourists, and it was in the company's interest to enable visitors to travel the Apache Trail and visit the cliff dwellings. Farmers in the Salt River Valley wanted to limit grazing upstream in the Tonto Basin to prevent erosion and silting, which they believed would degrade the quality of the water flowing downstream and thus threaten the long-term effectiveness of their new dam. Cattle ranchers wanted to continue grazing in the newly proclaimed Tonto Reserve, but to prevent access for sheep. The main role of the forest reserve during this early period—in keeping with the official "multiple-use" approach to managing lands reserved as forests—was to play referee.

The result was that from 1907 to 1933 no fencing marked the boundaries of Tonto National Monument, no known attempts were made to stabilize the ruins, and nobody kept the cows out. There were a series of dramatic clashes—between cattle and sheep ranchers, Tonto Basin ranchers and Salt River Valley farmers, and the Department of Agriculture and the Department of the Interior—but no documentation to show that any attention was paid to preservation. In 1934, when the National Park Service inherited responsibility for the monument, it also inherited the often contradictory perceptions and practices established between 1907 and 1933 that directly affected the condition of the cliff dwellings and the land area of the monument. National Park Service administrators could not provide immediate solutions: it took them until 1941 to procure funds to begin fencing, and until 1975 to eliminate grazing.

Figure 18: *Eastern entrance to the Apache Trail.* Courtesy Denver Public Library, Western History Collection, H. C. Tibbits, Z– 5846.

RAILS: THE SOUTHERN PACIFIC PROMOTES TOURISM TO THE TONTO BASIN

If Roosevelt was in fact as moved by the beauty of the Apache Trail as he said in 1911 after dedicating the dam, it is clear why the Southern Pacific added the Apache Trail to their list of places that travelers on the Sunset should visit. In characteristic hyperbolic style, Roosevelt said:

> The Apache Trail combines the grandeur of the Alps, the glory of the Rockies and the magnificence of the Grand Canyon, and then adds an undefinable mysterious something that none of the others has. To me it is the most awe-inspiring and sublimely beautiful panorama that nature has ever created.[3]

Second only to vandalism, the Southern Pacific had the greatest impact on the cliff dwellings during the Forest Service tenure because it launched a myriad of projects to transport and accommodate tourists to national parks and monuments. But the story is much bigger than transportation and tourists. The Southern Pacific was in the business of developing the West.

There was nothing new in the Southern Pacific Railroad's promotion of a national monument and nothing new in its partnership with a federal agency to promote tourism. To the contrary, the national railroads were partners in promoting the establishment of the national parks, the National Park System, and the National Park Service. The Northern Pacific Railway was the first railroad company to promote a national park, beginning in the 1880s with its Yellowstone Park Line and in the 1890s with its subsidies for rooms, dining facilities, and lobbies for socializing and dancing. The Atchison, Topeka & Santa Fe Railway followed Northern Pacific's example, encouraging the establishment of the Grand Canyon Forest Reserve in 1906 and Grand Canyon National Park in Arizona in 1919, as well as supporting construction of El Tovar and other structures at the Grand Canyon. The Great Northern Railway's "See America First" campaign was instrumental in the establishment of Glacier National Park in Montana in 1910. The Southern Pacific was an instrumental force in the development of national parks on the West Coast.[4]

The story that follows relies on information about how the Southern Pacific operated elsewhere to promote tourism to national parks and monuments; articles written for general audiences in its widely circulated magazines encouraging tourism; and information from early National Park Service administrators about the buildings, roads, and fences constructed by Southern Pacific that they inherited when they took over administration of Tonto National Monument.[5]

Between the 1880s and early 1900s, the Southern Pacific's passenger department emerged as a key engine for increasing company revenues from tourism while introducing potential residents to life in California, the Northwest, and the Southwest. The department published attractive booklets, maps, pamphlets, magazines, and books promoting travel, farming, and home-buying. In 1898, the department launched *Sunset* magazine, named after its overland train, the Sunset Limited, operating between New Orleans and Los Angeles. Volume 1, number 1 was dedicated to Yosemite. Subsequent monthly volumes promoted recreational opportunities, cooperative colonies, natural resource conservation, the creation of a national park movement, and the preservation of southwestern cultures and heritage. It was a convenient and powerful publicity machine for the Southern Pacific. In typically dramatic prose, it described the luxurious Sunset Limited as

> the most perfect example of the luxury of modern railway travel. Equipment consists of Composite Buffet Library Car, Ladies' Compartment

Figure 19: Southern Pacific Railroad brochure for the Apache Trail, 1924

and Parlor Car, elegant Double Drawingroom, [*sic*] Sleeping Cars and Dining Car. It is broad vestibuled throughout, gas lighted and steam heated, and runs solid from ocean to ocean.[6]

The Southern Pacific owned the Hotel Del Monte in Monterrey, California, and had working relations with other luxury hotels to accommodate train passengers in San Diego, Santa Barbara, Pasadena, Long Beach, and Los Angeles. Headquartered in a Mission Revival–style building, *Sunset* magazine featured naturalist writers, poets, novelists, and other aspiring writers and graphic designers, many of whom adhered to Progressive political and social values and conservationist impulses, and who expressed enthusiastic support for national parks and monuments. *Sunset's* coverage of the cornucopia offered by California's soil and climate was a staple of the magazine in its first two decades, with detailed success stories of ranching; sheep raising; rice farming; and the cultivation of prunes, olives, nuts, and citrus orchards. The magazine absorbed *Pacific Monthly*, which covered Oregon, Washington, Idaho, and Alaskan agricultural enterprises. In addition, the magazine inaugurated a home seekers' bureau and published local promotional pamphlets for counties, towns, and chambers of commerce throughout California, Nevada, and Arizona.

As part of its campaign to encourage western tourism and settlement, the Southern Pacific began to offer information and trips via the Apache Trail, including a stop at the Tonto cliff dwellings. In 1906, the company created a committee to name points of interest on the Apache Trail, and selected Sharlot Hall to head the panel, visit the trail, and decide upon "authentic and appropriate" place-names.[7]

There is insufficient documentation to explain the origins of the partnership between the U.S. Forest Service and the Southern Pacific Railroad—for instance, whether the Forest Service invited the company to partner with the agency or vice-versa. Nor is it known if the two entered into agreements setting the parameters for what the Southern Pacific could and could not do on monument acreage. But it is likely that the Forest Service welcomed what the company could provide: a custodian, on-site housing for the custodian, roads, trails, parking facilities, and fences. These afforded the government agency the ability to protect the monument while providing access and facilities for tourists.

By modern standards, the railroad provided highly limited access and facilities. In 1910, someone traveling between Globe and Phoenix could only travel three times a week. The trip required booking a stage ride with the OK

Figure 20: Southern Pacific brochure promoting side trip to the Tonto Cliff Dwellings

Daily Sleeper Service
APACHE TRAIL

STARTING at Globe the Apache Trail winds for 120 miles through the most interesting part of Arizona to Phoenix, the state capital. The trip over the Apache Trail highway offers the traveler a delightful break in the transcontinental journey over Southern Pacific's Sunset or Golden State Routes. The highway, which follows the old trail used by the Apache Indians during their centuries of warfare against the citizenry and soldiery of Spain, Mexico and the United States, is broad and smooth. The fine new motor stages are designed for comfort.

Here's what one writer said about the Apache Trail:

"If you've been fortunate enough to find the Apache Trail in the course of a transcontinental journey you'll think of it as something that rested because it was so entirely different from anything you'd ever seen before and because there your consciousness awakened to the reality of what you might have heard about or read about the 'lure' of the southwest."

The Apache Trail trip follows step by step the great reclamation project which began with the construction of the Roosevelt Dam (which the traveler has an opportunity to examine) has been followed by the construction of two other dams, the creation of three lakes and the conversion of 240,000 acres of desert into a garden of great and varied productiveness. Dams, Lakes and the Salt River Valley, are all on the Apache Trail trip.

The traveler also may see at Globe and Miami the great mines and smelters operated by power generated by the flow of water over the three dams. Along the trail is the strangest vegetation in America. Cactus of many varieties including the cholla, into which Apaches used to throw their captives, the Ocotillo or candlewood, and the giant sahuaro whose moisture has saved many an adventurer from death by thirst, whose thorns make practical phonograph needles and whose ribs furnished laths to the prehistoric builders whose cliff dwellings, occupied 2000 years ago, are among the interesting things you will see along the trail.

There are real Apaches on the trail and some of the famous battlegrounds of the bad old days.

The trail, always beautiful, is always interesting and has something for everybody, so you can make no mistake about routing passengers this way. It adds only a day to the transcontinental trip and immeasurably to its enjoyment.

WM. SPROULE
Traffic Mgr. S.P.-Streamship Lines (Atlanta Line)
New York, N.Y.

E. W. CLAPP, Traffic Manager
Chicago, Ill.

C. S. FAY
Traffic Mgr. Louisiana Lines
New Orleans, La.

J. T. MONROE
General Passenger Agent
New Orleans, La.

F. C. LATHROP
Asst. Pass. Traffic Manager
San Francisco, Cal.

C. K. DUNLAP
Traffic Manager Texas Lines
Houston, Texas

JOHN M. SCOTT
Asst. Pass. Traffic Manager
Portland, Ore.

H. LAWTON
Traffic Manager Mexican Lines
Guaymas, Mex.

W. C. McCORMICK
General Passenger Agent
Houston, Tex.

C. L. McFATE
Asst. Pass. Traffic Manager
Los Angeles, Cal.

F. S. McGINNIS, Passenger Traffic Manager
San Francisco, Cal.

Southern Pacific Lines

Livery Stable that left Globe at five o'clock and making a train connection at Kelvin. With the construction of roads for the Roosevelt Dam, entrepreneurs, including the Gila Valley Auto Transfer Company and the Globe-Phoenix Stage Company, began offering additional auto line services. Around the same time, the Southern Pacific Railroad wanted to stimulate traffic for its New Orleans–to–Los Angeles Sunset Route; it devised a plan to enable east and westbound passengers to take a rail-auto' detour from the main line to visit Globe, the Tonto cliff dwellings, the Roosevelt Dam, and Phoenix. The plan involved contracting with the Globe-Phoenix Stage line so that rail patrons arriving in Globe would be taken in seven-passenger automobiles to the Roosevelt Dam, the cliff dwellings, and Phoenix. Once in Phoenix, they boarded the train for Maricopa and reconnected with the Los Angeles train. The detour took eight hours and cost fifteen dollars. In 1915, the Southern Pacific began calling the route the "Apache Trail," and they advertised it heavily for the next thirty years, including at least a dozen editions of advertising folders in print runs of 50,000 each, plus one promoting the Apache Lodge. The brochures, complete with photographs, maps, prices, and information on accommodations, sometimes recruited nationally recognized graphic designers for covers or inside illustrations.[8]

For passengers, this was still the Wild West. Articles in *Sunset* between the years 1912 and 1940 give a glimpse of how the railroad made passengers feel safe about venturing through "Apache country," while portraying side trips to the Roosevelt Dam and the cliff dwellings as a once-in-a-lifetime adventure. "The only foes we have are the big mosquitos of the mesa, Apaches of the air!" expressed one author in 1912 when chronicling the first tourist automobile train from New York to Los Angeles. After making sure readers understood there was no danger from attacking Indians, the article went on to describe "one of the great automobile rides of the world," and encouraged them to "brave any desert with your car to reach this stretch; it's worth it."[9]

A 1916 *Sunset* article, "Through Apache Land: Riding on Rubber Tires over Geronimo's Trail," reveals that the railroad apparently still felt it necessary to make travelers feel safe about taking the trip. It uses the ruminations of a cattleman who answers questions posed by two women from Vermont traveling on the trail. The cattleman allays fears by saying

> I was just thinking how funny 'twas that you two ladies can go traipsin' right along the Apache Trail and pick posies on the stompin' ground of old Geronimo. Queer, ain't it, to see the bucks in overalls running the business end of a scraper, buildin' roads an' ditches where they used to

raise seventy different kinds of assorted hell? ... No, they won't hurt you; they'll eat outen your hand now. Trouble with the gov'ment or the settlers? Bless your heart, ma'am, ain't the blackest of Geronimo's black sheep fightin' right now with the soldier boys across the line? Ain't they been buildin' the biggest part of the big dam we're comin' to by-'n'-by? Why, nowadays you're safer on the San Carlos Reservation right in the heart of the Gila Valley among the Apaches than you are on Broadway, Los Angeles, dodgin' wild-eyed jitneys an' cowboys from the movies![10]

But the magazine was apparently less insistent upon historical accuracy. In 1916, another article used an already discredited notion of how and when the cliff dwellings were constructed and inhabited:

Long, long before the first pyramid was built; before Nebuchadnezzar reigned in wicked Babylon; long, long before the first prophet rose in Israel, eight, ten thousand years ago. In all Europe, in all Asia and Africa there has been found no relic of the Morning of Time, no habitation dating as far back in the unrecorded history of the human race as the ruins of the homes built by the vanished Little People of the mystic Southwest.

All of this could be reached "comfortably and inexpensively by the average traveler."[11]

This suggestion of ancient ruins, in a sense "classicizing" the site and its makers, was typical of a time when people thought of the ruins of the Southwest as equivalent to those of Greek, Roman, and biblical heritages. In addition, it distanced the ruins from having any connection to contemporary Indians.

By 1918 it was no longer necessary to make travelers feel safe. An article that year, titled "On the Warpath for Fun," compared the original cliff dwellers and the later inhabitants. After describing the civilization that constructed the chain of canals and cliff dwellings as bringing a "jewel of civilization" to a marvelous setting, the author expresses racial stereotypes, then acceptable, that today would be considered as outrageous as this writer's cosmology:

Savage tribal creatures who turned the cliff citadels into fortresses, who laid waste the fields, watering them no longer except with the blood of their enemies, and who inaugurated among the colorful peaks an era of warfare so cunning, relentless, and altogether barbarous as to set the whole world aghast. The Apaches! They outraged every tradition, every

Map of

Apache Trail Highway

Figure 21: Illustrated map of the Apache Trail Highway

aspiration of their vanished predecessors. It was as though they became the forced instrument of the devil himself to reverse the immeasurably uplifting influence of their natural surroundings.[12]

In 1926, another *Sunset* article extended an invitation to treasure-hunters:

In the little town of Roosevelt everybody is an archeologist of sorts. Excavating ruined pueblos in this part of Arizona is an exclusive privilege of the Smithsonian Institution and of those authorized by that august and useful organization. When the water in the lake is low, however, anybody so inclined has been allowed to dig among such ruins as lie below the normal high water line. Roosevelt's archeological interest was born when one of its residents, out trolling on the lake for black bass, sighted the head of a pottery duck sticking out of the bank near the lake edge. The duck, an ancient lamp, and a vase of graceful line rewarded

*T*HE side trip over The Apache Trail highway between Globe and Phoenix, Arizona, is a delightful one-day break in the transcontinental journey. Comfortable motor coaches, with roofs that can be opened to give passengers an unobstructed view of the spectacular mountain scenery, travel over the fine road which follows the old trail of the Apaches, through a region famous for scenic and historic interest. Giant Roosevelt Dam, Roosevelt Lake and three other great dams and lakes lie along the route. A feature of the regular trip is the visit to the prehistoric Tonto Cliff Dwellings with an Apache guide.

a few minutes digging. A few weeks later "a gentleman from New York" offered the finder $300 for one of these prehistoric pots and the town of Roosevelt went archeology-delirious. Men, women, and children soon were digging among the ruins that lie below the high water mark.[13]

It is beyond the scope of this administrative history to assess how these articles shaped the perceptions of visitors to the Tonto Basin, the Roosevelt Dam, and the cliff dwellings, but it seems probable that the language promoted and reinforced respect for the "original" cliff-dwelling civilization and the dam-building civilization, while displaying contempt for the contemporary "barbarous" Apache.

Once the Southern Pacific Railroad began promoting this form of tourism, it also had to make decisions about the preservation of and access to the cliff dwellings. Although the promotional efforts never attracted large numbers of visitors, those that did come needed paths to the dwellings as well as other facilities. In 1929 the Southern Pacific graded a road from the highway to a large parking area at the mouth of Cholla Canyon and constructed a trail to the ruins from that point and a large pit toilet. That same year they hired Ray Stevens, an Apache from the San Carlos Reservation, as caretaker. Someone from their advertising and promotion department also installed signposts to features on the monument, which "were in the form of an Apache's head which was pointed at the feature and, on the steel post, a rectangular sign to give the name this opium smoker had dreamed."[14] In 1932 the Southern Pacific expanded the facilities and added new ones, including a bridge and road to go farther up the canyon, a parking area, a caretaker's lodge, and a trail to the lower ruin. Each of the ruins was surrounded with a woven wire fence with locked gates.[15] From comparing photographs, we know that a lower cliff dwelling wall collapse occurred during the period of Forest Service administration.[16] Ray Stevens worked for the Southern Pacific for two years, then was succeeded by several other Apache custodians. The Southern Pacific paid them thirty dollars a month and provided housing. The stone caretaker's lodge was about 17 feet long, 8 feet wide, and had a fireplace and piped water. Although the stone building was built specifically for the caretaker, Ray Stevens built an adobe house in the arroyo just north of the housing provided by the Southern Pacific. Successive custodians also elected to live in the adobe, including Henry Padilla, who overlapped with the earliest NPS staff at the monument.[17] The stone lodge became the exhibit room when the National Park Service took over administration. The adobe became a tool and storage shed known as the Scorpion Shack.[18] There are no records indicating whether the Apache custodians who worked for the Southern Pacific interacted with visitors.

VANDALISM OF TONTO BASIN ANTIQUITIES

We can see from comparative photographs that the cliff dwellings suffered damage during the era of U.S. Forest Service administration. Evidence also comes from documentation left by Reverend Victor Stoner—a 1920 graduate of the University of Arizona in archeology who spent a day in 1935 checking drawings of the ruins that he had made in 1920—who reported that much damage had occurred in the intervening fifteen years. It is impossible to estimate the number of people who visited the cliff dwellings on Southern Pacific tours or to gauge their impact on the structural conditions and contents of the cliff dwellings. In fact, it is impossible to know the number of people who visited before the National Park Service gained administrative control in 1934.

Figure 22: *Two views of lower cliff dwelling, 1924*

What we do know is that, during the early twentieth century, a complex set of issues and behaviors controlled access to these and other antiquities.

Not all visitors treated archeological ruins with respect. For instance, Edgar Hewett's 1924 "Report on Illegal Excavations in Southwestern Ruins" suggested that, while the intent of the Antiquities Act was clear (making it a criminal offense to appropriate, excavate, injure, or destroy ruins and monuments), a lack of enforcement gave rise to illegal collecting in southwestern ruins. He suggested that residents of the Southwest considered it their "inalienable right" to dig for relics, and noted that "it is now extremely difficult to find a prominent ruin that has not been measurably mutilated." His report places much blame on the "Indian trader," whom he considers, "chiefly responsible for the present increasing traffic in artifacts from prehistoric ruins."[19]

Hewett was not alone in his concern. The American Anthropological Association appointed a committee to investigate illegal excavations in prehistoric ruins, because, as Hewett also noted, the illegal practices destroyed the evidence necessary for scientific investigation:

> That illicit digging in ancient ruins continues unchecked, especially throughout the southwestern United States, is well known to American anthropologists and others. Most of this vandalism is carried on in direct violation of the law, to judge solely by the clandestine methods pursued. The objects recovered find their way to dealers in curios and Indian artifacts and, ultimately, to individuals. In all such instances the related data are lost and the objects rendered useless for scientific purposes. Nearly every reservation trader is a primary aid to illegal traffic in American antiquities. These traders if not personally engaged in secret digging, encourage the Indians to do so through purchase of the objects recovered. Irreparable damage to the prehistoric ruins is the obvious result and the evidence upon which science depends is lost forever.

What was needed, he said, was enforcement of the law.

> As to the remedy: This committee is agreed that existing laws are entirely adequate to meet the conditions outlined above. The Act for the Preservation of American Antiquities, approved June 8, 1906 (34 Stat. L., 225) and the Rules and Regulations prescribed thereunder, clearly differentiate between legal and illegal excavations in prehistoric ruins and provide effective punishment for the latter. But the Act, if known, is generally ignored by those who profit through excavation and sale of American antiquities. Most ruins now subject to despolia-

tion lie within the Indian reservations in New Mexico and Arizona and on adjacent public lands, including those in southern Utah and southwestern Colorado. [20]

The committee recommended that superintendents of Indian reservations forward all antiquities that were illegally obtained to the national depository, that all traders cease traffic in antiquities, that copies of the rules and regulations of the Antiquities Act be posted throughout the Southwest, and that,

vandals, wherever found, should be effectively punished and collections illegally obtained should be confiscated. Otherwise there is but scant hope of realizing the clear intent of the Antiquities Act, namely, protection and preservation of that small portion of our once numerous prehistoric ruins still remaining under federal jurisdiction. The law stands but it is being constantly ignored, and with impunity.[21]

Not all the violators were strangers. In a survey on the archeology of Roosevelt Lake and the vicinity for the Bureau of American Ethnology, J. W. Simmons of Prescott, Arizona, documented that the custodian at Tonto National Monument was selling prehistoric pottery. It is unclear who was digging up the pottery and whether the pottery came from Tonto National Monument or from the surrounding Tonto Basin, but it is clear that illegal trafficking was taking place on Tonto National Monument property:

The Indian custodian at the Tonto Cliff dwellings was then visited where the pottery found by the Indians is sold to tourists at exhorbiant [sic] prices, the custodian acting as agt for the Indian diggers.

Only one B on White olla was seen, the balance having found a ready sale.

A mixed collection of 20 pieces, B on W, W on Red and plain food bowls had been sold to an El Centro, Calif. Man for $100.00. "I did not know their value at that time," was the custodian's comment on the sale.

A large number of smoke blackened food bowls remained on hand, also a few White on red on which the pigment had mostly disappeared. Also an intrusive little bowl from probably south of Holbrook.

About one dozen black food bowls had been reconstructed in such an amateurish fashion that the glue had spread all over the bowls which made them positively uninviting regardless of the price asked for them.

One set of 8 pieces consisting of two B on W pitchers, one B on W bowl, reconst. One red recurved olla and four good red bowls had been taken to Cottonwood, by a Camp Verde Indian.

For this set the custodian declared he could have received $150.00 dollars had they been left with him for sale.[22]

It is not possible to say whether the Forest Service or Southern Pacific was aware of the sale of antiquities at Tonto National Monument; however, the NPS superintendent of southwestern monuments in 1930 was aware of the situation. He noted that he was pleased that a complaint was going to be lodged about "the Indian who is in charge of the Tonto National Monument selling prehistoric pottery to visitors."[23]

RANCHING IN THE TONTO BASIN

The Southern Pacific Railroad operations clearly affected the archeological resources at Tonto National Monument, but the major environmental impact came from grazing. By the time of the designation of the Tonto National Forest in 1905 and the Tonto National Monument in 1907, the country had already undergone several decades of heated debate about whether the West's abundant natural resources should be in private or public hands. Meanwhile, environmental conditions on the western range had deteriorated, and dozens of bills had been offered in Congress to address both ownership and range conditions. Ranchers in the Tonto Basin area were outspoken participants in these issues. Their stock, which had previously grazed freely in the territory, became subject to regulations and fees when their grazing areas became part of the national forest. While ranchers bitterly fought these new restrictions, they gradually adjusted to a new era of collective decision-making about the best uses for the greatest good.[24]

Disagreements among sheep and cattle ranchers simmered through the mid to late-1800s, then erupted in the "Pleasant Valley Wars," which resulted in twenty-nine deaths by 1892. As this era receded, issues between the sheep and cattle ranchers were increasingly addressed not by violence-prone individuals but by bitterly opposed stock associations. The activities and influence of both the Arizona Wool Growers Association and the Arizona Cattlemen's Association grew after 1899, when the U.S. Department of the Interior threatened to exclude sheep from grazing on all forest reserves in Arizona. It seemed that the arguments over whether sheep or cattle did more damage to the soil and vegetation would be won by those who sided with John Muir's famous characterization of sheep as "hoofed locusts," but lobbyists from the Arizona Wool Growers Association and elsewhere fought to keep sheep on the land. Their cause was aided by the Bureau of Forestry's first grazing expert, Albert F. Potter, a Holbrook, Arizona rancher who ran both sheep and cattle and had worked closely with Chief Forester Gifford Pinchot. Potter convinced Pinchot that—Muir's influential view not withstanding—it could not be proved that sheep were more destructive than cattle.

Potter's opinions were respected by Arizona stockmen because they considered him to be well schooled and locally experienced. He argued that sheep and cattle could coexist if they were handled so that damage was minimized when sheep were moved between summer and winter ranges. He knew that, when bunched close together, sheep did more damage than when allowed to roam loose, and that cattle and sheep ranchers could work together effectively and minimize damage to the range if they could see the mutual benefits. As a result, at the turn of the twentieth century, the Black Mesa Forest Reserve allowed sheep grazing, while it was prohibited in other western reserves unless it could be shown that it would not interfere with timber supply and watershed conditions.[25]

In the spring of 1900, Pinchot toured the Mogollon Rim country, accompanied by members of the Arizona Wool Growers Association and the Salt River Valley Water Users' Association. Some among the party asserted that prompt action needed to be taken against grazing, which in their opinion, was threatening the forest's ability to store water for the territory. But Pinchot believed that careful regulation of sheep grazing, not total exclusion, would be sufficient. Pinchot and Potter, in turn, convinced President Roosevelt that a sheep ban in Tonto National Monument was unnecessary. Pinchot and Potter's pragmatism enabled access to the range by both cattle and sheep ranchers and supported the multiple-use approach to forest reserves.

The SRVWUA and the Reclamation Service entered the debate in 1905, both eager to prohibit grazing in the Tonto National Forest to protect irrigation in the valley below. Bureau of Forestry expert S. J. Holsinger paraphrased the farmers' and irrigationists' view of grazing, stating "every hoof which trods the range, and every mouth which crops the herbage or browses the foliage of shrub or tree is a distant enemy."[26] The SRVWUA proposed eliminating sheep grazing on Tonto to prevent overgrazing, which they believed threatened the watershed. But resolution wasn't going to be that simple. The sheep growers countered that all land without timber should be removed from the Tonto Reserve. Holsinger, whose job it was to weigh the demands on the forest reserve system, stressed the need for multiple uses and opposed an outright ban on sheep, suggesting that "it does not follow that the herd should be driven from the ranges" and called for "a careful study of the past and present conditions, cause and effect, in order that an equitable and economic balance be maintained."[27] He described that balance as "the status from which may be derived the greatest general good and the most substantial aid for conserving conditions most favorable to the greatest number of citizens, present and future." [28]

THE DEPARTMENT OF AGRICULTURE
VERSUS THE DEPARTMENT OF THE INTERIOR

Between 1907 and 1913, the challenges facing the Forest Service as it attempted to handle range conditions are reflected in correspondence among the secretary of the interior, the project director of the Interior Department Reclamation Service, the SRVWUA, and attorneys for the Department of Agriculture. The most daunting tasks were overcoming distrust between sheep and cattle ranchers, and between the Department of the Interior and the Department of Agriculture about who could best administer the Tonto Basin forest and grazing lands.[29]

The Department of Agriculture studied each of the national forests to determine timber resources, carrying capacity of the range, and suitability for cattle and sheep grazing. A. F. Potter and D. D. Bronson of the U.S. Forest Service, in cooperation with the Reclamation Service of the Department of the Interior, were assigned to the investigation. Gifford Pinchot wrote to the president of the SRVWUA in June 1908 about the need to study the situation:

> In all of these investigations the one object in view will be to protect the interests of the majority of the people, and the greatest care will be taken to cause no unnecessary injury to any minor interest. The results of these investigations will be made known as rapidly as possible. If the decision in any case shows that the grazing of sheep and goats or other livestock upon any particular area injures the water supply and does more harm than good, there will be no alternative but to carry out the law in the interest of the majority of the people, and for the development and welfare of the country.[30]

Potter and Bronson's study concluded that sheep had to be excluded from *some* parts of the forest. This meant Gifford Pinchot had to choose whether to protect the sheep industry, valued at $300,000, or the irrigation works of the Salt River Valley, valued at $6 million. Pinchot made his choice, and sheep were largely excluded from Tonto in 1909.[31]

The long-standing antagonism between the two federal departments over which would control the land—and indeed if government control was even appropriate—came to a head in the summer of 1913. At that time the Department of Agriculture came under criticism by stock growers for including unforested land in the national forests. In August 1913, the Assistant Secretary of the Department of Agriculture, Beverly Thomas Galloway, wrote a letter to the interior secretary, providing him a history of how and why the Tonto Forest was created:

At the time the Roosevelt Dam was projected, steps were taken to protect the large watersheds which drain into the main reservoir and the subsidiary works, such as diversion dams, canals, etc. It was realized that the water conserving powers of the drainage basins would have to be developed to the maximum; that every effort should be made to prevent torrential floods which would seriously damage the irrigation works; and that all possible precautions must be adopted to prevent erosion of the watersheds and the consequent accumulations of silt in the reservoirs and canals. There was no existing statute under which the Reclamation Service could directly accomplish these purposes and the act authorizing the creation of Forest Reserves offered the only means by which the project and its dependent interests could be adequately protected. The Forest Reserves were then under the administration of the General Land Office, and that bureau, presumably working in cooperation with the Reclamation Service, withdrew from all forms of homestead entry, large areas of land surrounding the headwaters of the Salt, Gila, and Verde Rivers and their tributaries.

On February 1, 1905, the administration of the National Forests was transferred to this department. The withdrawal from entry of the lands above mentioned was still effective, but no National Forests had been created to include the lands which in the opinion of the Reclamation Service should be retained and protected by the Federal Government. The Reclamation Service renewed its requests that the lands be included in National Forests, and subsequently the Tonto Forest was created to protect important parts of the Salt River drainage, and large additions were made to the Prescott Forest to protect the Granite Reef dam, the main canals of the project, and the interests of some small private irrigation enterprises dependent upon Cave Creek and other associated streams. These various additions to the National Forests were made between October 3, 1905, and October 7, 1910. [32]

Galloway noted that the Prescott and Tonto National Forests then contained two and a half million acres of land with no forest cover of commercial value but which were included to protect the Roosevelt project. He went on to assert why it would be wrong, as currently contemplated by the Department of the Interior, to return lands in the Tonto National Forest to public domain:

> The Roosevelt project represents so great an investment of public funds and the interests dependent upon it are of such magnitude that it would be wrong for the Federal Government to take any step which will endanger the success of the project or materially reduce its period of usefulness. At different times the elimination of these lands from the forests has received serious consideration but in each instance the water users who are dependent upon the projects protected, and the stock growers who have established themselves under the regulations of this department have protested warmly against an action which would hazard their interests and expose them to serious losses. [33]

Galloway also noted the impossibility of reforesting the lands already damaged by grazing, the difficulty of regulating use, and the heavy drain on the resources of the Forest Service caused by attending to conflicts among sheep, cattle, and irrigation interests. He added that the conflict

> presents many embarrassing problems of administration: and the inclusion within national forests of so large an acreage of land so obviously unfit for forest purposes exposes this department to a great deal of criticism, which is not wholly neutralized by the strong support given by the water users of the Salt River Valley. [34]

Essentially, Galloway was asking the Department of the Interior to understand how important it was for the federal government not to endanger the Roosevelt project, while also appreciating the concerns of the sheep and cattle ranchers when any actions were taken that could expose them to losses. Finally, Galloway wanted the secretary of the interior to decide whether the area should stay under federal administration, and if so, whether as part of the Department of Agriculture's national forest system:

> Inasmuch as these areas were included in the first instance on the initiation of the Reclamation Service, I would appreciate an expression of opinion from you whether you consider it necessary to retain the extensive area now included in the Tonto and Prescott Forests, for the protection of the irrigation projects of that section, and if so whether these lands should continue to be administered as a part of the National Forests.[35]

The position of the Department of Agriculture in favor of ending federal control is shown in a memorandum prepared by lawyers for the Department of Agriculture in December 1913. The document estimated the Tonto acreage at two and a half million and described it as devoid of forest cover of commercial value, unsuited for forest purposes, and impractical to reforest or attempt to reforest. The memo claimed that the original provision of the law authorizing the creation of forest reserves specifically required that the lands be wholly or in part covered with timber or undergrowth (which Tonto was not) and that the establishment of a forest reserve was primarily to protect the forest within the reserve. The memo argued that it was bad policy to withhold this vast area of land, and ended with a strong challenge to the SRVWUA and the Department of the Interior:

> Surely, the water users in the Roosevelt reclamation project, after having built for them by the government, at cost, this enormous and valuable irrigation and power plant, can not reasonable [sic] ask the United States to withhold from other citizens an area of two-and-a-half million acres simply because a little more silt will wash into the reservoir than might be the case if the lands were retained under government supervision. As to objections of the stock growers who, the Secretary of Agriculture says "have established themselves" upon the land, I submit that they naturally will object to the destruction of their monopoly because at present other livestock owners are debarred from the use of the lands and settlers can not enter thereupon. Personally, I believe the lands should be restored to the public domain, or, at least, that all of the area should be restored except comparatively small and limited areas [the word "areas" is changed to "amounts"] lying immediately adjacent to such water courses as connect with the government reservoirs or canals and may, therefore, be said to have a close and intimate connection with the use, protection, and control of these structures. Possibly, such a limited withdrawal may be made and maintained under the reclamation law.[36]

However confidently expressed, this Department of Agriculture view did not prevail. By November 1913, the secretary of the interior had already responded to the secretary of agriculture that all who investigated the matter concurred that the reservation of *all* the lands was essential to protect the works constructed by the Reclamation Service. He went on to note that the Interior Department could not withdraw the land for those purposes nor could it administer the land for those purposes, but if it were within his power to do so, he would relieve the Department of Agriculture of its difficulties. He also reported that Associate Forester Potter and A. P. Davis, chief engineer of the Reclamation Service, had decided in September that both cattle and sheep numbers would be reduced.[37]

The peculiar aspects of the creation of Tonto National Forest, the clashing views on federal control of the two relevant government departments, and the conflicting local views of how the land should be managed would resound for many years. In fact, they would not be fully resolved until 1974, when grazing on Tonto National Monument finally ended.

THE FOREST SERVICE RANGER: ON THE FRONT LINE BETWEEN POLICY AND PRACTICE

Once the Tonto National Forest was designated in 1905, the main resource available to users was a guidebook authored by the chief forester, Gifford Pinchot, which introduced the idea of the national forests, explained what they meant, defined what they were for, and provided guidelines on how to use them.[38] Pinchot's guidebook, tellingly titled *The Use of the National Forests*, began with an explanation of why the national forests were created and outlined arguments of those opposed to their creation. He recognized that mistakes had been made in the past when national forests were carelessly created without adequate examination of conditions or mapping. He addressed the common argument used against the national forests as places where the "resources of a region were at once locked up, industry checked, settlement prohibited, and future growth made impossible or very difficult."[39] But he countered by painting a picture of the homemaker, prospector, and miner as welcome, the timber and wood resources as available, the range as managed and accessible for livestock, and the flow of water made secure.

Pinchot's manual was one of many ways the Forest Service rangers combated the popular notion, especially in the West, that federal forests would exclude ranching, logging, mining, and settlement. On the contrary, as evidenced by the manual's title, multiple uses were encouraged, nurtured, and promoted—

including grazing, watershed protection, recreation, erosion control, and wildlife habitat. The U.S. Forest Service's mission was managing the forests for the permanent, most beneficial use by all the people.[40]

Before the Forest Service could do anything about addressing deteriorated soil, increased erosion, and generally degraded land conditions, it first had to overcome stockmen's resentment, particularly of the proposal to charge grazing fees. Longtime ranchers in the Tonto Basin were no exception to the national antagonism of stockmen toward the new rangers. They found new controls and fees unacceptable and, as John Cline, a longtime rancher, recalled, "When the Forest came in, I just laughed. I told them I would just like to see them come in and tell me. I thought I was boss."[41] Will Barnes characterized the situation as follows:

> The real blow, however, came in 1905, when word reached us that the Government was planning to charge us stockmen for the use of the forest ranges. Wow! How we did raise our voices in protest! To be sure, the fee was to be only a few cents a head for cattle in New Mexico and Arizona for the whole season's grazing, and still less for sheep. But what irked us all was the idea of having to pay a single penny for what we westerners felt was ours by right of conquest. It wasn't the money but the principle of the thing that made us want to fight somebody.[42]

Barnes went on to describe what they were up against:

> opposition to the new forestry plans fell flat before the dynamic backing given to them by Theodore Roosevelt, president of the United States. The movement went forward from its very inception. Gifford Pinchot, the man I had met in the mountains of northern Arizona several years before, was placed at the head of the newly created National Forest Service. He proved to be a very wise and far-sighted man. He seemed from the first to realize that the best way to overcome the prejudices of the old-time stockmen was to place the administration of the new system in the hands of western men who could talk their language, knew their ways, and understood their troubles. For his captain he picked a young Arizona sheepherder cowboy named Albert F. Potter, California-born, Arizona-hardened, who knew the smell of corral dust, the taste of sheep-dip, the difference between a lambing-ground and a bed-ground. Under Potter's supervision a group of young, wide-awake lieutenants trained in the school of their leader: cowboys, lumbermen, miners, and sheepherders, were picked out and dispersed over the West,

from the Canadian border to the Rio Grande, from the Sierras to the eastern slopes of the Rockies. Best of it all, they were absolutely fearless in their devotion to the new cause—forestry and range preservation. What a body of men they were! Warriors all, they believed firmly in the policy of Theodore Roosevelt—*speak softly and carry a big stick.* Great days were those for the Government grazing policy; for, say what you will, the grazing-men of the Forest Service were the shock troops who won the West for forestry.[43]

In 1909, the first ranger, Robert Thompson, arrived at Tonto. He was stationed in the Hackberry Ranger Station, located where Quartz Ledge Wash meets Tonto Creek.[44] U.S. Forest Service policy limited sheep in Tonto, which granted more access and less competition for cattle on the range, and the fees remained low. During the first decade of Forest Service administration, 1907–1917, these conditions held steady. Then pressure for beef production during World War I increased the need for more grazing, and the Forest Service responded by allowing larger herds. But when the war ended, the ranchers held on to their stock, and by 1924 Forest Supervisor T. T. Swift said, "Tonto National Forest is much overstocked. The Forest Service has finally decided that severe steps must be taken . . . to bring back the range to normal."[45] In 1926 Fred W. Croxen studied the change in grazing conditions on the Tonto and quoted one of the oldest ranchers, Florence Packard, as saying, "The range is not overstocked at present, it is just worn out and gone."[46]

Croxen's analysis in 1926 showed that the range conditions described by Packard, Watkins, and Griffin were but a memory. The creek bottom that Packard remembered as being filled with blackfoot and crowfoot grama grasses was now

little more than a gravel bar from bluff to bluff, most of the old trees are gone, some have been cut for fuel, many others cut down for the cattle during droughts and the winters when the feed was scarce on the range, and many have been washed away during the floods that have rushed down this stream nearly every year since the range started to deplete.

. . . the same condition applies to practically every stream of any size on the Tonto . . .

The Pine bunch grass grew all over the Sierra Anchas in the pine type and lower down than the pine timber on the north slopes. There were perennial grasses on the mesas along Tonto Creek where only brush grows at the present time. The first real flood to come down the

Tonto Creek was in 1891 after it had rained steadily for twelve days and nights. At this time the country was fully stocked, the ground had been trampled hard, much of the grass was short, or gone, gullies had started and the water came rushing down. This flood took a good deal of the agricultural land from the ranches along the creek and was so high that it filled the gorge where it entered the Salt River at the present site of the Roosevelt Dam and backed a house up Salt River about a mile.[47]

The range near Roosevelt was even more depleted, because it was used all year and stockmen never gave it a reprieve. D. A. Shoemaker produced an important study, also in 1926, detailing the forest's "carrying capacity." He described the severe erosion and reported an evaluation of only one successful allotment. He viewed the area near Roosevelt as the most damaged and over-used portion of the Tonto National Forest. The cumulative effects had taken their toll, and Shoemaker characterized needed policy changes as follows:

> Ending all grazing furnishes the only hope of restoring a cover of peren-nial grasses. Proper grazing methods, such as reduced numbers or only seasonal use, might transform a seriously depleted or an overgrazed range into a productive grassland. Nature could be trusted to revegetate if the Forest Service ensured the opportunity.[48]

In spite of the dramatically degraded conditions, Fred Croxen felt deter-mined to try something:

> It is up to us, the Forest Service employees, to whom this great area, this cattle range, a part of the watershed of the greatest irrigation system in the world, has been entrusted, to take and to do what we can as Forest employees, as servants of this great commonwealth. Can we do it? This remains to be seen.[49]

Despite attacks against massive nonforested acres being set aside as national forests, the national forest system was able to hold onto the boundaries, but no further changes or expansions were contemplated until the 1920s when the political climate was more conducive to such change.

By the late 1920s, Tonto National Monument had been under U.S. Forest Service administration for some twenty years, during which time the Southern Pacific Railroad largely controlled and administered access to the monu-ment. But the monument was a small part of a much bigger area of Tonto National Forest, which itself was caught up in an ongoing debate about the appropriation of western lands. The result was an uneasy truce among those who insisted on protecting the natural resources of this vital watershed and those who also wanted to make those resources available for ranching.

---

1. Proclamation No. 787, December 19, 1907, 35 Stat. 2168.

2. Ibid.

3. Cosner, A. J. et al. (1956, 1).

4. Marguerite S. Shaffer's *See America Firs: Tourism and National Identity, 1880–1940* is an excellent source of information on the connection between tourism and the search for American identity, the creation of the tourist landscape, and how tourism reshaped and redefined the built and natural environment of the United States between 1880 and 1840. Joan Michele Zenzen's dissertation (1997) on railroad promotion of the national parks is an excellent source of information on the role of railroad companies to promote the establishment, enlargement, and management of national park sites. Alfred Runte (1990) is an excellent source of information about the relationship of the western railroads and the national parks. Orsi (2005) chronicles the Southern Pacific's role in developing the American West.

5. In 1956 the NPS attempted to find out more about the history of the monument during the time when the Forest Service administered it. In June 1956, the Park Service requested the Forest Service supervisor at Tonto National Forest to furnish highlights pertinent to the time when the monument was under the administration of the Forest Service. Naturalist Dale S. King requested specific information, if available, about visitation, physical improvements, the names of the various rangers who patrolled the monument, and dates of interesting events and developments. Forest Supervisor Perl Charles responded quickly but, unfortunately, without much information. After looking for such information, only one file was found, containing a copy of the original proclamation and some correspondence back to 1925. Consequently, the Tonto National Monument history that was produced in 1956 revealed little additional information about the Forest Service administration and no details on whether there was a formal use agreement with the Southern Pacific Railroad. Sources for this section include TNM history file, correspondence among Dale King for the National Park Service and Perl Charles for the Forest Service, June 1956. On the subject of the Southern Pacific's alleged use agreements with the Forest Service to provide tourist facilities and visitation at the national monument there was also very little documentation available. *Sunset* magazine articles provided much context.

6. *Sunset*, vol.1, no. 1, February 1899, p. 82

7. Wright (1912, 33).

8. Myrick (1980) details the logistics of a trip offered in April 1917 as follows "Using westbound service as an example, passengers stepped off transcontinental trains at Bowie to board the regular passenger train to Globe, where they spent the night, probably at the Dominion Hotel, before taking the auto trip the next morning. Commencing October 1, 1916, and continuing for the remaining fall and winter months, a through Pullman sleeper on the Sunset Limited was operated three times a week from New Orleans to Bowie where a tri-weekly train, the Apache, took it to Globe, an arrangement which continued for many years. Arriving in Globe in the wee hours of the morning, passengers remained on the car until it was time for breakfast in the new restaurant at the station before commencing their tour of

the desert wonderland. Depending on the schedules, a lunch stop was made at Roosevelt Dam's Apache Lodge or further west at Fish Creek Station. Shortly after arrival in Phoenix, passengers boarded the waiting Pullman and rode to Los Angeles without change of cars. Similar service was offered eastbound passengers. (898) "After the name Apache was assigned to a Los Angeles–Chicago train, the Globe train became the Tonto" (899). Maynard Dixon's illustration is on the cover of the 1927 brochure. *Sunset Magazine, a Century of Western Living, 1898–1989*, is the best source for magazine graphics.

9. Eubank (1912, 194).

10. Woehlke (1916, 13).

11. Ibid., 15.

12. Steele (1940, 51).

13. Campbell (1926, 37).

14. Material by C. R. Steen for "Area History, Tonto National Monument," p. 1, TNM History file.

15. Vivian and Richert (1952, 3) indicate that the Southern Pacific received permission from the Department of Agriculture to fence both ruins for their preservation and estimate that the fences were erected between 1928 and 1930.

16. According to an entry in the Fact File, "Old Accession Cards and Survey Notes" file box at TNM, in January 1955 a man called Joe Stevens visited Tonto and said he was employed by the Forest Service with two other men for two months in 1916, and that they built the first trails to the ruins. It is not possible to distinguish precisely between the Forest Service and the Southern Pacific efforts to provide access to visitors. From NPS custodians and superintendents at Tonto National Monument we have a basic sense of what was provided during Forest Service administration between 1907 and 1933, including Forest Service patrols and improvements and operations by the Southern Pacific Railroad. According to the mid- to late-1950s area history produced by TNM, the Forest Service did not have sufficient personnel to station staff at the ruins, but did make periodic checks on patrol.

17. Ibid., p. 3.

18. This history of the Southern Pacific operations at the TNM comes from three TNM sources: (1) TNM Area History (1956–58, 6-7) and (2) Material by C. R. Steen for Area History, p. 2; and (3) Ramblings of "Old Man" Tonto, Supt. C. Sharp (1956, 1–3). According to Superintendent Sharp, Ray Stevens still lived on the San Carlos Reservation as of 1956. Tonto National Forest District Rangers from 1914 to 1939 listed in the TNM Area History are:

John W. Johnson	1914–1916
Charles Rak	1916–1918
Bent S. Benson	1918–1919
William M. Sherman	1919–1/15/1922
Monta R. Stewart	1/15/1922–9/19/1922
Arthur I. Hall	9/15/1922–4/30/1923
Albert L. Alexander	5/1/1923–10/12/1939

19. Hewett (1924, 428).

20. Ibid., pp. 430–31.

21. Ibid.

22. Simmons (1930, 5–6).

23. March 15, 1930, note in "Old Accession Cards and Survey Notes" file box, TNM.

24. Sheridan (1995) offers an overview of grazing in Arizona. Barbour (1999) and Croxen (1926) are major sources of information on ranching in the Tonto Basin, environmental consequences, the role of the Forest Service rangers in regulating use, and elimination of grazing from the National Monument.

25. Potter (1902, 236). S. J. Holsinger (1902) made a list of the animals by the extent of their negative impacts on the range (in descending order of destruction). The list was horse, sheep, goat, and cow. He reversed this order when describing the negative impact of animals in the forest.

26. Holsinger (1904, 14).

27. Ibid.

28. Ibid.

29. Louis C. Hill, supervising engineer for construction of the Roosevelt Dam (under the Department of the Interior Reclamation Service) was instrumental in determining the amount and location of acreage necessary to protect the irrigation works. He noted that "around the present reservoir site the land is reserved under the first form, preventing entry for any purpose whatever. This enables us to control the saloon business and other undesirable businesses from locating within a long distance of the reservoir. It would be very desirable to have this land remain as it is, and have the Forest Service have charge of the grazing over this reservation, so that it could be regulated and the grasses, which have grown up during the past few years, preserved" (Letter from L. C. Hill to Forest Service, October 9, 1907, NA/RG 115, General File 1902–1919, 783-1).

30. Gifford Pinchot, forester, to B. A. Fowler, President, SRVWUA, Phoenix, Arizona, June 28, 1908, NA/RG 115, General File 1902–1919, 783-1.

31. Antle (1992, 84–85).

32. Letter from Galloway, assistant secretary of the Department of Agriculture to the secretary of the interior, August 30, 1913, pp. 1–3, NA/RG 115, General File 1902–1919, 783.1.

33. Ibid., p. 4.

34. Ibid.

35. Ibid.

36. Memorandum to Mr. West by Mr. Finney, assistant attorney, December 10, 1913, p. 9, NA/RG 115, General File 1902–1919, 783.1.

37. Secretary of the interior to secretary of agriculture, November 5, 1913, NA/RG 48, Central Classified Files.

38. Pinchot (1907).

39. Ibid., p. 9.

40. It is interesting to note that in The Use of the National Forests, Pinchot comments that stores, hotels, residences, power plants, mills, and many other things could be built if they promoted appropriate land use. In the 1907 edition he included a full citation of the Antiquities Act and directed forest officers to arrest anyone who injured or appropriated monument objects.

41. Sowards (1997, 67), citing interview with John Cline.

42. Barnes (1941, 199–200).

43. Ibid., pp. 201–201.

44. LeCount (2003, 16).

45. Quoted in Sowards (1997, 69).
46. Croxen (1926, 11).
47. Ibid., pp. 1, 2.
48. Cited in Sowards (2000, 193–194).
49. Croxen (1926, 11).

chapter four

THE NATIONAL PARK SERVICE TAKES OVER, 1933-1953

The official history of Tonto National Monument dates from 1907, but its modern administrative history may be said to have begun in July of 1934, when the monument was transferred from the U.S. Department of Agriculture, Forest Service, to the National Park Service of the U.S. Department of the Interior in the wake of federal government reorganization. Effective August 10, 1933, the Department of the Interior gained responsibility for all national monuments previously run by the War Department and the Forest Service.

Interior set out to fulfill its new responsibility at Tonto along four parallel tracks. For the first two decades of NPS responsibility, from 1933 to 1953, the department sought to ensure visitors access to the site and provide an interpretation of its significance; to protect and study the cliff dwellings; to protect the land; and to improve the infrastructure. These four efforts, in turn, were undertaken amid three broad historical currents: a changing relationship between the Southwestern National Monuments—an umbrella field office for the fourteen southwestern national monuments—and the Washington, D.C. offices of the National Park Service; the impact of the Great Depression of the 1930s; and the home-front effects of the nation's involvement in World War II.

To a certain extent, accommodating visitors inevitably took precedence over the Park Service's three other, relatively long-range efforts, as it was imperative to greet and guide visitors from

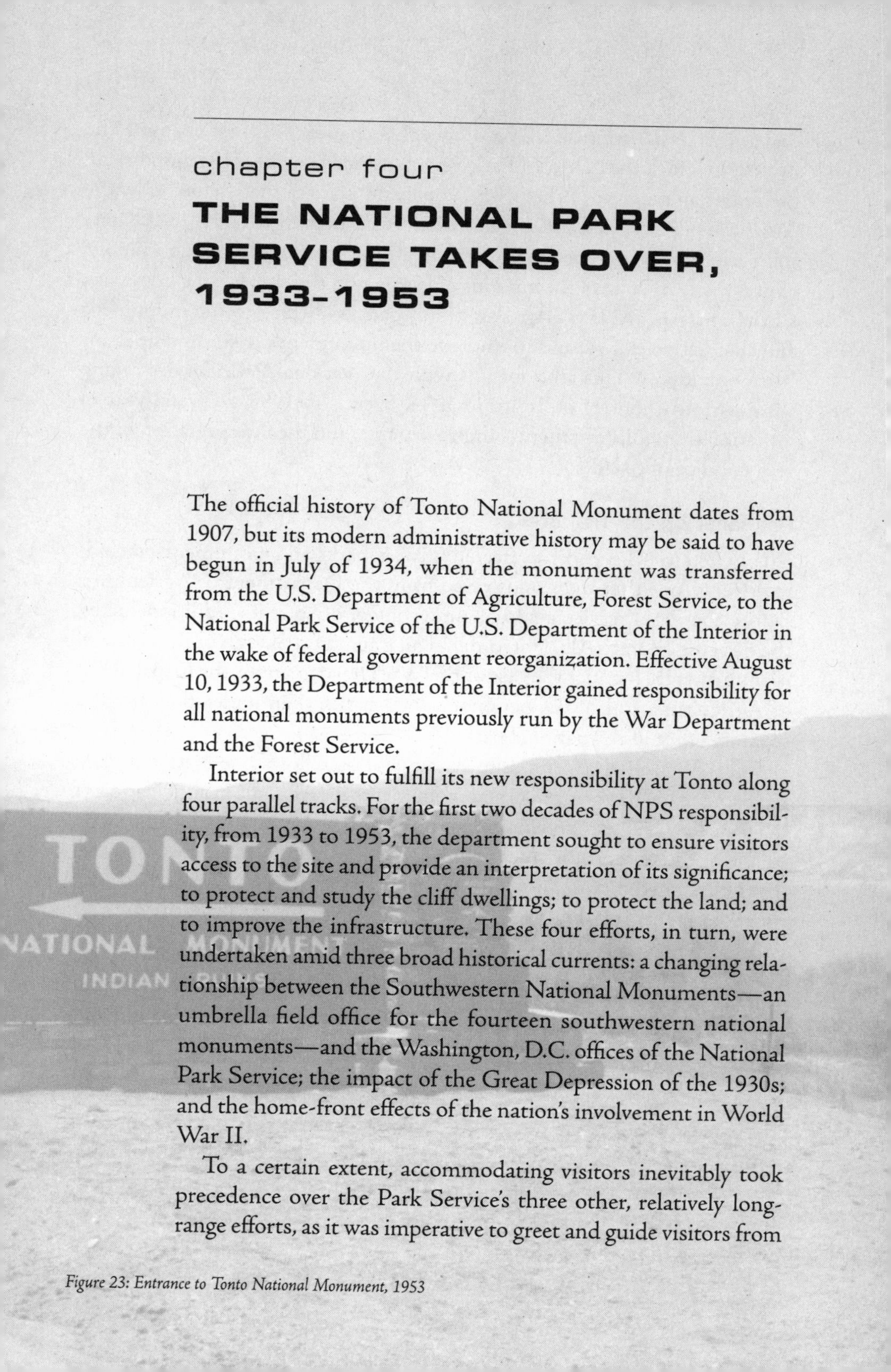

Figure 23: Entrance to Tonto National Monument, 1953

day one of NPS control. Accordingly, this chapter will first examine the context in which the National Park Service gained control of the monument, then offer an account of the NPS people and policies that shaped how the American public visited and understood the cliff dwellings. It further discusses the period's major archeological stabilization projects and the continuous efforts made to control the amount of grazing on the site. It concludes with a brief analysis of NPS efforts to build roads and trails to the monument and the cliff dwellings, and to improve the monument's basic amenities for NPS employees. This story begins with the National Park Service taking administrative control of Tonto in 1934. It ends in 1953, a pivotal year in visitation trends, infrastructure improvements, and the interpretation of the very concept of Salado.

Preparation for Transfer

The switch to NPS control affected fifty-six parks and monuments, including twenty-one that were transferred from the Department of Agriculture. Before the Park Service could assume control of so many additional sites, the director, Horace Albright, ordered an evaluation of each of the national monuments then under the care of the War Department or the Department of Agriculture, and of the national capital parks, then under the care of a separate office of the national parks.

Roger W. Toll, the former superintendent of Yellowstone National Park, evaluated many national parks and monuments for Albright in anticipation of the transfer. On February 26, 1932, Toll visited Tonto National Monument. While he did not meet with U.S. Forest Service officials, his report indicates . that he assumed they did not have adequate funds to administer and develop the monument. Toll reported,

> If it were practicable for the Park Service to secure an appropriation to employ a regular custodian and to undertake the necessary protective repair work it seems quite possible that the Forest Service would be willing to transfer the administration of this monument to the National Park Service.[1]

Toll rated the monument as of less interest to visitors than Mesa Verde or Bandelier, less important archeologically than Casa Grande, superior to Wupatki, and probably comparable to Montezuma Castle in terms of public interest.[2] Albright approved the transfer to the National Park Service on October 6, 1932.

Transition Time for Southwestern Monuments

Since its establishment in 1916, the National Park Service had been responsible for all national parks and some national monuments. Records indicate, however, that the Park Service considered national parks to be of more importance than national monuments; indeed, the former received more funding and staff. A 1920s study showed that the National Park Service spent 68.4 cents per visitor to a national park, compared to 9.2 cents per visitor to a national monument. Sometimes national monuments, such as Grand Canyon, Bryce Canyon, and Carlsbad Cave, were "upgraded" or "elevated" to park status, which brought them more funding and staff. In other words, the Park Service operated a two-tiered system.[3]

When Tonto was transferred to the National Park Service not only was the Park Service in transition, but, equally important, the regional Southwestern Monuments, an administrative umbrella over fourteen southwestern monuments, was also undergoing a period of change. In addition, in 1933, the director of the Southwestern Monuments, the colorful and controversial Frank "Boss" Pinkley, was in the process of falling out of favor with his superiors in Washington, D.C.

"Boss" Pinkley had an understanding of the value and significance of both national parks and monuments, and was a vocal advocate for a more generous distribution of funds to the southwestern region. Pinkley began his NPS career as caretaker and watchman at the Casa Grande ruins, which were set aside as a national reservation in 1892. He played an important role in orchestrating public support for monument designation for Casa Grande by enlisting the support of the Phoenix and Tucson newspapers, the University of Arizona's Department of Archaeology, and the Southern Pacific Railroad. Casa Grande was designated a national monument in 1918. Shortly thereafter Pinkley competed for the job as superintendent of Grand Canyon National Park. He was not chosen for that post, but in 1923 was appointed superintendent of the newly formed Southwestern Monuments.

Pinkley inspected all the monuments administered by the Southwestern Monuments field office, helped in restoration work, instituted reporting requirements for each of the fourteen monuments, and set standards for monument custodians. In the early 1920s, on a visit to Tonto National Monument, then under U.S. Forest Service administration, Pinkley reported that it was "not up to our standards of handling the public and giving information."[4] He believed that the Forest Service rangers were more suited to managing grazing lands and fire trails than caring for prehistoric ruins.

Figure 24: Frank "Boss" Pinkley—the first superintendent of the National Park Service Southwestern Monuments

At the time of the federal reorganization that led to NPS control of Tonto, Pinkley was still superintendent of the Southwestern Monuments but was losing favor with his superiors in Washington, D.C. He was outspoken in support of the ruins at Bandelier becoming a national park and was publicly opposed to its being designated a national monument. He also clashed with Washington over the mission of the monument museums and had openly criticized the NPS educational division personnel.

In 1934 Pinkley didn't help his situation when he failed to accommodate a friend of Interior Secretary Harold Ickes who wanted to tour the Casa Grande National Monument. Pinkley failed to acknowledge the man as a VIP and refused his request for an after-hours admittance and guided tour. While such awkward incidents contributed to Pinkley's downfall, it was the timing of the reorganization that exerted the major impact on Tonto's fortunes; the monument became a part of the regional Southwestern Monuments precisely at the time that Pinkley's national status was waning.[5]

The record of Pinkley's seven years of supervision of Tonto is mixed. On the one hand, Tonto benefited from its inclusion as one of the Southwestern Monuments, since Pinkley supervised and supported stabilization projects for the ruins, public speaking training for rangers, geological studies of the monuments, the writing of museum guidelines, and a number of natural resource studies that included bird banding. In contrast to his relationship with his superiors, Pinkley was beloved by Southwestern Monuments employees and had a tremendous impact in promoting an image of the ranger as competent, multitalented, in control, and worthy of respect. He was a charismatic and passionate leader—the staff he supervised was known as "Frank Pinkley's Outfit."[6] On the other hand, the Depression was hardly an ideal time for Tonto to become associated with a Southwestern Monuments leader who, due to troubled official relationships, could not lobby effectively in Washington for the funding necessary to enhance infrastructure, facilities, and programming.

TRANSFER TO THE NATIONAL PARK SERVICE

It might be assumed that the official transfer of responsibility over Tonto National Monument to the National Park Service would be complete, swift, and effective. However, as was the case with administration by the Forest Service, far more than mere formal authority was required to enable an agency to effectively serve as the new steward of a national monument. Notable among these necessities were additional funding and more staff. As it turned out, the Park Service provided neither to Tonto in significant quantities.

To begin with, it took a year following the federal reorganization for the monument to be officially transferred to the National Park Service. In July 1934, Pinkley selected the first NPS employee for Tonto National Monument, Charlie Steen, to serve as ranger in charge. During the transition period, the Southern Pacific custodians remained on site. But Steen was only there for a day before Pinkley transferred him to fill in for a ranger at Montezuma Castle for several weeks.[7]

As ranger in charge, Steen was responsible for filing Tonto's monthly report to Pinkley by the twenty-fifth day of each month. In the first entry in the July 1934 report, Steen wrote rather plaintively, "Here I am, trying to rate a little space in the monthly report, with less than 48 hours to my credit."[8] In the following several lines, he reported that during his only full day at Tonto, four autos carrying twenty-eight passengers stopped by. Many of the other early reports provide little more in terms of useful data, though they do offer a sense of who served in positions of authority—itself an apparently complicated topic. Steen files reports for 1934 and 1935. Woodrow Spires was reported as "in charge" in parts of 1935 and 1936; followed by Tom Onstott as "temporary" in 1937. Between 1937 and 1939, occasional reports were also filed by Park Rangers Roland Richard, Gordon Philip, Doug Frazier, and Ted Sowers, as well as Steen. After this, the record becomes more consistent. John Peavy, hired as the first official custodian in 1939, served through mid-1942, followed by Elmer Gipe, who served as the second custodian from the end of 1942 through 1947. Charles Sharp served as the first superintendent from 1947 to 1956. Relief rangers filled in on a seasonal basis. (See appendix C for list of superintendents.)

The monthly reports were rather informal during the 1930s and 1940s. They generally cited numbers of visitors, weather, flora and fauna, special visitors, perhaps a mishap or two, and often a story that the ranger felt was of interest. The reports were compiled at the Southwest Monuments headquarters, where supplemental reports were attached. Tonto rated a supplemental report as early as January 1935, and another in August of the same year.[9]

Taken together, these reports and supplements offer a glimpse of how the monument was administered during this initial period of NPS control. From them we know that efforts to install signage for travelers began in February 1935;[10] that during the following February, Park and Forest Service personnel tackled vandalism and pothunting at the Roosevelt Lake bed;[11] and that in 1941 the monument was still so woefully understaffed that when three museum cases were delivered in July they remained in the parking lot until September—until three able-bodied men could be found to move them into the museum.[12]

Occasionally a story of local interest was included in the reports. The following rather touching example gives a flavor of some of the tales then in circulation. Writing in November 1934, Steen included a story he heard and apparently was close to believing:

Two weeks ago I ran across a rather gruesome story concerning the cliff dwellings. Years ago, before the dam was constructed, a rancher named Blivens lived in the valley near here. His two baby daughters died of diphtheria and were buried on the ranch. Subsequently, Blivens moved out of the valley. While the dam was being constructed he heard that his old ranch would be covered with water, so saddled his horse, sent back to the old homestead, dug up the bodies, and carried them to one of the two larger dwellings here on the monument where the bodies were reburied. I have seen no traces of this recent burial, but have the story from two sources, so I am beginning to believe it to be true.[13]

ACCOUNTING FOR VISITORS AND THE VISITOR EXPERIENCE

The monthly reports do tell us how many people visited the monument as well as how they got there (see Appendix C for visitation totals). In September 1934 Steen spent his first full month on the job and compiled the first NPS statistic on monthly visitors: 305.[14] Before that Henry Stevens had estimated that there were several thousand visitors each year when the Southern Pacific employed him, reporting to Toll that he counted a maximum of thirty-one cars per day, mostly during the winter months, and that most visitors "are satisfied with a distant glimpse of the lower cliff dwelling and do not climb the trail to it."[15] The NPS reports show visitation ranging from approximately 7,000 in 1934 to 5,200 in 1940.

In addition to reporting the monthly numbers, Steen and other compilers explained their fluctuations. For example, Steen noted in his July 1935 report that there was a lot of traffic on the Apache Trail, but that cars weren't stopping at Tonto. He thought the weather had something to do with it, but ascribed more importance to reports that local filling station operators and cottage camp proprietors were advising customers that they could see the ruins from the highway and there was no need to stop.[16]

The monthly reports also provided a breakdown of visitors to the lower and upper cliff dwellings, and an indication of the international composition of those who passed through. In December 1934, for example, 266 people visited the monument, with 169 viewing the lower ruin, and 16 touring the upper ruin. Steen reported that the month's visitors came from as far away as Bogota, Honolulu, Kobe, Fairbanks, Bangkok, Frankfurt, Budapest, London, and Sydney.

In January 1936, Woodrow Spires, listed as "in charge" in the monthly report, furnished remarkably detailed visitor statistics. Between December 22 and January 25, 1935, Spires wrote 425 people visited; between December 26 and January 25, 1936, 757 people visited. The average was twelve a day in the 1935 period and twenty-four a day in 1936, representing a 100 percent increase. Spires broke down the numbers as follows: total visitor trips: 757, comprising 7,945 minutes; total visitors on field or museum trips: 536 on 93 trips, comprising 6,235 minutes; 67 minutes average per trip; average group size: 6; total museum visitors: 407 on 84 trips, comprising 1,710 minutes; 20 minutes average per trip; and average group size: 5.[17]

Thereafter, this level of detail became standard in the monthly reports. In September 1936, F. B. Horne, ranger in charge, surveyed where the visitors came from. He calculated that 30 percent came from Arizona and 25 percent from California, and travelers from outside Arizona hailed from twenty-five states and one foreign country.[18] While such reports provided information to the few NPS staff who read them, there is little evidence during the 1930s of monument staffers themselves trying to attract visitors. It is probable that visitation was still mostly generated by outside promoters. The Southern Pacific Railroad continued to operate the Apache Trail tours, and in fact mounted a new advertising campaign to attract visitors to the nearby Apache Lodge in November 1935. Beginning in October 1935, Tanner Tours offered trips along the Apache Trail; Pacific Greyhound offered tours in July 1937, AZ Motor Tours offered them starting in September 1937, and in February 1939 the Standard Oil Bulletin publicized the trail and the Tonto cliff dwellings.[19] Visitation reached more than 1,000 for the first time in February 1941, and 1,820 tourists arrived in March 1941.[20]

In the 1940s, NPS staff did become more involved in the publicity effort. In June 1941, for example, Dick Anderson of KPHO Radio in Phoenix invited the Tonto custodian, Ira Peavy, to write the script for a broadcast about the monument. Peavy wrote about a personal trip through the ruins, from which we get a sense of what he felt visitors needed to know—that the climb would not be too strenuous, that they would be rewarded with wonderful, panoramic views and a rich story about the people who built and inhabited the cliff dwellings, and that the visit to Tonto would be the highlight of a trip along the Apache Trail.[21] In addition, in September 1941, the industrious Peavy wrote a 3,000-word article for *Arizona Highways*.[22]

Gas was rationed during World War II, which might have been expected to reduce visitation. But Custodian Elmer Gipe noted that, while there was a trend toward people traveling together, presumably as a result of rationing, visitation did not decrease even when rations were cut for a second time.[23] Gipe's report for March 1944 comments,

A number of visitors this month have made this one of as many stops as they could get in, during a trip covering as many miles as their amount of gas would take them. Some thought they might be transferred and had better get here at once. Some had always lived around fairly close, but had never thought about coming here, until being curbed on gas had given them the urge to take as long a trip as possible.[24]

Indeed, Natt N. Dodge, the assistant naturalist for the Southwestern Monuments, reporting on his visit to Tonto in August 1941, asserted a need for a seasonal ranger at Tonto. Dodge described the 8,363 visitors to Tonto between October 1, 1940 and July 30, 1941 as "more than Aztec, Bandelier, Montezuma, or Tumacacori, each of which have two permanent men, and three of which has additional seasonal men."[25] Dodge urged that the museum should be staffed, "to handle the large number of visitors who make leisurely use of it while other members of their parties are at the ruins."[26]

Another account of conditions at the time comes from an August 1942 memorandum to Dodge written by Charles Sharp while the latter was serving as relief ranger. Describing the reactions of visitors to the museum exhibits, Sharp first addresses the pros and cons of the exhibits:

First, there are the exhibits to consider. Placed in three standing wall cases, about four and a half feet square and thirty inches deep, in usable space, they consist of pottery, artifacts, one skeleton of a child, some scraps of textile, some yucca sandals. In one case a very good Gila polychrome vase is the sole exhibit, and from an artistic standpoint the case is too empty, too white and unrelieved, but it does protect the vase, and fairly well. The publications case and two diagrams and a picture of a Gila monster, and a picture of Mesa Verde are the rest of the attractions. [27]

Then he comments:

Next, the visitor must be understood. I speak for Tonto only for the past two months. Two thirds of the museum contacts are with people from Globe-Miami, miners and others of not much schooling, not at all well-read. Their interest is, however, genuine, and reasonably thorough. Few of these know anything whatever of pueblo life, and must be instructed from the beginning.

There are a few, however, airmen from the fields near Phoenix, townsmen from Phoenix and Tucson, and a few out-of-state travelers who are enlightened, but many of these have not previously seen cliff dwellings near at hand.[28]

Finally, he describes the reaction of visitors to the information and experience presented:

The usual attitude is one of surprise at the organization, intelligence, amount of work performed, and degree of culture of the Salado Indians here represented. Cultivation of cotton particularly impresses most visitors. They are more familiar with the idea of pottery, which seems to be associated with the southwestern prehistoric in the minds of everyone. The specimens of cloth are quite interesting to most visitors. The skeleton draws the attention of practically all visitors, who usually ask, "Did that come from those ruins up there?"

Many think that the cliff-dwellers were Apache, a fairly logical assumption from the Apache Trail, and the natives over on the San Carlos reservation. . .

The sad amount of vandalism of this site is deplored by visitors of all types. There seems to be considerable consciousness of the value of preserving these things now, too late for Arizona. [29]

Sharp later served Tonto as superintendent from 1947 to 1956. In 1956 he wrote a piece titled, "Ramblings of Old Man Tonto," candidly recalling the monument facilities and the difficulties of accommodating visitors when he first arrived as a relief ranger in the summer of 1942:

In 1942, Tonto National Monument was a simple little area, with the present museum building (minus the aluminum shack built on for an office). Reached by a graveled entrance road on the same alignment as the present road, there was a small parking area, whose surface was higher than the top of the museum building ... This was not over 150 feet long, about 50–60 feet wide, with a 30 foot deep arroyo across the north (down-canyon) end, no guard rail, of which more anon. Visitors came down to the museum via a flight of steps and a short section of trail that was a little too steep, so some old ladies practically slid into the doorway. Whenever several cars were parked on the terrace, many incoming visitors could not see the museum, and did not always find it. The cliff dwelling trail started up a flight of stairs from the corner of this parking area, and control was difficult.

At that time, the chain link fence erected by the Southern Pacific RR around 1929 was in place with a gate which could be padlocked. It was the practice for whoever was stationed here to make the trip to the ruin with every party, if it was humanly possible. Since the area was usually lucky to have one man as the total force, little else than guiding visitors was accomplished during much of the year. Various

Figure 25: Current site of visitor center parking lot, pre-1950

practices were followed as to keeping the ruins gate locked. After a few experiences of puffing and sweating up the trail with a party, and finding that one had left the key down at the office, the gate would be left unlocked for a while. Then some party would go up after hours and perhaps defecate in the storeroom or the room with the roof, which would make the ranger or custodian so mad that he would lock the gate after every party for awhile. Following this phase, some very nice and trustworthy group or person would come along, right when some other job had to be done, and the ranger would want to send them up on their own, but the gate would be locked, so he would have to go along. This usually resulted in another period of leaving the gate unlocked. Each incoming man would usually go through these several phases for his own edification, before finally deciding to leave the gate unlocked and to hell with it.[30]

The rangers', custodians', and superintendents' reports offer a clear picture of monument personnel frustrated by staff shortages and their inability to both accommodate visitors and perform preventive maintenance. At the same time, their writings reveal resourcefulness, an intense sense of responsibility to and affection for the monument, a willingness to perform duties at all hours of day and night, a reliance on employees' spouses to perform a variety of tasks, and a sense of resignation that there was nothing they could do to change the situation.[31] Not unlike elsewhere in the country, "getting by" was the prevailing ethos during both the Depression and World War II. Then things began to change. After the war, visitation increased to the point that tours to the upper cliff dwellings had to be suspended because the staff was stretched too thin to accommodate the demand. The heightened traffic also led Superintendent Sharp t o conclude that the wear and tear caused by large numbers of visitors required a rethinking of how to handle the public: "It was only a question of time, and not much time, until the volume of visitors will force us, at least in the January to June period, to make a radically different approach to the whole undertaking of interpretation and preservation."[32]

There was even some consideration given to closing the ruins to visitors. In 1954, however, such pressures were eased when an admission charge was introduced and visitation declined. Robert Viklund, who served as a seasonal ranger for two winters in the early 1950s, recalled that visitors were amazed by how remote the monument was and wondered what staff did on their off-work hours. Viklund wrote that the standard reply was that "their entertainment was the store at Roosevelt where they would go and watch the bacon slicer."[33] He remembered the constant need during visitor hours for staff to be either leading a tour to the lower ruin or waiting there for other visitors to come up the trail. While they did have an army surplus hand-cranked telephone at the lower ruin that connected with the office below, they would usually simply rely on knowing when it was time for the archeologist, the superintendent, or the seasonal ranger to relieve whoever was on duty at the lower ruin.

PROTECTING THE CLIFF DWELLINGS

Charlie Steen's presence at the monument might have been sporadic in the early 1930s, but the record he left behind is a solid one. Steen's documentation of the excavation and stabilization of the upper cliff dwellings, combined with that of William Duffen on the lower cliff dwellings and the subsequent work of Malcolm Bull, Gordon Vivian, Roland Richard, Lloyd Pierson, and others are our best sources on the first two decades of NPS administration of the cliff dwellings and archeological sites.[34] But this work is best understood in the context of prevailing archeological theories and practices, which set the stage for fieldwork at Tonto.[35]

In 1924, A. V. Kidder published *An Introduction to the Study of Southwestern Archaeology*, which established rules for naming and describing pottery based on a binomial approach—the first word signifying where the pottery was found and the second word describing the pottery. "Black Mesa Black-on-white," for example, would identify pottery first found in Black Mesa, Arizona, with black designs on a white background. Kidder thus organized the existing, disparate descriptive systems in use for characterizing southwestern antiquities and also provided a chronology of ancient southwestern cultures.[36] Archeologists from all over the Southwest adopted his rules after sorting through the existing names, schemes, and pottery-sherd-based chronologies and classifications at the 1927 Pecos Conference at Forked Lightning Ruin near Pecos Pueblo, New Mexico.

This was a period of growth and consolidation of archeological information as archeologists found employment at several institutions, founded between 1928 and 1937, that provided bases for multiyear fieldwork. These institutions included the Gila Pueblo Archaeological Foundation of Globe, Arizona (founded in 1928); the Museum of Northern Arizona in Flagstaff, Arizona (founded in 1928); the Laboratory of Anthropology in Santa Fe, New Mexico (founded in 1930); and the Amerind Foundation of Dragoon, Arizona (founded in 1937).[37] The Gila Pueblo was especially important because of its close proximity to Tonto. Harold Gladwin and his wife, Winifred, directed Gila Pueblo; two important archeologists, Emil Haury and E. B. Sayles, were associated with the site. The Gladwins, Haury, and Sayles also provided expertise, services, and advice to Tonto.

In the late 1920s, the development of tree-ring dating techniques enabled archeologists to precisely identify construction dates for southwestern ruins. It also gave rise to the naming and dating of the Basketmaker and Pueblo chronologies. Through the dating of wood used in the construction of ruins— and in combination with new methods of understanding stratigraphy (the layering of artifacts) and seriation (the sequencing of artifacts)—tree-ring dating allowed the development of a "time-space" classification system. Gladwin and others characterized southwestern cultures and their growth and change as being like that of a tree with "roots" (old, deep patterns) elaborated into "branches" and "stems." They identified the four major roots of southwestern culture as the Hohokam, Anasazi (now called ancestral Puebloan), Mogollon, and Patayan.[38] It was in the context of this immense deepening of understanding of southwestern cultures that the National Park Service began efforts to preserve, stabilize, and study the Tonto ruins.

CONTENTIOUS CHANGES IN THE CONCEPT OF SALADO AND THE POLYCHROME PEOPLE

Harold and Winifred Gladwin are usually credited with introducing the term *Salado* in the 1930s to describe the people who inhabited the Tonto Basin. The Gladwins suggested the name Salado to refer to a people in the upper Salt River drainage basin who inhabited multistoried adobe structures, created a polychrome pottery, and buried their dead in an extended position. According to the Gladwins, the Salado were Puebloans who had moved from the upper Little Colorado River area into the Tonto Basin between AD 1150 and 1200.[39] Some say the word *Salado* comes from the Spanish word for salt, relevant because the Salt River runs through the basin. Others say that *Salado* refers to the conjunction of the Salt and the Colorado. In fact, neither past generations of archeologists nor contemporary ones have agreed on much about the term. *Salado* has been used to describe people descended from those indigenous to the Tonto Basin. It has been used to describe influxes of people from the north (the Mogollon). It has been used to describe influxes of people fro m the southwestern Phoenix basin (the Hohokam). It has been used to refer to a set of artifacts and architecture found in southern Arizona and northern Mexico; the artifacts, architecture, and other traits, it is generally agreed, occurred in three phases: the Miami Phase, AD 1150–1250; the Roosevelt Phase, AD 1250–1350; and the Gila Phase, AD 1350–1450, while the three diagnostic pottery types include Pinto, Gila, and Tonto polychromes.

The Tonto staff's acceptance of the contemporary concept of Salado is reflected in Louis R. Caywood's 1946 guide to the cliff dwellings subtitled *A Brief Resume of the History, Ecology, Geology and Archaeology of Tonto National Monument in Southern Arizona*.[40] Caywood synthesized the work of contemporary archaeologists, ethnologists, geologists, historians, and astronomers in a publication intended for a popular audience. He offered drafts to Tonto staff for review and edits. His guide offers the best overview of what Tonto staff at that time endorsed in terms of a portrait of the Salado; a chronology for how archeologists pieced together their knowledge of the Salado; an introduction to Roosevelt Black-on-white, Gila, and Tonto polychrome; and the construction and significance of Salado textiles and baskets.

By the early 1950s, however, NPS archeologists became divided over the prevailing concept and term *Salado*. Albert H. Schroeder, archeologist for Region Three, doubted the description of Salado that continued to be used by Lloyd Pierson, archeologist at Montezuma Castle.[41] Pierson was continuing to write that the Salado moved into the Tonto Basin and developed their distinctive culture with the "aid of close contact with the Hohokam." But Schroeder believed that the highly developed weaving, use of posts to support roof beams, and mud with rock-fill walls indicated the presence of a Hohokam-Sinagua culture. Schroeder believed that Pierson was ignoring the evidence that was beginning to complicate the concept of Salado. Pierson disagreed with Schroeder on the specifics, but acknowledged the term needed further clarification. Pierson proposed, "a 'bull' session on this problem in Flagstaff at the Pecos conference. I know the Salado is vague, ill defined and in need of a purge, and I am in hopes we can come to some conclusions with the help of those who are interested."[42] Through all of this, however, the controversy and confusion among archeologists about the term did not find their way into Tonto National Monument interpretations provided to the public, who continued to be offered the Gladwin definition of Salado.

GETTING TO KNOW THE RUINS

Because the Forest Service kept incomplete records, when the National Park Service gained control of the archeological ruins in 1934, it was impossible to piece together enough evidence to document precisely when major changes or damage occurred to the ruins. It was clear, however, that much had been lost. By that time, in fact, the ruins were in a severely compromised state—future visitation and vandalism had to be controlled and stabilization was essential.[43]

A variety of informal sources offer evidence as to when and how the cliff dwellings were damaged before NPS control. For example, an account gathered by a local resident who saw the ruins in 1888 indicates that some of the roofs had been burned by people robbing bee colonies located in the dwellings.[44] Additional destruction likely occurred between 1917 and the mid-1920s, according to a letter written by C. F. Barry to Superintendent Sharp in March 1953 after seeing a story about the Tonto ruins in the October 1952 issue of *Desert Magazine*. Barry noted that in September 1916 he went to Globe to visit his brother, and visited and photographed the ruins in 1917. At that time "there was not even a foot trail leading from the highway to the foot of the cliff, and very few visited the ruins."[45] In the mid-1920s he visited again, by which time a good road had been built from the Apache Trail and the "ruins had been almost completely destroyed by vandals, souvenir hunters and other wreckers."[46] He never returned. In 1953, Barry offered his 1917 negatives to the Tonto superintendent, but it's not known if they were accepted.

Some formal sources also support when and how the cliff dwellings suffered destruction prior to NPS control. For example, Bandelier's 1883 examination of the dwellings found them in excellent structural condition, but with many rooms burned by the Apaches.[47] It's probable that further destruction occurred between 1920 and 1935, based on reports on two trips to the ruins by archeologist Victor Stoner from the University of Arizona. When Stoner compared observations he made in 1935 with a map he had made in 1920 he concluded, "A great deal of the ruins have been destroyed since then," and that the previously sealed Room 19 had been broken into and vandalized.[48] Elaine Guthrie's overview of archeological and stabilization work at the upper and lower cliff dwellings notes, "The entire monument, especially the Lower Ruin, had been heavily disturbed by vandalism and pot hunting long before archeological investigations began in earnest in the 1930s."[49]

When the National Park Service assumed control, it almost immediately began various projects of bracing, stabilizing, and excavating. In October 1935, Woodrow Spires detected the need for emergency bracing in the upper dwelling. He wrote to Pinkley,

> On my last trip to the upper dwelling I found one section of a two story wall has weakened to such extent as to be unsafe. To save it we should brace it as soon as possible as a good strong wind would blow it over. When Dale comes up we will work out some means of bracing it. This should be done as soon as possible if we wish to save the wall.[50]

After completing that task, which required using galvanized wire in Room 9, Spires faced another emergency situation in the lower cliff dwelling that required a different approach. He sketched a solution suited to the special circumstances of another wall that needed bracing:

> The wall being braced was not true so I could not use 4 long pins as they would not contact enough wall surface (had to use 8 short pins) and the wall forming room 13 was higher than the ceiling level of the wall being braced. Tying into the cave wall on an angle would defeat its purpose.[51]

Spires wrote in May 1936 that he "expected to get started bracing the walls in the lower ruin which apparently is going to be a rather tedious job." Soon thereafter, in June 1936, he wrote that even though June was the "dullest month I have witnessed here, nevertheless, I have accomplished quite a lot especially in the strengthening of the walls in the Lower Ruin."[52]

Efforts to determine the dates of occupation of the cliff dwellings began as early as April 1935, when Emil Haury gathered fifteen samples of juniper, pine, piñon, and fir from the upper and lower cliff dwellings for study. He reported on May 10, 1935, that only one log, which was lying loose in the north end of the upper ruin, "has given a possible date of 1346. However, it is not a particularly strong date, and, if used, it should be stated as tentative."[53] He added that he was sorry that "out of fifteen specimens, only one piece gave results, but we cannot always expect a high percentage of datable material."[54]

The routine nature of life at the ruins was interrupted in February 1938 when rain exposed a mummy in the upper dwelling. Junior Park Naturalists Dale S. King and Charlie R. Steen, temporary Ranger Woodrow Spires, and Ranger Don Erskine found the body of a child, wrapped in cloth, lying extended on its back with its cranium to the east. They exhumed the skeleton and placed it on exhibition in the museum and added it to the catalogue. King's notes end with the suggestion that "the physical characteristics should be thoroughly studied, and combined with a study of the weaving found therewith."[55]

It is clear from the information available to the National Park Service about past conditions of the ruins that the Park Service had inherited a site that had suffered severe deterioration. More important, the site was continuing to deteriorate, meaning that much had to be done to understand and protect the dwellings and their archeological evidence.

Two Decades of Excavation and Stabilization Projects

So the National Park Service got to work. Previous projects had mainly addressed emergency situations, but Southwestern Monuments financed labor and materials for Tonto National Monument's first major excavation and stabilization project, which took place in the lower dwelling from May 27 to June 30, 1937. William Duffen, a graduate student from the University of Arizona, led the project and filed a report on its completion. His notes record the sequence of work, which involved excavating all rooms in the lower cliff dwelling except Room 16, as well as his efforts to create a chronology of original cliff-dwelling construction. The notes are quoted here at length,

Figure 26: Archeologists and laborers building retainer wall after fence removal at the lower cliff dwellings, 1952

because this extensive excavation and stabilization project had a significant impact—both positive and negative—on subsequent archeological work.

Work began May 27 and continued until June 30th.

The working crew consisted of the writer, who was in charge, two laborers and two burros, the latter being used for transportation of water and adobe from the ranger cabin up to the ruin.

This period of work was wholly upon the lower group, which was really in a bad state of repair, and consisted of the rebuilding of retaining walls and cleaning of rooms which had been dug out at earlier times. In many cases the debris had just been mulled over in the quest for "antiques." The slowest part of the job was the rebuilding of the rear wall of Room 2.

The first unit of work accomplished was that of rebuilding the retaining wall in front of the cave, and the continuation of the same across in as near level manner as possible until it reached the remnant of the south wall of Room 1. This latter chore also added much strength to the front wall of Room 2. The dry masonry retaining walls now in place, we had a place to put the debris from the rooms.

Figure 27: Trained laborers performing stabilization work, lower cliff dwelling, 1952

The second work unit was removal of the aforementioned accumulation of trash in excavated rooms. All rooms of the ruin had been gutted before it was put under protection of the National Park Service, with the exception of Room 16 which we left undisturbed. Removal of this debris brought to light features that had not been reported to date as well as some very interesting artifacts. Room features will be included in the section of the report on room descriptions; artifacts were entered in the catalog of Tonto National Monument museum and will be described in a future Southwestern Monuments report.

In some cases only a couple of inches of dust would be found on the floor and in several cases as much as two feet of trash was removed. Even though the room had previously been "gutted" great care was taken by the writer in the removal of this material and as a consequence the artifacts were removed in good shape. In most cases the floors, which have been left as such, are in reality false floors which are the result of careless housekeeping by the ancient dwellers. The fire pits will however in all cases be filled in save one which is in Room 15. This room will not be entered by visitors. However, its features may be observed from Room 16. This is a safety measure as well as one of exhibition, in that the room may be seen in its original floored condition with fire pit, metate, etc.

The third work unit was the removal of the old ramp that used to lead from the cave floor to Room 7. Its removal allowed much more space and was in reality unnecessary in the exhibition of the site. The slats of a cradle were uncovered at the base of this ramp.

The fourth chore was to get good adobe for the reconstruction of a wall of Room 2. It was necessary to go as far as Windy Point, several miles from the ruin, to obtain the material. The adobe then had to be handled a second time. The transportation of same from the parking lot to the ruin was a slow tedious one. The beasts of burden would balk when one pound too much was hoisted upon their lazy little backs. The trip up was then very slow, as only a burro can make it. Five-gallon oil cans were used as containers for getting water to the site. All materials now being in place, the last task was ready to begin.

This consisted of cutting down to bed rock and obtaining a good foundation on which was laid dry masonry on which to build the wall. The steps built by the Southern Pacific Railroad Co. leading to the little court, or Room 11, were moved to the spot where the door once penetrated this room.

It was found necessary to build up the wall in courses not much over a foot in height and let this set before the next layer was put on. The wall was constructed a trifle higher than beam height and then stepped off gradually down to about a foot high, the stepping commencing just beyond the beam axis. The large beam that had for years lain in Room 10 was replaced for exhibition purposes as well as to strengthen the newly built wall and to support the roof timbers which had for so long projected into Room 10. This part of the work really added much to the appearance of the ruin. It was the writer's wish to clean up and strengthen so far as such work would stabilize the ruin and yet not polish it up to the extent of looking too new or artificial. He hopes that will be satisfactory.[56]

Duffen then provided room-by-room descriptions. His report concluded with a "hypothetical building period reconstruction" and drawings of its four periods.

Figure 28: Trained laborer opening a prehistorically closed doorway between Rooms 8 and 14 in the lower cliff dwelling

While Duffen's notes might suggest a carefully planned and executed project, later archeologists had other opinions. Roland Richert's stabilization reports for work conducted in March 1957 refrain from condemning Duffen's digging in the ruin, but pointed out the consequences of his extensive excavation. Richert reports that

> sub-floor excavations and subsequent backfilling were extensive, which, together with earlier vandalism probably reaching its height around the years following the beginning of construction of Roosevelt Dam in 1906, have resulted in a well-churned fill condition beneath the present surface. At the time the Indians were living there, most of the rooms had well-compacted clay floors, and although resting in some places on earlier refuse or on scaly portions of the cave floor, were nonetheless stable. Once these floors were penetrated by excavation, and even though they were backfilled, this exposed the foundations to erosion, loosened the fill layers, and increased the undercutting of wall bases and shattering of the soft spots in the cave floor.[57]

Guthrie's 1994 analysis of Duffen's excavation was less forgiving, charging that.

> the documentation was poor and the exact locations and amounts of disturbance are ambiguous.
>
> Material provided by Steen (n.d.:4) for an area history report (Cosner n.d.) indicates his opinion of Duffen: "Duffen, a graduate student at University of Arizona, worked at the Lower Ruin more or less under my supervision. At least I hired him and should have fired him."[58]

Duffen's excavation of the lower ruin in 1937, Steen's excavation at the upper ruin in 1940, Pierson's excavation at the lower ruin and annex, and additional studies were published in 1962 as *Archeological Studies at Tonto National Monument, Arizona*.[59]

Coincidentally, at the same time that Steen and Duffen were excavating at Tonto, an NPS committee was compiling information about ruins stabilization to shape future policies. In 1940, the "Report of the Director's Committee on Ruins Stabilization" presented seventeen policies and made sixteen recommendations. The report begins with an appraisal of the previously inadequate funds and techniques applied to stabilization of ruins, excepting the work of the Civilian Conservation Corps (CCC) Indian Mobile Unit, which was set up by inter-bureau agreement between the National Park Service and the Bureau of Indian Affairs in 1937. It goes on to describe the preference for Indian workers:

> Indians were deemed preferable as workmen because of their familiarity with living conditions in isolated locations, and their native patience and artisanship. They have proved eminently satisfactory.
>
> It was envisioned that the unit would move from area to area, to accomplish emergency stabilization. Projects were set up and approved at Chaco Canyon, Aztec Ruins, Wupatki, Tonto, and Casa Grande national monuments.
>
> Southwestern Indians cling tenaciously to their native localities, suffer weakened morale when removed from them, and desert their jobs. In addition, it is felt that although the Navajo Agency allows continuance of the present unit for particular purposes related to its own administration, the Agency will look with disfavor upon the establishment of additional units, nor would other agencies be interested.[60]

More relevant to Tonto, policy number 3 prohibited excavating sites:

Obligations to Science as well as to the public necessitate a firm policy
of no modifications of unexcavated sites. Maintenance of those sites
unmodified may involve, however, limited stabilization. Unexcavated
ruins must be protected and should receive *Related Stabilization* as
required, *Emergency Stabilization* when needed, and, at the most *Limited
Stabilization*. *Comprehensive Stabilization* should not be applied to unexcavated ruins.[61]

Policy number 16, another forward-looking finding that would have
implications at Tonto, stated that

Restoration is essentially an interpretive function, not a form of stabilization. Replicas are preferable to type restoration, in that they do not
modify the actual site. Restoration in situ may be permitted at historical
areas only if fully documented and defensible. They should, in general,
not be utilized in archaeological areas.[62]

The recommendations outlined specific needs for annual reports, and the
need for preliminary surveys and sound budget estimates. The report also
concluded that experimental survey projects should be conducted to determine model procedures, and that in-group training should be provided by
the National Park Service.[63]

The report had immediate effects on how Tonto officials assessed the
monument's stabilization needs. Custodian Peavy outlined the stabilization
work needed in the lower ruins and included a condition assessment estimate
of man-days and material needed.[64] Stabilization of the upper ruin by Charles
Steen, Paul Ezell, and six laborers from the Chaco Canyon Mobile Stabilization Unit began in 1940 with construction of a buttress wall on the outside
of and perpendicular to the east wall of Room 9. In 1945, Caywood braced
the lower cliff dwelling walls again because they were considered a threat to
visitor safety. Gordon Vivian and Roland Richert managed a stabilization
project in the lower ruin in 1952.

Yet however well intended, these efforts may have done Tonto more harm
than good. Analyses made decades later revealed the shortcomings of these
early stabilization projects,[65] but by the late 1950s it was obvious to at least
one archeologist that the projects between 1933 and 1953 had, collectively,
disastrous results. Archeologist Joel Shiner reported that,

A history of the stabilization that has been necessary has been staggering
... work was done by Duffen in 1937, Caywood in 1945 (a considerable
project), by Pierson in 1950, by Vivian and Richert in 1952 (another large
project), and again by Richert in 1957 and the most recent by Richert
and Shiner in 1958. Each job meant that there was a little less of the
original structure left. Continued stabilization is not the answer. In addition to the expense, the result would soon be a ruin consisting entirely
of reconstruction thus impairing its interest and significance.[66]

Cosmetic changes were also made at the monument. In 1940 the Park Service
removed the fence installed by Southern Pacific at the upper cliff dwellings
since it was "unsightly, serves no useful purpose, and unnecessarily mars the
photographic quality of this ruin,"[67] and erected a four-strand barbed-wire
fence on the slope below to protect the ruin from range cattle. In 1952 the
Park Service removed the fence installed by the railroad at the lower ruin and
replaced it with a retaining wall. Elimination of the two fences may have rid
the monument of symbols of the pre-NPS period, but nothing could undo
the damage done by negligence, vandalism, and—unintentionally—excessive
stabilization. What Superintendent Sharp could do was begin to address
the inherent conflicts between preserving the archeological resources and
providing access for the public.

Recognizing the Conflict between Ruins Preservation and Visitor Access

In a 1952 memorandum, Charles Sharp laid out several specific issues concerning the often-conflicting goals of preserving the cliff dwellings while also
maximizing visitor access. The tone of his memorandum suggests he felt
Tonto was at a crossroads—he believed visitors should continue to approach
as closely as possible to the dwellings, but the question remained whether
people could continue to enter them.

The pressures on the monument, Sharp noted, were many. These included
the increases in nationwide travel and in the local population and volume of
winter visitors, the improved road conditions, and the expansion of publicity
about the monument via *Arizona Highways* magazine, local chambers of commerce, films, and word-of-mouth. He described the natural desire of visitors
to visit the cliff dwellings directly upon their arrival, with little or no pause for
orientation. The result was a continuous procession going up the trail rather
than orderly tours through the ruin. Sharp believed that, since the monument would be "compelled to adopt a greatly changed method of responding

to greatly increased visitation, it would be wiser to work with the natural tendencies of the visitor instead of against them."[68] He went on to say

In this case, I believe we would find little objection to a plan which allowed the people to walk across the front of the cave, stop as long as they wished, ask questions of the ranger (who should be there during periods of heavy travel), and see the dwelling at close range, but not actually go through it. In this manner protection could be accomplished, increasing rate of visitation would not be a severe problem, and more time could be devoted to interpretation at the headquarters area where all instead of about 50 percent of the visitors could be contacted. Even now, a few of our better informed visitors express surprise that unlimited access to the dwelling is allowed.

Throughout this memorandum, and in previous reports and other communications, I have stressed the gain and rate of gain in travel, and the probable future increase, for only one reason, to try to carry out my responsibility to the future of the area, and enable my superiors to plan intelligently for that future. I am not proud of the increase, not interested in setting records, nor promotion-minded. In fact, because we are lagging in staff and physical facilities to meet even the present rate of visitation, I have refrained from making a number of contacts, sponsoring local show-me days, making talks to civic and school groups, and putting up more conspicuous signs . . .

Some eminent Park Service man has been credited with the statement that "For the past twenty years, the automobile has done our thinking for us." I only hope that here at least, we can perceive and act on the problem in time to forestall the automobile.[69]

Shortly after explaining the conflict between ruins preservation and visitor access to the lower cliff dwellings, Sharp extended his analysis to the question of where to construct a trail to the upper ruin. He originally suggested creating a trail from the lower ruin to the upper ruin, but later revised his opinion. Sharp was convinced that a trail should not be built between the two ruins, stressing instead the need to build the trail through Cholla Canyon. According to Sharp,

I know from over six years experience here that whenever the upper ruins is mentioned, immediate and strong interest is aroused in everyone within hearing, and they forget about the dwelling they are visiting, in the stronger attraction of something that is out of sight and therefore

Figure 29: Monument staff using a tractor on the trail to the lower cliff dwelling, 1953

mysterious. So, much of the time, the ranger on duty in the lower ruin would be answering questions about "where does that trail go, can we go there, how long will it take," and so on. This would be fine at an information desk, but it is a disrupting factor at an interpretive station. I believe that a trail over the mountain in sight of the lower ruin would be principally a rat race to one more thing to see, for a considerable number of our visitors.

. . . and though it is impractical to try to "hide" the upper ruin, we still should not seek or encourage publicity any faster than it will naturally occur.[70]

By 1954, in other words, twenty years of stabilizing ruins and accommodating visitors gave staff a clear understanding of the inherent conflicts between these twin goals. It also gave them a clear perspective on how to use their experience and plan for the future, which would come in handy during Mission 66 planning, the subject of the next chapter.

PROTECTING THE LAND

On April 1, 1937, President Franklin Roosevelt's Proclamation No. 2230 (50 Stat. 1825) transferred an additional 480 acres from the Tonto National Forest to the Tonto National Monument "for the proper care, management and protection of the said historic ruins and ancient cliff dwellings."[71] Up until that time, a portion of the entrance road was on U.S. Forest Service land. The transfer was asked for and obtained by the National Park Service so that they could extend control over the entire entrance road. This brought the total acreage to 1,120.

First Attempts at Fencing, Eliminating Grazing, and Protecting Water Sources

The Park Service now had the authority for the care, management, and protection for the monument—on paper, at least. Practically speaking, it was bound by a series of traditions and permits that allowed grazing on monument lands. In the 1940s, NPS policy supported the elimination of grazing on its parks and monuments, as well as fencing to protect the most vital features. At Tonto, this policy marked the beginning of a series of disputes over grazing permits and fees, water rights, and boundary lines. Resolution came neither quickly nor easily. The negotiations demanded tremendous patience and doggedness on the part of Tonto staff over a thirty-five-year period, for although some progress was achieved by the 1950s, it would take until 1975 to eliminate grazing and until 1981 to finally fully fence the monument.

Figure 30: Tonto National Monument boundary fence and notice

Joint Jurisdiction over Grazing Permits and Fees

When the National Park Service took over the monument, confusion reigned between the Park Service and the Forest Service over land-use control, grazing permits, and grazing fees. The 1934 reorganization should have made it clear that the Park Service took over control of monument acreage, and the 1937 proclamation referred specifically to withdrawing land from the Forest Service for transfer to the National Park Service. Still, confusion persisted over which of the two federal agencies was to administer grazing permits.

In 1907, when the monument contained 640 acres (Section 34), the U.S. Forest Service extended grazing allotments to various ranchers. Two allotments were still in effect in 1934 when administration switched to the Department of the Interior. These allotments, numbers 60 and 66, should have switched to joint agency jurisdiction, but the matter was never adequately addressed. The result was that none of the parties, including those with U.S. Forest Service grazing permits, was clear about who was responsible for permits, fees, and water rights.

Since the Park Service did not fence their acreage, the Forest Service assumed that the area was under joint jurisdiction. That being the case, it might follow that the permits the U.S. Forest Service administered during the period 1934–1941 would have been coadministered; however, the issue was not addressed and the forest service simply continued to offer ten-year renewable permits to graze on what was NPS acreage.

It was only in retrospect that the Park Service recognized the confusion born of the lack of communication and collaboration between the two agencies. A memorandum of agreement between the National Park Service and the U.S. Forest Service "Relating to Issuance of Grazing Permits within the Boundaries of the Tonto National Monument" became official on July 17, 1942. According to its terms, the Park Service was to receive "a proportionate part of the grazing fees collected; said revenues to be divided between the two Bureaus in proportion to the amount of monument land involved as compared to the amount of forest land and according to the number of stock grazed thereon."[72] No new grazing permits would be granted on lands within the monument, though several stockmen were grandfathered in and permitted to continue grazing on the unfenced portions.[73]

Fencing Fights, Water Rights

In 1941 Tonto National Monument secured funds and created a plan to begin fencing boundaries, in keeping with the National Park Service objective to protect monuments from grazing. But Custodian Peavy approached the project without realizing how much resistance it would generate. In fact, the plan was vigorously opposed by ranchers—two in particular—who feared the fences would interfere with their grazing and water rights. In the early 1940s, two cattlemen grazed and watered their stock on almost all of the monument acreage. Dwight Cooper's allotment number 66 permitted him to graze on 11,851 Tonto National Forest acres. Overflow water from the Tonto seep supplied water for Cooper's cattle, although there were no formal agreements that extended water rights to Cooper. Neil Lyall's allotment number 60 permitted him to graze on 400 acres of the monument, and overflow water from the Tonto seep watered his cows, although there was no formal agreement to supply water for this purpose. Both stockmen viewed Peavy's fencing program as a major threat, not so much because it would restrict grazing acreage, but because it would restrict access to water.

Cooper, the U.S. Forest Service, and the National Park Service corresponded and met frequently over these issues, but the more they explored the situation the more complicated it became. In 1941 Peavy and others at the Park Service discovered that the federal government had never filed for water rights for Section 34 (the original monument acreage). They feared it would be disastrous to let the cattlemen know about this because it might have placed the latter in a stronger legal position to receive rights to the water because they had been using that water source for grazing for generations. The fencing issue was, thus, intricately intertwined with the matter of water rights and with the Park Service's reluctance to take direct legal action.

In early 1941, Peavy had an encounter with Cooper that revealed the depth of the rancher's opposition to the fencing. The two men met by chance at a doctor's office, and Cooper disclosed his displeasure with the Park Service's plan to fence off 1,120 acres and a spring. Peavy said that Cooper got angrier the more they talked about it, saying that the old-timers should have "blown out the cliff dwellings years ago and then we wouldn't be bothered with them now," that "who knows when those dwellings might be struck by lightening some night," and that "something will be done about it," and finally that, "us cattlemen know how to handle our business without the government telling us."[74] Following this apparent threat, members of the Gila County Cattle Growers Association, which met on November 10 in Globe, registered a protest against the proposed fence. Although Peavy addressed the group and tried to explain NPS policy, the association passed a resolution against further fencing.

After a series of meetings between Cooper and Peavy, as well as a flurry of communications between the Gila County Cattle Growers' Association and figures as influential as U.S. Senator Carl Hayden of Arizona, the U.S. Forest Service, the National Park Service, and Cooper agreed by the end of 1941 that Cooper would not object to a fence if a water line was extended from the Tonto seep to the northern park boundary near Arizona State Route 88, where a watering tank would be installed. The Park Service would furnish pipe and pay for labor, except for $50, which was to be supplied by Cooper, to install a water pipe from the seep to the northwest boundary. With this agreement in place, fencing of Cave and Cholla canyons was completed and a cattle guard installed by February 1942. Custodian Peavy's memorandum to the regional Southwest Monuments superintendent suggests the satisfaction he must have felt when the first fence was constructed. He wrote,

> A boundary fence was constructed Oct. 1941 to Jan. 1942 with Soil and Moisture Funds. This operation provides for the fencing of Tonto National Monument along the boundary. The monument vegetative cover is now protected from the grazing by livestock that has been going on for the last 60 years.
>
> This action should stop incipient gullying and sheet erosion which was becoming evident in heavily grazed areas. These areas will now have a chance to become reestablished, and the spread of certain objectionable plants which are overgrazing indicators will be stopped.[75]

For the first time, a fence would keep cattle off of approximately half of the monument's land. The fenced area contained the visitor center, a road, and the ruins, but it was not installed along monument boundary lines, which led to later confusion and further disputes. It become increasingly clear that, along with the monument itself, the National Park Service had inherited from the Forest Service the same contentious relations with local cattle grazers. The ranchers weren't about to give up their grazing rights without a fight; the clash over values simply took on new depth when USFS land became NPS land.

Shortly after fencing was completed, the Park Service took steps to establish its rights to water in Cholla Spring and Cholla Canyon. Charles A. Richey, assistant superintendent of Southwestern Monuments, applied to the state of Arizona,

> For permission to appropriate water from Cholla Spring (Number One Drain) (Permit No. A-1829) and a spring in Cholla Canyon

(Permit No. A-1830) for two purposes: the park needed a water supply for residential and general use; and the two ranchers wanted water for their cattle. Under Permit No. A-1829, 182,500 gallons a year were allotted for domestic use, and 40,000 gallons a year for stock watering. Permit A-1830 allotted 730,000 gallons a year for domestic use and 365,000 gallons a year for stock watering. A 700-gallon tank served Lyall's herd, while Cooper's cattle were supplied via a trough.[76]

After 1947, the records suggest the Park Service began to recognize the interconnection among grazing, water, and fencing issues, even though it continued to deal with them separately and acted on a piecemeal basis.

Food for War Versus the Efforts to Eliminate Grazing

In March 1942 the Department of the Interior asked the National Park Service to summarize the potential for grazing in southwestern monuments in order to increase food and fiber supplies for the war effort. The summary was based on reports from individual monuments. Tonto's contribution, completed that same month, provides the following statistics: 1,120 acres—the total acreage of the monument—were considered browse/brush (the categories included nonvegetated, grassland, browse, woodland, and forest); the area provided feed for 192 animal months (an animal month is one month's feed for one head of livestock of the kind under discussion). The report also presented the probable adverse effects of grazing: "Heavy damage would result to archeological values. Cattle would be nuisance in pollution of water and heavy damage would result to already overgrazed landscape."[77] In the space marked for additional remarks, the following was inserted: "Service has just completed fencing the monument at cost of $3,818.12 to prevent the damage mentioned above."[78]

During World War I, grazing increased on lands controlled by the U.S. Forest Service and the Department of the Interior, including acreage on NPS parks and monuments. Land managers, having seen the negative impact of this policy, did not want it repeated during World War II. The National Park Service, based in Chicago during World War II, issued a memorandum in February 1943 that deftly supported the need to hold intact the features of the national parks and monuments without belittling the need to increase the food and fiber supply for the war effort. This memorandum gave custodians and superintendents at places like Tonto a clear sense of the direction that the Park Service wanted to go and of how their sites fit into the policy changes being encouraged. For example, the memorandum noted that there were opportunities for "moderate increases on some types of areas."[79] However, an adjoining statement added,

> It has also confirmed our conviction that no new areas should be opened to grazing in the great scenic parks that have been established as the last and best examples of the Nation's landscape. The damage to these holdings would be out of proportion to the slight addition they would make to the total of the Nation's food supply. We believe that the highest public interest would be served, even in these war times, by holding intact the outstanding scenic parks without disturbance of the natural balance of factors that contribute to their greatness.[80]

The memorandum recommended reaffirmation of the goal of eventual elimination of grazing on NPS sites, and that no new grazing should be introduced in national parks that did not already permit it. It also proposed that, at sites that allowed grazing under permit—which included Tonto—grazing should continue for the duration of the emergency situation, but without extension to new ranges or increases in the number of stock.[81]

Indeed, the move to eliminate grazing in the national parks was far from new. Its supporters could point to a series of directives, including one in 1918 from the secretary of the interior to the director of the National Park Service:

> In all of the national parks except Yellowstone you may permit the grazing of cattle in isolated regions not frequented by visitors, and where no injury to the natural features of the parks may result from such use. The grazing of sheep, however, must not be permitted in any national park.[82]

Another, in 1925, stipulated, "In national parks where the grazing of cattle has been permitted in isolated regions not frequented by visitors, such grazing is to be gradually eliminated."[83] Yet another in 1939 suggested, "It is a part of sound national park policy not to permit grazing by domestic livestock in areas set aside for preservation and recreation."[84]

A March 1943 communication from NPS headquarters details the reasons why grazing, while sometimes permissible, should be eliminated from the NPS sites. Negative consequences of grazing are cited in five areas: to scenic and aesthetic values, to historical and archeological values, to biological values, to general recreational values, and finally to structures and other physical investments.[85] Of particular relevance to Tonto, a March 1943 memorandum from headquarters to the regional directors stated,

> The Service will continue to hold grazing to a minimum and eventually eliminate it from the national parks and all other areas, except for certain historical units wherein livestock may have historical significance and recreational areas where it does not interfere with human use. As an emergency measure in order to meet critical wartime demands for food and fiber, concessions authorizing grazing may be made in the Director's discretion.
>
> Experience shows that developments made and held by a permittee frequently lead to an assumption that he has a perpetual right to the use of the area, thereby making it harder to terminate his use. Capital investments and maintenance of improvements on park land, as a matter of sound policy, should be made by this Service.
>
> By issuing permits on a three-year rather than on an annual basis, it should be possible to overcome the frequently encountered indifference of the permittee toward our principles of conservation. With a three-year tenure the permittee would have far more reason to be sympathetic to the Service's position and thus be more willing to cooperate in making conservative use of the range. This action should strengthen the Service in enforcing necessary controls, and, in some cases, it may be possible to work out a progressive reduction and elimination of livestock. These three-year grazing permits should be a medium for greatly improving mutual understanding in achieving the best in range management of Service areas.[86]

This planned move to a new grazing program would clearly be a difficult and time-consuming one. It was even viewed by some as anti-American because it was not supporting the war effort. To that end, the memorandum was accompanied by talking points for use by employees when discussing the undesirability of grazing in the National Park System. These talking points were characterized as

> possibly being help to you in discussions that may arise concerning the steadily strengthened policy of the Service to exclude grazing and the reasons for the extension of grazing at this time as a step that involves a sacrifice to be made only as a last resort and because of the war emergency.[87]

These policy directives may have bolstered resolve at Tonto among caretakers confronted by cattlemen who had enjoyed access to monument acreage for many years. But there is no evidence that Tonto experienced a drastic change in relations or conditions because of the long-range plans to eliminate grazing from the National Park System. Quite to the contrary, Superintendent Sharp had a 1951 conversation with cattleman Cooper that reveals how the argument favoring increased beef production during World Wars I and II simply reappeared during the Korean War. Sharp writes,

> During the interview, Mr. Cooper consistently used the 'raise beef for the boys in Korea' motif, and had the incredible gall to tell us that we were merely sitting here doing nothing "while them boys was over in Korea" and we were blocking his patriotic desire to raise more beef for them. It was necessary to remind him that we were both overseas veterans. It would be pointless to recite further the abuse and insults irrelevantly poured on us by Mr. Cooper.[88]

Boundary Disputes

In 1944, it was found that "the west boundary was over one-fourth mile west of the location which everyone, including the local permittees, considered to be the boundary . . . since Section 34 was never surveyed . . . it is felt that a boundary survey should be done of this area after the war."[89] Just before the war ended, there was also another push to eliminate grazing. Ben H. Thompson, chief of the National Park Division, Branch of Lands, wrote a memorandum in 1945 to the regional director of Region Three that characterized the change:

> It is believed that our long-time policy should be directed toward the total exclusion of grazing in Cholla Canyon within the Monument. It is questionable whether there is any real need for the Lyall cattle to enter Cholla Canyon in the southeastern corner of the Monument . . . or whether there is any real need for the fenced corridor down in the bottom of Cholla Canyon extending from the south boundary of the Monument to the watering trough below Cholla Springs No. 1.[90]

No formal changes were made at the site through the rest of the 1940s and early 1950s. As in the past, each Tonto National Monument custodian or superintendent inherited the results of their predecessor's actions, inactions, and continuing disputes. By 1954, Superintendent Charles Sharp summed up the cyclical nature of the situation as follows:

> In the seven years during which I have been in charge of Tonto, there has always been one phenomenon which is apparently as intrinsic a harbinger of approaching winter as falling leaves, migrations of wild fowl, and frosty weather. This is the annual discussion with our neighboring rancher, Mr. Cooper, on the subject of turning off the water to his stock tank so that we may drain the line before it freezes. This discussion is occasionally amicable, sometimes not.[91]

Sharp was aware of the need to bury the water line to preventing freezing, but this idea was complicated by both rocky ground and a lack of funding. His other solution was for the Park Service to ensure that it possessed senior water rights and thus had no obligation to furnish water to Cooper. While Sharp endorsed this as a practical solution, he noted that such a course "would cause such repercussions, and be such bad public relations, that I would hesitate to recommend it."[92]

In taking over control of Tonto, the National Park Service faced a lengthy challenge in establishing new relationships with the Forest Service, and an even lengthier one in changing the long-standing traditions and perceptions of area ranchers, which were supported by the stockmen's organization. Water rights, grazing permits, fencing restrictions, boundary lines—conflicts over these and other issues punctuated the first twenty years of NPS administration and would carry on for many more.

Wildlife and Wildfire

The National Park Service conducted its first survey of national park wildlife in 1929, and for the next ten years its wildlife division promoted what today would be called ecological awareness. A 1933 publication by the division's wildlife biologists argued for research to become part of NPS management, but accommodating ever-increasing numbers of visitors continued to take precedence over protecting or restoring natural conditions.[93] Accordingly, from 1934 to 1954, staff at Tonto, like other parks and monuments, was not able to study wildlife conditions on a systematic and sustained basis. However they did conduct a number of small-scale studies of birds, the health of the giant saguaros, and fire dangers at the monument.

One of the earliest studies of wildlife in Tonto National Monument was conducted in 1920 by H. S. Swarth, as part of a comparative study of birds of Papago Saguaro National Monument and Tonto National Monument. Swarth observed that western tanagers and Palmer's thrashers were abundant at the point where the park trail led from the stage road to the cliff dwellings: "I had been hearing complaints of the lack of birds and of bird music in this region, but surely no one could wish for anything finer than the chorus produced by these two species alone."[94] The first bird report exclusive to Tonto was conducted by Gordon G. Philip, who provided a list of birds seen within the monument's boundaries between November 4 and December 26, 1938. It was published as a park monthly report supplement for January 1939.[95] Tonto was also part of a study of migratory birds in 1939. A wildlife census began in 1942, and a study of bacterial necrosis in the giant cacti in 1943.

Efforts to evaluate wildfire potential increased in April 1942, although it took until 1948 for the monument to obtain all the necessary fire-fighting equipment. During the 1940s, fire patrol became a regular part of staff duties. Workers attended fire-fighting schools, erected signs on the monument to help prevent fires, and worked with the Forest Service to extinguish fires near the upper cliff dwelling in 1947 as well an electrical fire in the custodian's house that same year.

While Tonto can point to several studies and increased ecological awareness during this period, the demands of serving visitors, stabilizing the ruins, and improving infrastructure far outweighed the amount of time, energy, and funds devoted to formal study of flora and fauna and the ecological systems of the Tonto Basin.

IMPROVING INFRASTRUCTURE

The two main types of infrastructure improvements during this period were access routes, including roads to the monument and trails to the dwellings, and staff accommodations.

Roads and Trails

The first road improvement projects began almost immediately after the National Park Service gained control of Tonto National Monument, and for most of the years between 1933 and 1953, much of NPS employee time was devoted to keeping the roads and trails open. During 1934 a road was graded from the entrance to the stone building built by Southern Pacific, which the Park Service used as a museum. The first NPS trail improvement

Figure 31: Tonto National Monument museum and administrative headquarters, 1938

project began in 1940 with the reconstruction of the trail to the lower cliff dwellings. Road and trail maintenance increased after each rain and especially after heavy rains, particularly those in 1941–42. Custodian Peavy's monthly report for November 1939 is typical:

> A good percentage of my time this month has been spent in repairing the entrance road. The maintenance men for the Hwy. Dept. have allowed me to utilize their gravel pit located on the Apache Trail 2½ miles east of the Tonto entrance. I have been hauling surfacing and filling up pot holes and gullies most of the month expect during the time that Dodge 8113 was out of commission between the 13th and 23rd. I put in about four hours work on the trail after the first rain, filling in incipient gullies and removing rocks.[96]

In March 1940, Hugh M. Miller, acting superintendent for Southwestern Monuments, inspected Tonto. In reference to the entrance road, he wrote,

> The maintenance on the entrance road was better than I have ever seen it. Certainly this road cannot be called good and such maintenance as the custodian is able to give it goes apart after very heavy rain. Tovrea was requested to prepare revised estimates on the relocation and grading

of the entrance road and plaza in accordance with master plan, so that a proper future construction sheet might be submitted. Only feasible method of construction would appear to be contract under Roads and Trails appropriation but item should be given a reasonably high construction priority because the development of a small administration building and headquarters units must be deferred until after relocation of the entrance road and proposed plaza grading, which will be, presumably, a part of the contract when let.[97]

Miller refers here to a "master plan"; the next suggestion of master planning occurred in April 1941.[98] During 1941–42, Tonto National Monument was examined for road alignments, a parking area, and potential residential sites. It was clear that Tonto's plan needed to integrate the entrance road, parking area, headquarters, water system, and residences, but World War II intervened and nothing was done until it ended.

Prewar conditions were complicated by the fact that the graveled entrance road leading to the museum building ended in a parking lot whose surface was higher than the top of the museum building. This caused some visitors to miss the museum entirely. While the need for road and trail improvements was obvious and well documented, Sharp's writings remind us that,

> During the 1942–46 period, about all that could be done in most NPS areas was to hold them together, without much money or anything else, and accomplish whatever could be done by just hard work. Tonto was no exception. Custodian Doc Gipe maintained the entrance road by use of Mormon culverts, a series of ditches dug transverse to the roadway, starting just past the center line and angling across the road. There were 120 of these in the 1 mile of road when C♯ came back in 1947. The effect was terrific, as the ditches were around 4 to 6 inches deep at the road shoulders, giving a super-washboard effect. Doc had a ditch and ridge of dirt just above the cattleguard, to keep it from washing full of gravel, which was guaranteed to throw any unwary drivers clear into the lake if they hit it over 10 mph. [99]

Several years after the war, a NPS publication called attention to the desperate conditions of the national parks and monuments. In 1949 Newton B. Drury, director of the National Park Service, issued a report, "The Dilemma of Our Parks," that documented deterioration, the need for repairs and replacement, and the funding gap between what was needed and what

Figure 32: Tonto National Monument parking area and ranger housing, 1941

was appropriated.[100] At the same time, a campaign highlighted the dire situation of southwestern NPS facilities, their chronic maintenance needs, and understaffing. *Sunset* magazine published an article in February 1949, and the *Arizona Republic* wrote one on the Arizona national parks and monuments in June 1950. The *Arizona Republic*'s research revealed that the worst problems at Arizona parks and monuments were the lack of parking, sanitary facilities, picnic areas, and other public facilities. Ben Avery's article, "Historic Arizona Shrines Run-Down, Tourist Trade Imperiled by Long Neglect," described Arizona's parks and monuments as neglected, unsightly, and overcrowded. About Tonto he wrote,

> Tonto National Monument near Roosevelt Dam, which draws heavily on the sightseers using the Apache Trail between Phoenix and Globe, needs an enlarged parking area, a wider road, additional sanitation facilities, picnic areas, a campground, and office space.[101]

The power of the press might have had something to do with the quick action that occurred at Tonto shortly after the negative publicity. Tiffany Brothers was awarded a contract about which Sharp recalls,

> In the summer of 1950 a contract was let to construct the present parking area. Not any too soon. The old area would hold 18 Model

T's, or six or eight Hudsons, and was getting to be quite impossible on weekends...

Since it was right in the middle of the visitor use area, it upset operations all summer long, but made things more interesting for the visitors. When completed, this gave us a lovely parking area and approach curve, with a narrow bridge and a nasty turn at the bottom of it, which pointed up the need for improvements to the entrance road. It also left Pierson's house (exp. Trailer) really exposed, with cars parking within 14 feet of the trailer, and damn little privacy at any time. Parking area was finished in September of 1950.

Completion of the parking area inaugurated a new phase in the development of Tonto. For the first time, something was built here according to the master plan, a propadeutic step from which orderly design and development could proceed. This of course sparked a series of moose calls to superior authority for developments which were badly needed here.[102]

The Tonto Entrance Road Project was detailed in a completion report, dated August 1, 1953, and accompanied by before-and-after photographs. For the first time, the project brought the one mile of entrance road from State Route 88 to the parking area at monument headquarters to an acceptable standard. It widened and raised the road, improved grades, and installed large multi-plate culverts covered by several feet of fill. At the same time, a new water system was installed to bring water from Cholla Spring, a task that required construction of a 10,000-gallon concrete water-storage tank as well as 3,500 feet of pipe. A road to the staff residences and one to the utility area were also roughed in, followed by liquid asphalt, sealing, gravel chips, and oil.[103]

Staff Housing

Tonto staff lived for a while in the museum building, but the pressures of living constantly in the public eye led Custodian Peavy to construct a tent house in 1940 just south of the museum for himself, his wife, and his daughter. This structure was made up of two tents end-to-end complemented by a sheltered gas refrigerator and hot plate.

In March 1940, Hugh M. Miller, acting superintendent for Southwestern Monuments, inspected Tonto. Referring to the custodian's quarters he wrote,

Figure 33: Tonto National Monument entrance road, 1953

The master plan location for employees' residences is in a side canyon. The tiny house erected by the Southern Pacific is hopelessly inadequate as family quarters, especially since certain artifacts derived from the site are exhibited in one small room. The custodian, his wife, and infant child live, sleep, and eat in a space not more than 10 x 12 feet. Peavy prefers tent quarters and he was authorized to retain the tent cabins erected for the convenience of the Mobile Unit detachment, upon withdrawal of the detachment. He will move into these two tents, remove the flimsy partition in the little stone building, and utilize all of it as a public contact and exhibit space. This arrangement, while subjecting the custodian to some inconvenience, is at least in line with policy in separating family activities from the immediate contact point and the resulting confusion and embarrassment both the family and to monument visitors. Construction of a permanent custodian's dwelling should be given high priority on the future construction program. Water is already available from the spring, sewage disposal facilities may be limited and inexpensive.[104]

In November 1941, the acting regional director for Region Three reported on a trip he made to Tonto the month before. What he saw impressed him both positively and negatively:

> It was my first opportunity to inspect Tonto National Monument since a permanent custodian, Mr. John Peavy, was assigned to Tonto. I was impressed with the way he has taken care of his area and handled the visitors without assistance … but greatly shocked at the conditions under which he has to live … one can not appreciate the conditions under which our custodian has lived and worked for nearly two years without seeing-it for themselves.[105]

The memo described the Peavys as having no privacy, and although Mr. and Mrs. Peavy did not complain, "continued existence under the conditions which prevail at Tonto seems more than we can reasonably expect from anyone." It was "hard to imagine any more urgently needed physical improvement, or 'more justifiable, within the Service."[106]

Superintendent Sharp's notes on the housing situation give a further sense of how little separation there was between the public and the private lives of staff. He recalled,

> When the Peavys left for Saguaro, Mrs. C♯ and I cooked in the tent-house, used the refrigerator, and slept in our 11 foot trailer on the parking area for about 3 months. This was a bit public too, and we always had to get up early, as one never knew when an early visitor would come roaring in. Travel was light in the hot weather, about 300 per month, almost all very interested visitors, and there were even quite a few days when no one came in.

Figure 34: Tonto National Monument maintenance headquarters, 1953

That was when I developed "Tonto ears." One would start out in fatigues, get all sweaty doing some trail work or road work, then hear a car coming up, and run to get into more presentable clothes. Since you could never be sure whether a car would come in (on week days) and hated just to sit and wait for visitors, quite a bit of this monkey business went on. The Tonto Ears were very useful too for taking a bath. In warm weather, the bather stood on the back steps of the museum, turned a hose on himself, and got cleaned up, listening meanwhile for cars. This was a sporting hazard, but not too hard, since the road was rough and the cars slower and noisier than they are now. Even so, a few stories about Tonto being a nudist camp got around.[107]

These conditions prevailed until Custodian Gipe built a house in 1943. According to Sharp's recollections,

Doc Gipe excavated the site with pick, shovel, and wheelbarrow, from the tough rocky bank, poured the concrete in slabs after mixing it by hand (for the floor slab), and built the cabin almost single-handed. Rancher Neal Lyall helped him occasionally with jobs that took 2 men, and I imagine Mrs. G helped also. They built the cabin hell for strong.[108]

Supplies were so tight that Sharp said they had to get authorization from Washington for nails to finish the job. Doc Gipe's construction was made from used lumber. It was 32 feet long, 22 feet wide for half its length and 16 feet wide over the rest. Situated on a small terrace dug from the hillside, the structure's back wall was built into the hill. Ten years later, in 1953, a request for emergency funds for residential construction at Tonto described the superintendent's quarters as

> a one-room cabin built from salvage materials ten years ago. This cabin is considerably below National Park Service standards, and was constructed as a temporary expedient pending a building program, at a period of time when the whole Monument was far below present standards of public use and development.
>
> It has no bedroom, and no adequate storage space. It would be quite inadequate for permanent residence of a family with children, but would be adequate for seasonal ranger quarters if the proposed residences are built. Present quarters for the seasonal ranger is a tenthouse in the utility area.[109]

The archeologist's accommodations were even less favorable, as described in a 1953 report:

> The present archaeologist, his wife, one two-year-old child, and one baby, exist in the trailer now. I wish to emphasize that in this area, it is considered necessary that the children sleep in screened cribs to protect them from deadly scorpions, centipedes, and other poisonous animals which cannot be kept out of housing here. The two screened cribs now in the trailer take up all the space normally used in trailers as a living room, and cause fantastically crowded conditions. The archaeologist has been forced to build a small screen-house outside under the tree, but even this is necessarily used largely for storage of necessary household items, and is scarcely available for living room. This condition has endured here for two years.[110]

It is probable that the negative publicity of 1949–50, as well as a 1951 fire that destroyed the archeologist's army surplus trailer, spurred approval of emergency improvement plans. Suddenly, conditions that had been tolerated for twenty years were no longer acceptable. In 1950 a telephone system was installed. In 1952 electric lights were installed in the museum. In 1953 the Salt River Water Users' Association entered into a new agreement to supply electric power. By the end of 1953 new roads, a parking area, a water system, staff residences, and a comfort station were installed at Tonto.

During the first twenty years of NPS administration, Tonto National Monument remained understaffed and underfunded. Its remoteness, coupled with the financial hardships caused by the Depression and World War II, conspired to keep Tonto's archeological resources in a precarious state, its visitor accommodations spartan, and its infrastructure insufficient. Indeed, the monument survived because of the hardiness, initative, and determination of its staff. By the early 1950s, the end of the war combined with negative publicity likely helped secure emergency funds to bring Tonto National Monument's infrastructure up to acceptable standards. For most of this early period, however, the National Park Service—despite its best intentions— proved ultimately unable to protect the cliff dwellings or provide adequate accommodations for staff and visitors. But times, finally, were changing. Over the next ten years, Mission 66, a national project of immense proportions, would enable Tonto to begin to reach its potential as a national monument.

---

1. Toll (1932, 2).

2. Ibid., p. 3.

3. Rothman (1985, 226).

4. Rothman (1985, 210–411) presents on the NPS during the period of the 1920s through WW II. Rothman (1986 and 1989) are both excellent sources for information about Pinkley's changing role and status in the park system.

5. Rothman (1985, 288).

6. Shortly after Pinkley's death, the SWMA monthly report for February 1940 included the following tribute to Pinkley: "You know, a fellow never is appreciated fully until after he has gone away. We are just beginning to realize the importance of some of the things that you have done for the National Park Service and for us. As an organization, we have always been mighty proud of our Esprit de Corps and of our loyalty to you and to each other. Your transfer hasn't weakened that loyalty a bit, in fact it has strengthened it immeasurably. No matter what happens, as long as the Southwestern National Monuments is an organization, we will be known as Frank Pinkley's Outfit. Through your persistent work, your determination, and your everlasting belief in and loyalty to the ideals of the National Park Service, you built up the strongest unit in that Service, and, God willing, we are going to keep it the strongest. One of your most difficult accomplishments was impressing the Service, as a whole, with the fact that national monuments are not second-rate parks. You went even further, and brought that fact to the attention of part of the public. We alone realize how much it worried you to feel the misunderstanding which people had as to the meaning and function of national monuments" (SWMA monthly report, February, 1940, pp. 1–11).

7. Material by C .R. Steen for Area History, Tonto National Monument, 1956, p. 3.

8. SWMA monthly report, July 1934, p. 30. In December 1934, the monthly report of the SWMA reflected the various NPS personnel who were in charge of the 25 southwestern monuments. One monument had an acting custodian; 14 had custodians, 6 had no custodians, 3 were in the charge of park rangers, and 3 people in positions of responsibility were, like Steen, listed simply as "in charge."

9. SWMA supplement, January 1935 pp. 41–42; SWMA supplement, August 1935, pp. 147–149.

10. SWMA monthly report, February 1935, p. 61.

11. SWMA monthly report, February 1936, p. 111. Woodrow Spires reported running across "semi-professional" pothunters who knew the difference between local types of pottery. He let them know he represented the federal government, and they reported they were out of work and had to feed their families. After promising they would never do it again, Spires let them go. He notes "thrashing out the matter" with the Forest Service so that they could curb pothunting in the vicinity.

12. SWMA monthly report, September 1941, p. 32.

13. SWMA monthly report, November 1934, p. 229.

14. SWMA monthly report, September 1934.

15. Toll (1932, 2).

16. SWMA monthly report, July 1935, p. 26.

17. SWMA monthly report, December 1934, p. 279.

18. SWMA monthly report, September 1936.

19. SWMA monthly report, February 1939, pp. 96–97.

20. SWMA monthly report, February 1941, p. 70, and SWMA monthly report, March 1941, p. 153.

21. *My Trip through the Tonto National Monument*, Ira Peavy, June 3, 1941. National Archives, Laguna Niguel, Box 4 433-01 to 630-640, Folder #501, Publicity 1936–1951.

22. SWMA monthly report, September 1941, p. 32.

23. SWMA monthly report, February 1943, p. 15, and SWMA monthly report, November 1943, p. 14.

24. E. C. Gipe, Custodian, Report to SWMA, March 25, 1944.

25. Assistant Naturalist Natt N. Dodge, Memorandum to the Superintendent, reporting on his visit to Tonto National Monument on August 28–30, 1941, September 2, 1941 (NA, Laguna Niguel, Box 1 06–250, Folder #204-20, Inspections and Investigations by Headquarters Office 1936-40).

26. Ibid.

27. Charles C. Sharp, Acting Custodian, Memorandum to the Superintendent, Southwestern National Monuments, August 26, 1942 (NA Laguna Niguel, Box 9 D3415-K2615, Folder #K18, Museums and Nature Trails 1937-53).

28. Ibid.

29. Ibid.

30. Sharp (1956, 1–2).

31. In 1951 the special skills of the archeologist at Tonto were listed as first aid, skier (not professional but skilled), usage of topographic maps, photographer, equipment operator, auto and airplane mechanic, fire suppression experience with NPS and Forest Service, fire lookout experience, blasting dynamite (both fuse and electric caps. Superintendent Sharp's

skills were listed as equipment and tractor operation, riding and packing, rifle and pistol shot, supervision and maintenance of vehicles, driver (light duty trucks and pickups), aerial observation (some experience), and pilot (light planes, in extreme emergency only.) Training was done with employees to meet, direct, guide, or inform the public; training should be a matter of course on physical aspects of the areas, routine of highways, distances, and general travel info, and should stress requirements of courtesy, helpfulness, and genuine friendliness. (NA Laguna Niguel Box 6 840.02.02- 883, Folder 840.020.02: Libraries 1940–53).

32. Sharp to general superintendent, SWMA, February 23, 1952, NA Laguna Niguel, Box 5 660.01-833.02, Folder 833.02: Natural Resources 1935–36 (actual materials span 1935-1957).

33. Telephone conversation with Robert Viklund by author, 10/26/05.

34. Louis Caywood (1962) edited four scientific papers about excavation work at the Tonto National Monument in one volume, including the work of Steen and Duffen. See Archeological Studies at Tonto National Monument, Arizona, published by the Southwestern Monuments Association, Gila Pueblo, Globe, Arizona, Technical Series vol. 2.

35. Several sources for the history of southwestern archeology that affected this time span include Fowler (2000) and Reid and Whittlesey (1997). This section borrows heavily from the work of Chris Downum, an archeologist at Northern Arizona University, who created a web course, especially lecture 2 on The Discipline: History and Methods of Southwestern Archaeology, as well as his 1993 article in Expedition Magazine on the past, present, and future of Southwestern Archaeology.

36. Kidder (1924)

37. Downum (1993, 13).

38. Ibid., pp. 1–25.

39. Houk (1992, 3). Reid and Whittlesey (1997, 236–238) credit four archeologists with enriching our early understanding of Salado: Erich Schmidt, Gladwin, Florence Hawley, and Emil Haury.

40. Caywood (1946).

41. Memoranda between archeologists Schroeder, Pierson, and Steen 1952–54, NA Laguna Niguel, Box 9 D3415-K2615, Folder H2215, National Park Service Areas 1935–61

42. Ibid.

43. At the National Park Conference held in Yellowstone National Park in 1911 there was a note about the Tonto cliff dwellings that indicates that Park Service personnel might have already begun to question whether the condition of the ruins rendered them less significant. The note reads, "The ruins are not of the first class, but they are located so close to what is fast becoming a large urban and agricultural population that their reservation as a monument is believed to be in the public interest." Albert H. Schroeder sent this note to the Superintendent at Tonto as part of compiling the area history information. (Schroeder to superintendent at Tonto, July 13, 1956, Tonto History File).

44. Cosner (1956, 5).

45. C.F. Barry. letter to Charles Sharp, Supt Tonto Cliff Dwelling, March 16, 1953, NA Laguna Niguel, Box 5 660-01 to 833-02, Folder 833.02: Natural Resources 1935–1936 (materials in this folder actually extend to 1957).

46. Ibid.

47. Bandelier (1892).

48. SWMA monthly report, October, 1935, also quoted by Guthrie (1994, 2).

49. Guthrie (1994, 2).

50. Spires to Pinkley, October 11,1935.

51. SWMA monthly report, May 1936, p. 334, and SWMA monthly report for June 1936, p. 446.

52. Ibid.

53. Emil Haury letter to Charles R. Steen, May 10, 1935, NA Laguna Niguel, Box 5 660-01–833–02, Folder 833.02 Natural Resources.

54. Ibid.

55. Dale S. King, park naturalist, Memorandum to Archaeology File, Tonto National Monument, March 11, 1938.

56. William A. Duffen, draft notes for Tonto Ruins Stabilization, May 27 to June 30, 1937, published in Caywood (1962, 69–70).

57. Richert (1957, 2).

58. Guthrie (1994, 8–9).

59. Caywood (1962).

60. "Report of the Director's Committee on Ruins Stabilization, September 27–October 2, 1940, Santa Fe, New Mexico," pp. 7–8, NA Laguna Niguel, Box 5 660-01-833-02, Folder 833.02, Natural Resources.

61. Ibid., p. 26.

62. Ibid., p. 30.

63. Ibid., pp. 31–36.

64. John Peavy, Cust., Tonto NM letter to Hugh Miller, Supt. SWMA, outlining stabilization work needed at Tonto within the next 12 months, November, 27, 1940, NA Laguna Niguel Box 5 660-833-02, Folder 833.02, Natural Resources.

65. Guthrie's analysis in 1994 of the research and stabilization projects at Tonto reveals the shortcomings of Steen's 1940 excavation, but she reserves her harshest criticism for Pierson's 1950s excavation in the Lower Ruin and the South and North Annex. Guthrie (1994, 8).

66. Joel Shiner, archeologist, memo to regional director, January 7, 1959, NA Laguna Niguel, Box 5 660-01-833-02, Folder 833-02: Natural Resources 1935–36 (actually involves cultural resources and spans to 1959). Shiner wrote this memo in response to fears that visitors' abuses needed to be curbed, which will be addressed in the following chapter.

67. Hugh M. Miller, acting superintendent, Memorandum for files, headquarters, Southwestern Monuments, March 19, 1940, NA Laguna Niguel, Box 1 06–250, Folder 204–20, Inspections and Investigations by Headquarters Office 1936–40.

68. Memorandum from Superintendent to General Superintendent, Tonto, July 12, 1952, NA Laguna Niguel, Box 5 660.01-833.02, Folder 833.62: Natural Resources, Ruins Stabilization, p. 3.

69. Ibid., p. 4.

70. Memorandum from Superintendent to General Superintendent, Tonto, Re: Proposed Trail to Upper Ruins, Tonto, October 19, 1953, NA Laguna Niguel Box 5 660.01-833.02, Folder 833.62, Natural Resources, Ruins Stabilization, pp. 2–3.

71. The transfer included T.4N, R12E, Sec. 26 SW ¼; Sec. 27, SE ¼; Sec. 35, NW ¼.

72. Memorandum of Agreement between the National Park Service and the United States Forest Service Relative to the Issuance of Permits for Grazing within the Boundaries of the Tonto National Monument Located in Gila County, Arizona, NA Laguna Niguel, Box 7 883-901-01, Folder 901-01, Grazing Permits, Correspondence concerning Forest Service Experimental Plot and Collecting Permits 1942–53. This file contains a series of letters between the Southwestern Region of the Forest Service and the NPS that refer to considerable confusion the two agencies had in arriving at even the appropriate form for the agreement. After the memorandum of agreement was signed, it became clear that the NPS and the USFS had used a form for similar situations in the Coronado National Forest involving the Chiricahua and Saguaro national monuments. This form eliminated the clause that called for proportionate sharing of the grazing receipts to the Park Service since the amount involved was insignificant. Regardless of using a non-preferred form of agreement, the terms were agreed to as of July 17, 1942.

73. Barbour (1999, 26).

74. Letter from John Peavy to Superintendent Hugh Miller, SWMA, October 19, 1941 (McChristian (1999) refers to it as being in HF headquarter files).

75. John Peavy, Custodian, Tonto NM, Memorandum to the Superintendent of Southwestern Monuments, June 13, 1942, NA Laguna Beach Box 8 S2623-D30, Folder D-30, Roads and Trails 1940–51.

76. Ibid., p. 27.

77. "Summary of Potential Grazing in Southwestern National Monuments," NA Laguna Niguel, Box 7 883-901-01, Folder 901-01: Grazing Permits, Correspondence Concerning Forest Service Experimental Plot and Collecting Permits 1942–53.

78. Ibid.

79. Memorandum to the Secretary, United States Department of the Interior, National Park Service, Chicago, February 15, 1943, NA Laguna Niguel, Box 7 883-901-01, Folder 901-01, Grazing Permits, Correspondence Concerning Forest Service Experimental Plot and Collecting Permits 1942-53.

80. Ibid.

81. Ibid.

82. Department of the Interior Secretary Lane to Mather, NPS, May 13, 1918. NA Laguna Niguel, Box 1 06-250, Folder 204-20, Inspections and Investigations by Headquarters Office 1936-40.

83. Department of the Interior Secretary Lane to Mather, NPS, March 11, 1925, NA Laguna Niguel, Box 1 06-250, Folder 204-20, Inspections and Investigations by Headquarters Office 1936–40.

84. Department of Interior Secretary Ickes, February 16, 1939, NA Laguna Niguel, Box 1 06-250, Folder 204-20, Inspections and Investigations by Headquarters Office 1936–40.

85. "Reasons Why Commercial Livestock Are Undesirable in the National Park System," NA Laguna Niguel, Box 7 883-901-01, Folder 901-01, Grazing Permits, Correspondence Concerning Forest Service Experimental Plot and Collecting Permits 1942–53.

86. Memorandum to the Regional Directors, March 25, 1943, NA Laguna Niguel, Box 7 883-901-01, Folder 901-01, Grazing Permits, Correspondence Concerning Forest Service Experimental Plot and Collecting Permits 1942–53.

87. Ibid.

88. Memorandum from Superintendent to General Superintendent, Tonto, Request of Rancher Chester Cooper to graze stock on Monument., NA Laguna Niguel, Box 7 883-901-01, Folder 901-01, Grazing Permits, Correspondence Concerning Forest Service Experimental Plot and Collecting Permits 1942–53.

89. Cited by Barbour (1999, 25–26).

90. Barbour (1999, 28) cites memorandum from Ben H. Thompson to Regional Director, May 8, 1945.

91. Charles Sharp to general superintendent, SWMA November 11, 1954 (quoted by McChristian)

92. Ibid.

93. Sellars (1997, 91–112).

94. Swarth (1920, 18).

95. SWMA supplement, January, 1939 pp. 71–73.

96. SWMA monthly report, November 25, 1939.

97. Hugh M. Miller, Acting Superintendent, Memorandum for files, headquarters, Southwestern Monuments, March 19, 1940, NA Laguna Niguel, Box 1 06-250, Folder 204-20: Inspections and Investigations by Headquarters Office 1936–40.

98. SWMA monthly report, April 1941, p. 202.

99. Ibid., pp. 9–10.

100. Everhart (1983, 26).

101. *Arizona Republic*, June 18, 1950, section 2, p. 3.

102. Sharp (1956, 9).

103. "Completion Report—Project 323.04,Entrance Road—Tonto National Monument," August 1, 1953, NA Laguna Niguel, Box 5 660.01–833.02, Folder 713: Birds 1954–1956.

104. Hugh M. Miller, Acting Superintendent, Memorandum for files, headquarters, Southwestern Monuments, March 19, 1940, NA Laguna Niguel, Box 1 06-250, Folder 204-20, Inspections and Investigations by Headquarters Office 1936–40.

105. SWMA Superintendent Memorandum to the acting regional director, Region Three, November 1, 1941, NA Laguna Niguel, Box 1 06-250, Folder 204-20: Inspections and Investigations by Headquarters Office 1936–40 (actual materials span 1936–1953).

106. Ibid.

107. Sharp (1956, 4).

108. Sharp (1956, 5).

109. Superintendent, Tonto National Monument, Memorandum to general superintendent, SWMA, June 26, 1953, NA Laguna Niguel, Box 1 of 3 transferred from Denver, Subject: Need for Residences 1952–53.

110. Ibid.

chapter five
A TIME OF TRANSITION: MISSION 66, 1954–1966

During World War II, National Park Service funds—like most domestic resources—were limited. Maintenance was restricted to such an extent that by war's end, many Park Service roads, buildings, and other facilities had seriously deteriorated. Nor did the financial picture immediately improve after the war. By 1950 funding was 25 percent lower than before the war, despite the fact that there were twice as many visitors to the parks and twenty-one new parks for them to visit. [1]

This was no secret to the American public. Bernard DeVoto, a prominent historian and journalist, captured the essence of the NPS dilemma in a 1953 *Harper's* magazine article provocatively titled "Let's Close the National Parks." DeVoto charged Congress with treating the Park Service like an "impoverished stepchild," or like a widow who "scrapes and patches and ekes out," using "desperate expedients" in an effort to survive.[2] The article popularized phrases such as "people loving the parks to death" and "patch on patch no longer possible" to describe the condition of the parks. It grimly detailed the challenge facing the National Park Service: the need to revitalize overcrowded, deteriorating parks and monuments suffering from long-term neglect. Clearly, it was time to act.

Enter National Park Service Director Conrad Wirth. Beginning in 1952, Wirth developed an ambitious multiyear effort that would bring momentous changes to Tonto National Monument and virtually all other park properties. Wirth proposed to repair, rebuild, construct new buildings and housing, hire new employees,

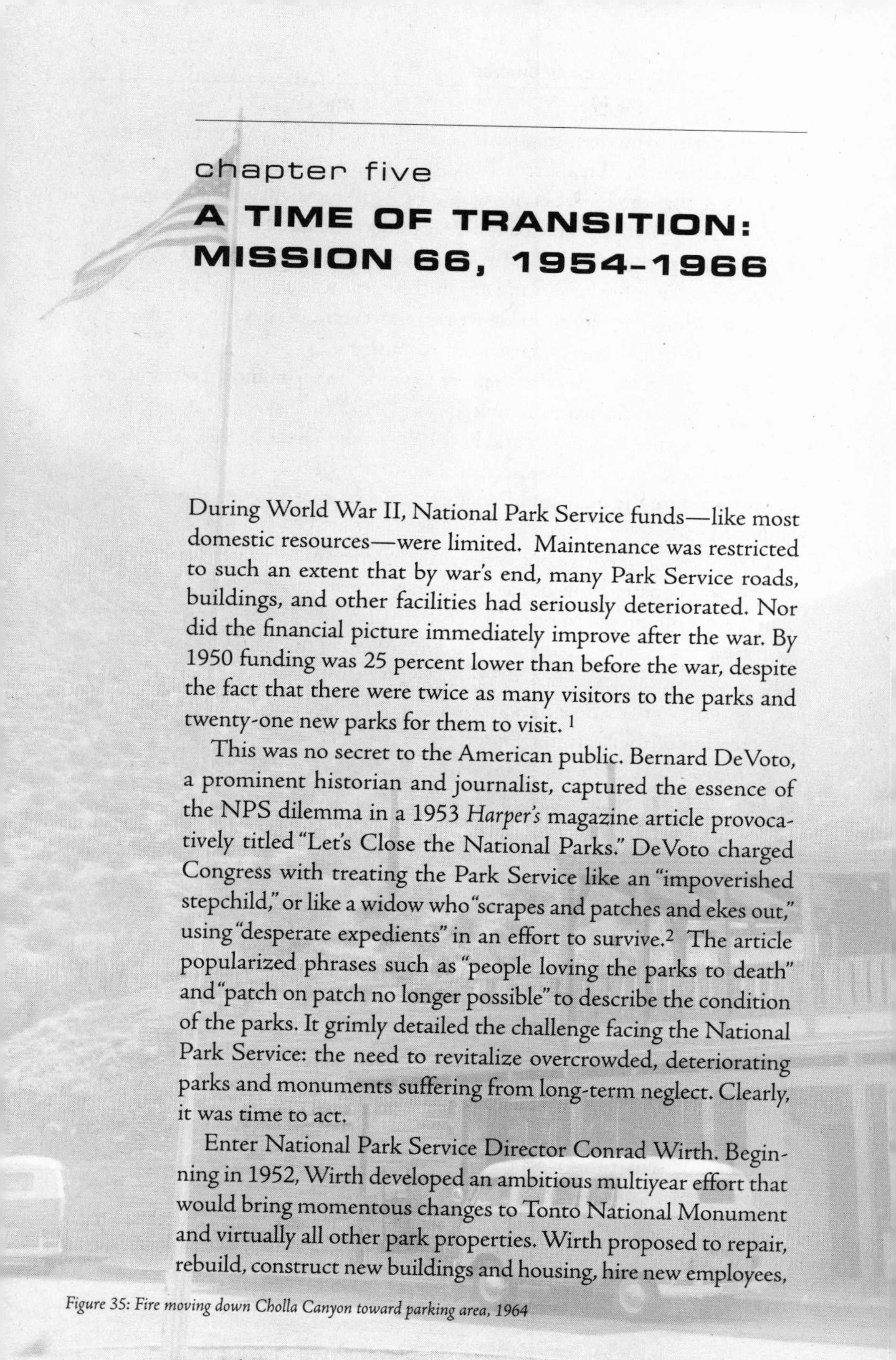

Figure 35: Fire moving down Cholla Canyon toward parking area, 1964

raise the parks to modern standards of comfort and efficiency, and at the same time conserve natural resources. He called the plan Mission 66 because estimates were that the Park Service would be handling eighty million visits per year by 1966. Wirth's proposed ten-year budget included a remarkable array of projects—park roads, trails, airport runways, parking areas, campgrounds, picnic areas, campfire circles and amphitheaters, utilities, administrative and service buildings, employee residences, comfort stations, interpretive roadside and trailside exhibits, and marina improvements.

The National Park Service then set to work. Superintendents formulated detailed Mission 66 plans at meetings in 1952 in Glacier National Park, 1953 in Yosemite National Park, and 1955 in the Great Smoky Mountains National Park. Wirth led a successful campaign of both publicity and politics to promote the plan, and President Dwight Eisenhower approved it in January 1956.

One of the immediate outcomes was the creation of eastern and western design and construction offices to oversee construction of the 109 visitor centers recommended to be built between 1956 and 1966. Horace Albright, who served as assistant to the first superintendent of the National Park Service and as superintendent until 1933, ranked Mission 66 as one of the "noblest conceptions in the whole national park history,"ranking in importance" with the creation of the National Park Service itself."[3]

Prior to Mission 66, the National Park Service had planned on an annual basis only. That made Mission 66 a novel approach not only in the breadth of its content but also in its forward-looking vision. It also introduced a significant change in the NPS philosophy of visitor management. Planners analyzed visitation needs for an entire park area and designated special zones for maintenance, employee housing, administration, and visitor services. The visitor center became the "hub" of a park's interpretive program—drawing visitors inside and providing them with information, maps, audio-visual programs, museum exhibits, and whatever else necessary before sending them outside to the park's major attractions.[4]

These changes in visitor management practices also led to a change in park architecture. The rustic style used previously throughout the system was rooted in nineteenth-century English landscape traditions and called for designs that harmonized structures with their surrounding natural landforms. Materials native to the local area were used, and they usually gave the impression that they had been constructed by craftsmen. After the war, however, with changes in both architectural trends and in the functions of the park buildings, rustic architecture was no longer thought to fit the parks' needs.

In its place, Mission 66 created a distinctive new type of NPS architecture that is now referred to as Park Service Modern. Rather than designing buildings to be picturesque elements of the landscape, the new approach designed them to be as unobtrusive as possible, with low horizontal profiles and flat roofs. Composed of textured concrete and other cheap materials, the new buildings aimed for an image of modern efficiency, as they fostered visitor flow among exhibit areas, auditoriums, restrooms, and lobbies.[5]

At Tonto National Monument, Mission 66 planning and implementation activities dominated for ten years, from the beginning of planning in 1955 to the opening of the new visitor center on February 21, 1965. This chapter chronicles Tonto's Mission 66 experience in detail, not only because it resulted in major physical and interpretive changes at the time, but also because these changes set the physical structure and framed the visitor experience at Tonto for the following forty years.

MISSION 66 PLANNING AT TONTO

In 1955 Tonto was in a good position to respond to the challenges and opportunities offered by Mission 66. Tonto had already addressed the basic inadequacies in infrastructure and employee housing. By 1954 the monument boasted new residences, adequate quarters for the first time for regular staff, a cabin available for a seasonal ranger (previously only a tent was available), a comfort station for visitors, and a power line link. The move of the Southwestern Monuments office from Casa Grande to Globe was also of considerable benefit for Tonto because it placed the regional office in close proximity for administrative and technical help.

In May 1954 the main deficiencies in infrastructure at Tonto remained cramped facilities, including the 12 x 22 foot museum building, the attached 7 x 19 foot lean-to that served as office space, and the vehicle shelters.[6] At the same time, other factors—both natural and human-made—complicated matters. An admission fee, imposed beginning July 1, 1954, proved unpopular with visitors, many of whom chose to leave without seeing the museum and cliff dwellings. Morale was further damaged by the seasonal malady of bug bites, resulting in a lethargic staff who "showed the usual Tobacco Road syndrome, which is characterized by general malaise, weakness and lack of zip, headaches, and itching at the locus of the puncture."[7]

Preparation of the Prospectus

But Mission 66 left little time for lethargy. In memos written in February and March of 1955, Wirth notified NPS superintendents—including Sharp at

Figure 36: Old museum and new parking lot, 1949

Tonto National Monument—of the upcoming changes and goals. In July 1955, superintendents were required to submit a park or monument prospectus, consisting of a narrative plan for protection, development, interpretation, and operation, as well as an eleven-year budget for proposed construction projects. This was not to be business as usual. Superintendents were to "disregard precedent and give full play to imagination in an effort to arrive at new approaches to old problems," and to "disregard existing limitations of existing development outlines, master plans, policies and practices, etc."[8] Superintendent Sharp complied, and his prospectus was received enthusiastically by John M. Davis, general superintendent of the Southwestern Monuments, and by Robert Hall, the acting chief of the Western Office, Division of Design and Construction. The only revision they suggested was relatively minor. Sharp had suggested a closed-circuit television as the best way to give visitors who could not make the climb a sense of the ruin; reviewers instead suggested using a less-expensive film projector.[9]

Siting and Planning the New Visitor Center

In September 1955 the NPS regional director based in Santa Fe, New Mexico, questioned the feasibility and suitability of the proposed site for building

Tonto's headquarters. His questions were prompted by regional archeologist Charles Steen, who argued—not for the first time—that the proposed site at the base of a steeply sloping canyon (today's site) was inappropriate. Steen described it as follows:

> The present parking area, and the area proposed for headquarters development, is conspicuous and is built partly on fill in a steeply sloping canyon. The area involved is restricted in size and the whole arrangement is obnoxious and obtrusive. From the lower ruin, which is the focal point for most visitors, the parking area stands out glaringly and any additional structure will add to the disfigurement of the monument.[10]

Steen urged reconsideration of one of his previous proposals: that all construction at Tonto be located just below the mouth of the canyon and that the then-current parking area be torn out. Citing the Mission 66 concept that freedom for revised thinking should be encouraged, the regional director asked the Tonto superintendent to reanalyze the issue. Sharp was quick to respond. Steen's argument that future development should occur just below the mouth of the canyon was hardly a new point of contention between the two. They had argued the issue several years before, and Steen had reluctantly agreed to Sharp's view. But Steen saw the Mission 66 planning process as a opportunity to revisit the question. Sharp, on the other hand, did not. On October 5, 1955, he responded,

> Having been here off and on since 1942, I have heard, thought of, and considered just about everything in the way of possible development, short of installing wings on the visitors, that I believe could be suggested. The idea of placing all construction and building development outside the canyon is not new to me, and this idea had considerable merit if it had been followed from the beginning.
>
> For reasons given below, and in the light of present development and conditions, I strongly urge that it be disregarded now, that the location recommended by myself and by the General Superintendent be approved, and our efforts concentrated on trying to obtain the public use building.
>
> Listed below are the things which would have to be done in order to return the canyon sufficiently near to its pristine glory to justify demolition of the developments recently made:
> 1. Obliteration of a $25,000 parking area.
> 2. Removal and obliteration of a $7,500 comfort station.

3. Removal of about $2,000 worth of power lines.
4. Removal of Quarters #2, replacement cost $5,000.
5. Obliteration of .1 mile of road and disassembly of an $8,000 set of multi-plate culverts.
6. Obliteration of the present Southern Pacific building, which would meet with no objection here.

Even though all that were to be done, the residence and utility area would show up very well, practically all the way up the ruins trails. A very conspicuous part of the view from the ruin is Roosevelt Lake, which is far more attention-compelling than Cholla Canyon. This is of course an artificial lake which has irretrievably altered the primeval scene which the Indians knew.[11]

Steen argued that the parking lot could be washed out by a violent rain. Sharp countered that this scenario was as unlikely as an earthquake that would bring the cliff crashing down on the dwelling—possible, that is, but not probable. Sharp prevailed. Over the next several years the prospectus was revised and amended, but Sharp's original planning for Mission 66 proved remarkably durable. Although he was transferred to Chaco Canyon in February 1956, his initial proposal for Mission 66's physical layout at Tonto National Monument was adopted and remains to this day.

The job of steering Tonto through the rest of the Mission 66 experience fell to Wiffler Oakes, who became superintendent in July 1957. A document produced shortly thereafter, the September 1957 Prospectus Brief, remains the clearest record of how Tonto presented itself and its Mission 66 planning. The brief defined Tonto's major problem as inadequate interpretive facilities to cope with the increasing volume of visitors, and insufficient safeguards to protect and preserve the ruins--not only from the 36,572 visitors who came in 1956, but also for the 85,000 projected to arrive in 1966.[12] But the brief was just the start of the task. Between 1957 and 1962, Tonto National Monument staff compiled and documented a wide range of information, objectives, and policies concerning park organization, design, interpretation, forestry, soil and moisture conservation, buildings, utilities, and other matters; these became the 1964 Tonto National Monument Master Plan.

The 1957 Prospectus Brief placed prime importance on construction of a new visitor center that would serve as the "central point from which all interpretation will stem," and "will house the exhibit room, lobby, storage and work space, and administrative offices."[13] The exhibit room was deemed of special importance, as it would provide the background information necessary about the area; it would also "carry the visitor step by step through the everyday life of the Salado Indians and will display the artifacts of their handiwork and craftsmanship."[14]

Ruins stabilization was another pressing concern. The brief stated that so many of the walls in the upper ruin were unstable that visitation had to be restricted, and that a complete stabilization would be required before the public could be readmitted. It also noted that work in the as yet unexcavated rooms was expected to add to the artifact collection and aid the interpretive story in the museum. The lunch area and the water system were to be expanded. Two new apartment-type residences would be constructed to house new staff and seasonal employees. The 1957 brief was quickly approved, though with reduced budget and staffing projections.

The July 7, 1958 version of the brief offers a glimpse of contemporary thinking on visitor management. It ranked the principal visitor interests at Tonto as (and "will always be") archeology, photography, nature rambles, hiking, and bird watching.[15] Visitors had to learn three things to understand the true significance of Tonto:

> (1) learn how the Indians built for the environment, through the archeo-logical remains; (2) learn how prehistoric man modified the environment (physical changes the Indians must have wrought in the terrain, such as irrigation dams, planted areas, etc.); (3) learn how the Indians used the existing environment and its products (the fruits, berries, nuts, fuel, minerals, etc.).[16]

To achieve this, it was necessary that visitors have a variety of ways to experience the park: a trip to the principal ruins with guides, a trek along self-guided natural trails with emphasis on ethnobotany, exhibits at or near the parking area, and sufficient natural history information for visitors to identify the birds and animals they saw.

From Rustic Style to Park Modern

The Southern Pacific Railroad's custodian house, built in the rustic style in 1932, served as the NPS museum and office for Tonto from 1934 to 1965. Despite this longevity, the museum, and especially the office located in a lean-to attached to the museum, were inadequate as Park Service facilities. Mission 66 ended this long-standing deficit by providing Tonto a new visitor center. The timing was right: because Tonto's new construction was scheduled toward the end of the Mission 66 era, it benefited from NPS experience in putting up other new centers throughout the country.[17]

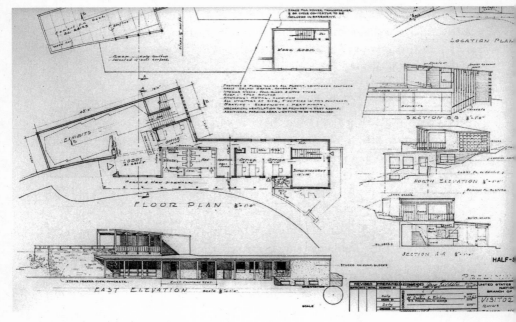

Figure 37: Floor plan for Mission 66 visitor center

Visitor center components were generally based on the Park Modern design principles. The new structure usually included a lobby, which focused on an information desk where visitors could wait and gather for trips; an exhibit space that explained the area's features; an auditorium for audio-visual presentations; restrooms (usually with outside access); and office space. The center's aim was to attract visitors inside, encourage them to approach the information desk, watch an audio/visual program, get a map, see the views, and go on to the major attraction. Serving as a one-stop service unit, the centers were designed to increase efficiency, control visitor flow, and in general, to enhance the visitor experience.[18]

One of the principal architects of Mission 66 visitor centers—including Tonto's—was Cecil Doty, a long-time and prolific NPS architect. He first visited the monument on July 21, 1954 along with Thomas C. Vint, chief of the Division of Design and Construction; Dick Sutton, chief architect, Ralph Lewis of museum division's Washington office; architect Lyle Bennett of the Western Division of Design and Construction in San Francisco; and architect Kenneth Saunders of the Regional Office. Doty prepared preliminary drawings for Tonto in July 1962, visited again in December 1963, and prepared working drawings from 1963 to 1965.

Doty's Mission 66 buildings used standard manufactured building materials, working within the constraints of both budgets and building codes. His consistent approach to visitor center design is characterized as follows:

> Two assembly areas would be typical. One would be an outside terrace, partly under cover. Restrooms, phone, and vending machines would be located here. Entry to the inside lobby, the second collection area, would be directly off the terrace. Large glazed panels between the inside and outside assembly areas enhanced the sense of connection. Sometimes similar paving materials would be carried from the outside into the lobby. The auditorium, exhibit spaces, information desk and book sales (a minor Mission 66 function that expanded in later years) opened to the lobby. A drinking fountain, seating, and a few special exhibits would be in the lobby as well. The lobby was the major public orientation space. Doty liked to make this and the exhibit rooms spacious enough so that people would not feel crowded or encouraged to move on before they were ready.[19]

The visitor center became a central component at NPS parks and monuments, and of the new effort to control visitor flow:

> One of the intentions of Mission 66 preservation was to control where visitors would go. They were no longer meant to wander about wherever they pleased. Instead, paved walkways and terraces directed people to the visitor center front door or to other approved places where their impact could be controlled. As a result, buildings could have public and non-public sides that could be treated differently.[20]

At Tonto, Doty used laminated beams and glass-paneled walls in an upper deck. One end of the east elevation consisted of stone veneer over concrete, while the other was stucco over concrete blocks. He used finer materials around the entrance, which was typical of his designs:

> The parking area, walks, terraces, and everything in and around the building are part of the visitor center ensemble, and are on exhibit as something constructed by the National Park Service. They can be more important than the exhibits themselves.[21]

Trails and Archeological-Site Planning

But once visitors left Tonto's new visitor center, where should they go? This period also witnessed a debate about where to build trails to the ruins. As part of his effort to avoid paths in Cholla Canyon, Steen had argued that the trail to the upper cliff dwelling should be tied to the lower cliff dwelling trail. Sharp had favored separate trails. In September 1957, it appeared that Steen's plan would prevail, as Superintendent Oakes supported the trail to both ruins to form a loop:

> The present self-guiding nature trail to the Lower Ruin will be improved to the extent that it will provide for less strenuous walking and physical exertion. Easy access to the Upper Ruin will be provided through construction of a trail system leading from the Lower Ruin and returning via Cholla Canyon, thus completing a loop walk. The trails will be so laid out that either one or both ruins can be visited in one trip. A short nature trail will also be provided in the vicinity of the visitor center.[22]

However, this was the last time that a loop trail was formally proposed. In the end, Sharp's ideas again prevailed, and the trails to the dwellings were constructed separately.

In September 1957 Earl Jackson from the Southwest Archeology Center inspected open site ruins (not the cliff dwellings) on the monument. Following his examination, he and Superintendent Oakes discussed a proposed trail to these ruins in the saddle east of the parking area. On November 4, 1957, Oakes requested that the trail sketches be modified to include an extension to the open site ruin.[23] In May 1958 a preliminary study and mapping of the village sites was conducted, the details of which were outlined in the monthly narrative report:

> A preliminary study and mapping of the Open Village Site east of the parking area in the saddle was made. It appears that it is late Pueblo II or Pueblo III. This would date the site from around 1000 AD to about 1250 AD There has been considerable discussion and preliminary planning done to excavate the site and put a trail in to it. Although this type site is quite common in the area, none of them have been excavated. Work on a site such as this should aid us materially in giving a more adequate interpretation of the Salados and their movement from the river homes to the cliff dwellings. It is planned to include a trail to this site and the site excavation in the master planning for the area.[24]

The July 1958 prospectus called for additional archeological research to determine the relationship of the recently surveyed open sites to the cliff dwellings. It also noted recent discoveries of several open sites not previously reported.[25] This was the first time that any sites other than the cliff dwellings were formally proposed to be made available to visitors to the monument.

Over the next several years, however, Oakes abandoned the idea of a trail to the open village sites. He referred to these sites at Tonto National Monument as "small, unspectacular open pueblo sites," that "do not seem to fill the need as they are quite small and would require excavation and, possibly, some degree of reconstruction to be worthwhile from the visitor's standpoint."[26] Indeed, Oakes in 1960 expressed continued disappointment that many visitors could not visit the ruins, lamenting that, regardless of the excellence of the exhibits at the new visitor center, "we still will not have provided the majority of the visitors with a means of visiting an interesting Indian ruin while at Tonto, which was their primary purpose for entering the area in the first place."[27] His new proposed solution was to expand the monument by adding three nearby surface sites, then on Forest Service land, which offered easier access for visitors. Working with archeologists from the Southwest Archeology Center and the acting archeologist at Tonto, Robin Dempster, Oakes proposed the addition of School House Point Ruin, Griffin Point Ruins, and Tonto Basin Ruin.[28] He characterized the large sites close to Roosevelt Lake as appropriate for addition to Tonto because they

would satisfy the visitor desire for the feeling that they have visited an interesting Indian ruin. These sites are large enough that a visitor could wander on the unexcavated, or nearly so, floor plan with considerable satisfaction. These sites are also acccessable [sic] without an arduous hike. Further, excavation at some future time, in the deep material of the large sites would almost certainly bring to light more interesting features as far as visitors would be concerned.

Detached sites would serve the following purposes: 1) provide an area which would give those visitors unable to climb to the cliff dwellings a chance to visit a ruin; 2) aid in the interpretation of the prehistory of the area by providing a means of showing the transition of architecture and associated culture from the earliest occupation near the river through the large and small open pueblos to the defensive cliff dwellings; 3) provide protection of valuable sites from vandalism and thereby insure their value for future archeological investigation; 4) provide for the dispersion of the visitors which would reduce the strain placed on the Lower Ruin at present. [29]

Oakes was seeking more than just visitor satisfaction. He argued that, by including an off-site experience, visitors would gain a fuller understanding of Salado chronology, at least as far as it was understood at the time. He was aware that the cliff dwellings represented the end stage of the Salado in the Tonto Basin, and suggested that another site from a different time frame would afford the visitor a more complete picture of the Salado:

> The Roosevelt Basin has not been as fortunate as some other south-western areas in the matter of scientific investigation, since only the site called "Roosevelt: 9:6" and the Lower Ruin at Tonto have been completely excavated and the Upper Tonto Ruin partially excavated. There is a considerable time gap as well as architectural difference between these sites. "Roosevelt:9:6" is recognized as Colonial Hohokam and is dated as circa 900–1000 AD. The Tonto cliff dwellings are dated as approximately 1300–1400 AD. The gap in our knowledge of the local architecture from the Hohokam pithouse to the Pueblo cliff type of construction has never been adequately explained or adequately defined. Nor, for that matter, has the confused cultural sequence of the area received the adequate study it deserves.
>
> The large pueblos outside the monument undoubtedly hold an important part of the Salado story as do primitive village sites and small masonry pueblos, none of which have been excavated. Archeological problems concerning these ruins, such as the presence of "compound walls" and their meaning, whether some of the sites are multi-storied structures or villages on mounded earth, while important to the scientific interpretation of the local prehistoric picture, are only side issues to the real need to supply visitors with a more complete enjoyment and understanding of the part played by Tonto National Monument in the reconstruction of the prehistory of the area.[30]

However, Oakes's superiors at the National Park Service declined to try to shift the sites from U.S. Forest Service control. In fact, the only joint planning between the two agencies was on the advisability of having a panel or exhibit in Tonto's new visitor center that would point out the differences between the two services.

Stabilization work during the Mission 66 era included the installation of kick-plate stones below doorsills to keep visitors from scuffing bases of walls in the lower ruin, and the strengthening of the dangerously weak two-story wall in the upper ruin's Room 9. For this project, which was carried out from March 13 to March 30, 1957, archeologists Gordon Vivian and Roland Richert employed six Navajo laborers from the Ruins Stabilization Mobile Unit; area ranchers provided pack horses for rent. In 1958 Joel Shiner and five Navajo laborers from the mobile unit made emergency repairs to lower cliff dwelling walls. Several years later, in January 1960, the telephone in the lower ruin was removed to eliminate an eyesore as well as a nuisance to interpreters. In 1962 the Park Service published a handbook on stabilization of prehistoric ruins with information on materials, techniques, and recording methods.[31]

Planning Exhibits and Interpretation

Exhibit planning for the visitor center required staff to analyze the monument's geology, plants, animals, and natural history. To design the exhibits, Oakes in 1958 sought the services of a geologist who could communicate in everyday language about the geological significance of the area. Charlie Steen, the former archeologist at Tonto then based in Santa Fe, New Mexico, requested the assistance of the American Geological Institute on behalf of Oakes. As a result, Robert B. Raup Jr. studied the area and submitted a geologic history of Tonto National Monument in 1959, including information on the origin of the caves and a description of the exposed rocks.[32] Robert Burgess conducted a study at Tonto between 1961 and 1965 on the botany, vascular flora, and use of desert plants by native peoples. His study drew on the flora collections begun by John Peavy around 1940; the collections by archeologist William Bromberg starting in 1958; and the studies by temporary employee Charles Strong in 1961.[33] Mission 66–era projects also included Vorsila Bohrer's studies of ethnobotanical materials at Tonto, Lyndon Hargrave's identification of archeological feathers and birds, Henry Jones's study of saguaros, and Philip Welles's report on mammals.[34] Louis Caywood edited four scientific papers on special projects that resulted from excavation work at Tonto from 1940 through 1958, including studies of archeology and ethnobotany, and an analysis of cotton textiles from Tonto.[35]

Museum exhibits require artifacts, and the Western Museum Laboratory, hired to create the exhibits at the new visitor center, became aware of the famous "Tonto shirt." Correspondence on the subject between the laboratory and the Arizona State Museum aimed to clarify its provenance. The exchange began on June 29, 1960, with the following request from Western Museum Laboratory:

Planning of the exhibits for the new Tonto Visitor Center is well under way, and it begins to look as if this may be one of our best small museums, at least insofar as quantity of good exhibit specimens is concerned.

We have quite a number of small bits and pieces of cloth for the textile exhibit, plus several fine weaving tools, but the key specimen for this case is not immediately available. This is the beautiful embroidered (if this is the proper term) Tonto shirt, found a few years ago by Dr. Emil Haury in the Upper Ruin at Tonto, and now in the Arizona State Museum at Tucson. The shirt would undoubtedly be the finest single specimen in the new Tonto museum if it could be returned to Tonto, and is one of the best finds to come from any NPS archeological area. At the present time we are showing a photograph of it in the little museum at Tonto.

Our details surrounding the finding of the shirt are hazy and second-handed, coming from Superintendent Oakes, but Lee Abel's recollection of his account is that Dr. Haury, while visiting the Upper Ruin with a photographer, found a bit of the textile uncovered in the dust, pulled it out, took it to Tucson, and put it in the State Museum. Superintendent Oakes would like to see the shirt returned to the monument for display, as would we.[36]

In September 1960, Emil Haury of the Arizona State Museum researched the provenance of the lace shirt from Tonto and responded,

It was found by the Rupkey brothers in 1923 which puts it about 16 years after the Tonto National Monument was set aside. It was given to the Museum about the same time by the finders. The circumstances seem to have been as follows. The front wall of one of the houses had fallen away, exposing the refuse beneath the floor, and it was in this refuse that the coiled basket, cut in half with the halves folded over each other, was found. The basket contained the remains of a baby, and wadded up in a bundle under the head was the shirt. The notes we have do not make clear whether it was found in the upper or the lower ruin. In fact, the records we have merely say "from a cliff dwelling near Roosevelt Dam, Arizona."

I would still like to leave the matter open awhile as to what we would finally do about your suggestion. Elizabeth King, a graduate assistant in the Museum now and a textile expert from the Textile Museum in

Washington, D.C., is going to look it over, first to see what, if anything, needs to be done for better preservation. Parts of it are quite fragile. And secondly, I suggested to her that maybe she would be able to make a replica of it—which elicited something of a yelp.[37]

A number of exhibit plans were proposed and revised between 1957 and the final installation in 1964. Eric Reed, the regional chief of interpretation, believed that the original 1957 plan was much stronger than the one proposed to him in 1961 by the Western Museum Laboratory. The following excerpt shows Reed's strong preference for the original:

Since Tonto is primarily an archeological unit, natural history is of secondary importance. Nevertheless, many people who visit the Monument are interested in desert biology, and natural history, per se, would have a place in Tonto interpretation. It is intended to develop this phase of Tonto's values through wayside exhibits or other devices outside the museum. More interpretation of the natural history features of the Monument should be included however in the museum through ethnobiological exhibits ...

For example, Tonto is rich in bird life and many people who are "bird-watchers" from other parts of the world are interested in the bird life of the desert as exemplified on the Monument. The only bird mentioned in the entire exhibit plan is the turkey. Admittedly, this particular topic is one which can be covered, more or less adequately, by an outdoor exhibit—and is at present by a temporary one.

Yet, an ecological exhibit should have a place in Tonto's interpretive plan. By including prehistoric man as a part of the scheme of nature, an exhibit indicating the relationship of his environment might be considered with some coverage of natural resources, perhaps including birds. [38]

His specific comments on the proposed exhibits were as follows:

Exhibit #7, "Hunting" is merely a discussion on bows and arrows without mention of the animals the people hunted. Rather than a detailed dissertation on how an arrow was made, perhaps this exhibit could be broadened to tell what animals were hunted and how the animal products were used as food, for clothing, in making tools, etc.

Except in Exhibit #6 there is no mention of the geology of Tonto yet the prehistoric people built with stone, had stone tools and implements, and used earth substances in making pottery, wall plaster, and mortar. Something of the geology of the Monument might well be included in the exhibits which refer to the caves in which the pueblos were built.

I am simply going to refer you back to the original Tonto prospectus which this exhibit plan deviates from considerably . . .[39]

The list of proposed exhibit cases in 1957 included the following:

Case 1: Geology: The Caves are Natural
Case 2: The First Indians
Case 3: Early Peoples of the Southwest
Case 4: The Cliff-Dwellings Six Hundred Years Ago
Case 5: Farming and Cooking
Case 6: Gathering and Hunting
Case 7: Pottery
Case 8: Baskets
Case 9: Weaving of Cotton
Case 10: Costume and Ornament
Case 11: Funeral Customs
Case 12: How the Age of the Ruins is Known
Case 13: What Happened Afterwards
Case 14: The Modern Tonto Indians
Case 15: Plants and Animals of the Desert[40]

Reed's views did not prevail. Six of the original fifteen proposed exhibit cases remained in the final installation plan, including Desert Gardening; Foods from Wild Plants; Salado Hunters; Stone, Clay & Wood; Dress; and Weaving: Their Finest Art. These decisions had long-lasting consequences: The final exhibits are still on display today, although at the time of this writing new exhibits are being designed.

The controversy among archeologists over the term *Salado* became quite contentious in the mid-1950s, but these differences of opinion did not affect Tonto's interpretation. In 1955 Regional Archeologist Al Schroeder wrote a memo to the superintendents of Tonto, Montezuma Castle, Tuzigoot, and Casa Grande in an effort to integrate the varied interpretive stories of each monument. The memo set out the few ideas about the Hohokam that he contended everyone could agree upon: that present evidence pointed to Hohokam occupation alone in the Verde Valley up to about AD 1125, in the Gila Basin up to AD 1150, and in the Tonto Basin up to AD 900.[41] Shroeder stated firmly that Gladwin's original definition of Salado had to be revised

Figure 38: New visitor center displays, 1964

based on new evidence, and that the term *Salado* would probably need to be redefined as a branch of the Hohokam, not of the Anasazi. In the memo he proposed that, for the time being, the term *Salado* should continue to be used when referring to the Tonto Basin because

> it has been so employed for a long time, and perhaps will help to serve as a 'handle' in separating the Tonto and Verde areas for discussion purposes. However, it may be well to explain that the relation of the Salado to the Sinagua was probably very much like the present relation of the people of New Mexico to those of Arizona. Basically they are the same with slight variations either due to environment or neighboring contacts.

As to the "Salado invasion" into the Gila Basin around 1300 AD, as proposed by Gladwin in the 1930s, the lack of any detail on the period between 1150 and 1300 hampers interpretation along this line. A good majority of the traits Gladwin made us aware of, to present his hypothesis of a 1300 AD invasion into the Gila area from the Tonto Basin, were either traits of wide distribution not restricted to any one culture or traits that occur among the Hohokam as early as 1150 AD However, several of the 1300 to 1400 AD traits of the Tonto Basin also may have occurred in the period prior to 1300.

We have neither a tangible trait list nor pattern for this latter period. For this reason, it is felt that the so-called Salado invasion should not be stressed, but should only be mentioned as a hypothesis that has been advanced. It is difficult to imagine that the Tonto Basin at 1300 AD was so heavily populated that a large group moved into the Gila Basin, particularly when the great number of sites that did exist in the Tonto Basin between 1300 and 1400 AD are taken into account. If the large number of Salado had moved out at 1300, the population of the basin would have been phenomenal.[42]

Two months later, however, Schroeder retracted his suggestion that the term *Salado* continue to be applied to those who occupied the Roosevelt Basin before AD 1150, urging instead that the reference be employed as a geographical area only, not as a culture.[43] Schroeder not only wanted to reflect the archeological evidence that was then challenging the notion of Salado, but also to ensure that visitors at the various monuments got the same story about prehistoric people and events. Unfortunately, this latest interpretation of the archeological findings did not alter interpretation offered at Tonto's new visitor center.

New Technologies

The policy on use of audiovisual technology in NPS visitor centers changed during the Mission 66 project and had an effect on the exhibits at Tonto National Monument. In the early years of Mission 66, the National Park Service viewed audiovisual equipment in visitor centers with skepticism, and rejected Tonto's request for audiovisual programs. However, as new visitor centers came on line throughout the park system, the Park Service's attitude changed, as reflected in correspondence in 1962 from NPS Public Affairs:

> In the early years of Mission 66 the need for audio-visual rooms in visitor centers was viewed with skepticism by some park people; it was a new idea and no one really knew how important it was to become. Today the majority of Park Service people are enthusiastic about the contributions being made to park interpretation by audiovisual installations. Visitors have been enthusiastic from the very beginning.

Reviewing the Preliminary Drawing for the Tonto Visitor Center it was noted that no audio-visual room was provided. Recalling his conversation with Supt. Oakes at the Park Mr. Erskine remembered that only 37% of Tonto visitors walk up to the Lower Ruin—63% viewing the ruin from the parking area. He remembered Mr. Oakes' stressing the importance of "bringing the ruin down to the visitor" in some way. He also recalled that many visitors, unable to make the trip to the ruin, have to wait while others in their party make the hike. All this is recognized in the Tonto Interpretive Prospectus.

Thus it would seem obvious that Tonto, even more than other parks, should have an audio-visual room in its visitor center.[44]

Work on Tonto's first audiovisual program began in May 1964; installation came in March 1966. In a ten-minute projection of forty-three slides of the lower ruin, the program did what Oakes earlier urged: "bring the ruin down to the visitor."[45]

CONSTRUCTION AND OPENING

Tonto's makeover—construction of the trails, visitor center, roads, and extensions of water lines—took place between 1961 and 1965. In March 1964, a one-hundred-person civil defense fallout shelter was added and stocked. The Schulz Fire, which ignited south of Tonto National Monument on June 27, 1964, burned 540 monument acres on July 1. The visitor center was completed at the time, but was spared. The fire denuded the slopes below the ruins however, and damaged the interpretive stations along the lower ruin trail. Robert Burgess, making the best of the calamity, proposed a fire ecology study; the staff then shifted the focus of the interpretive installations from the microclimates created by the canyon to the effects of fire.

Tonto National Monument enjoyed several other major infrastructural upgrades during the Mission 66 era. Beginning in 1957, State Route 88 was moved and paved, providing increased access to the monument. Telephones were installed in the office and superintendent's residence in August 1961 (phone number: Pinto Creek #1). In 1957 monument staff informed the Salt River Project, which supplied their power, of their need to switch from 25- to 60-cycle power. The Salt River Project generated 25-cycle power for the local mines and made that available at Tonto National Monument. Anything that heated, such as an iron or a stove, would work on 25 cycles, but anything requiring a more powerful motor would not. Staff thus relied on propane refrigeration and battery-operated radios. Monthly reports were filled with guesses about when the 60-cycle power would come to the monument. It finally arrived, at Tonto and to the town of Roosevelt, on December 9, 1964.

Figure 39: Dedication ceremony for new visitor center, 1965

In 1963 Tonto National Monument drilled its first well, and between April and August 1963, a 50,000-gallon concrete water tank was constructed in Cave Canyon; a 4-inch line brought the water to the residential area and the visitor center. On December 14, 1964, the old museum building was finally removed. Two months later, on February 22, 1965, 800 people attended the visitor center dedication ceremony. This physical upgrade was followed by an official one: on October 15, 1966, as a consequence of the National Historic Preservation Act, the Tonto National Monument was automatically placed on the National Register of Historic Places.

The Mission 66 era resulted in increased accessibility in various forms: improved roads and parking, a visitor center, museum exhibits, and improved trails to the upper and lower ruins. The era went a long way to address the issues of how best to accommodate visitors and their cars. The next several decades would focus attention on gaining control over the monument's natural and cultural resources.

1. Wirth (1980, pp. 234, 237).

2. Cited in Sellars (1997, 182).

3. Cited in Sellars (1997, 205). Sellars (1997, 180–203) details the need to improve the parks' physical facilities, the ambitious size and scope of Mission 66, and objections to it because it favored recreational tourism development over ecological concerns.

4. Allaback (2000, pp. 22, 26, 30).

5. Ibid.

6. Superintendent's annual report to the Director, May 22, 1954. NA/RG 79, Stack 570,/ Row 80,/Compartment 02,/She lf 05,/Box 78. A26 Reports, Tonto National Monument, 1954–59.

7. SWMA monthly report, June 1955.

8. Memo No. 3 from Director to Washington Office and all Field Offices, Subject: Mission 66, Progress and Procedures, dated June 27, 1955, received at TNM July 9, 1955, NA Laguna Niguel, Box 1 of 3 from Denver, D6215: Planning, Preparation and Maintenance and Presentation of Museum Exhibits. According to his monthly report for July 1955, Superintendent Sharp received the memo on July 9, which was inadequate time for him to prepare the prospectus by the due date, July 20. He spent considerable night time hours preparing the document and delivered it to Globe for review on Monday, July 18.

9. No copy of the original prospectus submitted by Superintendent Sharp in July 1955 is available; however, subsequent versions submitted throughout 1955–1958 were based on this original submission. In July 1956 Superintendent Theodore Thompson built a plywood folder for copies of the master plans for Mission 66, since it became obvious that these reports would be numerous and weighty.

10. Memo from regional director to chairman, Mission 66, Subject: Comment on Prospectus, Tonto National Monument, September 12, 1955, NA Laguna Niguel, Box 1 of 3 from Denver, D6215: Planning, Preparation and Maintenance and Presentation of Museum Exhibits.

11. Memo from superintendent, Tonto NM, to general superintendent, Subject: Comment on Prospectus, Tonto, from Regional Director to Chairman, MISSION 66, w/copy to Tonto, October 5, 1955, NA Laguna Niguel, Box 1 of 3 from Denver, D6215: Planning, Preparation and Maintenance and Presentation of Museum Exhibits.

12. Mission 66 Prospectus Brief, Tonto National Monument, September 1957. NA/RG 79, Stack 570,/Row 80,/Compartment 32,/Shelf 02,/Box 735, A98 Conservation and Preservation of Areas for Public Enjoyment, Mission 66, Washington Office, Prospectus, Tonto National Monument, 1956–57, p. 3

13. Ibid., p. 4

14. Ibid.

15. Mission 66 Prospectus, Tonto National Monument, July 7, 1958, p. 2, NA Laguna Niguel, Box 1 of 3 from Denver, D6215: Planning, Preparation and Maintenance and Presentation of Museum Exhibits

16. Ibid.

17. For instance, according to Allaback (2000, 30), by 1958 thirty-four visitor centers were completed and twenty more were under construction.

18. Allaback (2000, 30).

19. Monroe (1986, 92).

20. Ibid., pp. 96–97.

21. Allaback (2000, 34).

22. Mission 66 Prospectus Brief, Tonto National Monument, September 1957, NA/RG 79, Stack 570,/Row 80,/Compartment 32,/Shelf 02,/Box 735, A98 Conservation and Preservation of Areas for Public Enjoyment, Mission 66, Washington Office, Prospectus, Tonto National Monument, 1956–57, p. 4.

23. Superintendent, Tonto NM memo to director, NPS, Subject: Master Plan, Tonto National Monument, November 4, 1957, NA/RG 79, Stack 570,/Row 80,/Compartment 03,/Shelf 01,/Box 1002, D18 Planning Program, including Development Outline and Master Plans, Tonto National Monument 1954–59

24. Superintendent's Monthly Narrative Report, April 1958, p. 3.

25. Mission 66 Prospectus, Tonto National Monument, July 7, 1958, p. 8, NA Laguna Niguel, Box 1 of 3 from Denver, D6215: Planning, Preparation and Maintenance and Presentation of Museum Exhibits

26. Memo from superintendent, Tonto to regional director, Region Three, Subject: Possible additions to Tonto National Monument, July 3, 1960, p. 1, NA Laguna Niguel, Box 2 of 3 from Denver, L58: Proposed Areas.

27. Ibid.

28. Ibid. The Forest Service site numbers were School House Point Ruin, T.4.N-R.11.E-S.35/26; (2) Griffin Point Ruins, T.5.N-R.11.E-S.17; and (3) Tonto Basin Ruin, T.4.N-R.13.E-S.22.

29. Ibid., p. 2.

30. Memo from superintendent, Tonto to regional director, Region Three, Subject: Possible additions to Tonto National Monument, July 3, 1960, p. 2, NA Laguna Niguel, Box 2 of 3 from Denver, L58: Proposed Areas.

31. NPS (1962).

32. Memo from acting regional chief, Division of Interpretation to director, Region Three, Subject: Request for Assistance of American Geological Institute at Tonto National Monument, November 4, 1958, NA Laguna Niguel, Box 1 of 3 from Denver, D6215: Planning, Preparation and Maintenance and Presentation of Museum Exhibits. Raup (1959).

33. Burgess (1965).

34. Bohrer (1962); Hargrave (1959/62/63); (1964); Jones (1963); Welles (1955).

35. Caywood (1962).

36. Memo from chief, Western Museum Laboratory to regional director, Region Three, Subject: The Tonto Shirt, June 29, 1960, NA/RG 79, Stack 570,/Row 80,/Compartment 32,/Shelf 02,/Box 1228, D6215: Museum and Exhibit Activities, Planning, Preparation, Maintenance, and Preservation of Museum Exhibits, Tonto National Monument, 1958–61.

37. Letter from Emil Haury to Dr. Erik K. Reed, September 15, 1960, NA/RG 79, Stack 570,/Row 80,/Compartment 32,/Shelf 02,/Box 1228, D6215: Museum and Exhibit Activities, Planning, Preparation, Maintenance, and Preservation of Museum Exhibits, Tonto National Monument, 1958–61.

38. Memo from regional chief of interpretation to chief, Western Museum Laboratory, Subject: Visitor Center Exhibit Plan, Tonto, October 5, 1961, NA/RG 79, Stack 570,/Row 80,/Compartment 32,/Shelf 02,/Box 1228, D6215: Museum and Exhibit Activities, Planning, Preparation, Maintenance, and Preservation of Museum Exhibits, Tonto National Monument, 1958–61, p. 2.

39. Ibid.

40. Ibid., pp. 3–4.

41. Memo to superintendents, Tonto, Montezuma Castle, Tuzigoot, and Casa Grande from Archaeologist Schroeder, March 22, 1955, p. 1. NA/ WACC.

42. Ibid., pp. 6–7.

43. Memo to Archeologist Cattanach, through superintendent, Montezuma Castle from Archeologist Schroeder, May 17, 1955, p. 1, NA/WACC.

44. Memo from assistant director, Public Affairs to assistant director, Design & Construction, Subject: Preliminary Drawing, NM-TON 3110A, Tonto Visitor Center, December 10, 1962, NA/RG 79, Stack 570,/Row 80,/Compartment 32,/Shelf 02,/Box 1116, D3415: Buildings, Construction and Maintenance, Tonto National Monument, 1954–49, pp. 1–2.

45. Ibid., p. 2.

THEODORE
ROOSEVELT
LAKE
ARIZONA

TONT-85A
TONTO NATIONAL MONUM

— - — Monument Boundary
4•   Recorded Site
— - — Dirt Road

chapter six

TAKING CONTROL: FENCES, SCIENCE, AND SURVEYS, 1967-1985

There's little doubt that the National Park Service Mission 66 era of construction and expansion achieved its aim of both attracting and accommodating more visitors. In 1955 about five million people visited national monuments; by 1974 the total had more than tripled to approximately seventeen million. But Mission 66's accomplishments came at a price: detractors observed that the program did comparatively little for the environment. Indeed, if the 1950s brought criticism of the National Park Service for allowing visitor accommodations to deteriorate, the mid-1970s saw complaints that the Park Service had gone too far in favoring recreational tourism over protecting natural and cultural resources.[1] As historian Richard Sellars cited, "some believed that the bulldozer was the appropriate symbol for Mission 66, and one individual had asserted that the Park Service needed a 'Mission 76 to undo the harm done in Mission 66.'"[2]

Another significant change was occurring in National Park Service management of their parks and monuments, previewed by the nation's general shift in popular environmental consciousness and by several NPS reports of the 1960s and 1970s. Just as the Mission 66 plan was approaching completion, the 1963 Leopold Report called for the infusion of science into national park management. In 1967 a Conservation Foundation publication called for an emphasis on managing plants, animals, and wilderness in the park. A 1972 report on the future of the parks challenged the agency to reassert its role as a leader in the conservation of the country's natural resources. The NPS response included the

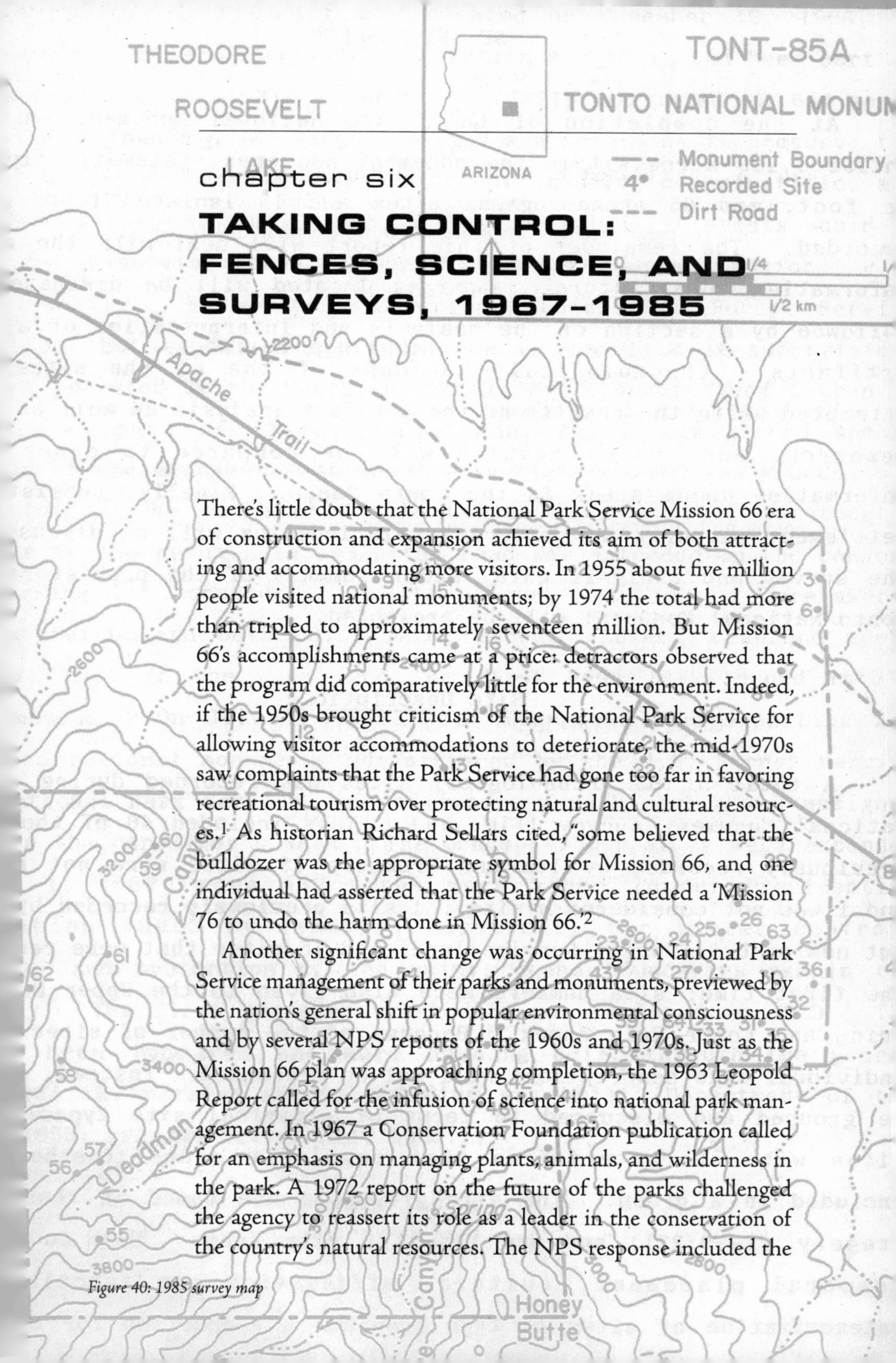

Figure 40: 1985 survey map

172 ■ AT THE CONFLUENCE OF CHANGE

development of natural resource management guidelines, which would shape how each unit would prepare for resource management; institute national environmental education development programs at Harpers Ferry; and establish cooperative park study units, which were formed in 1973. In addition, federal legislation required the National Park Service to comply with the 1964 Wilderness Act, the 1966 National Historic Preservation Act, the 1967 Air Quality Act, the 1969 National Environmental Protection Act, the 1972 expanded federal water pollution control act (later known as the Clean Water Act), the 1978 American Indian Religious Freedom Act, and the 1979 Archaeological Resources Protection Act.

Tonto, having benefited from the construction dollars of Mission 66, went on over the following twenty years to accomplish two milestones, one natural and one cultural. The *natural* milestone was gaining physical control of the monument's land by eliminating grazing and erecting a fence marking monument boundaries. The *cultural* milestone was completing a 100 percent archeological survey, which professionally recorded sixty-five archeological sites on the monument to current standards. This chapter chronicles these two efforts, together with an account of other organization and management decisions that affected operations.

A NATURAL RESOURCE MILESTONE: CATTLE GRAZING ENDS AND BOUNDARY FENCING BEGINS

In 1966 Superintendent Jack Broadbent broached the three crucial and interrelated issues of grazing, water use, and fencing at the monument with the regional director of the Southwest Region. His reasons for doing so are not documented, but records reveal that his actions laid the foundation for later efforts to eliminate grazing, settle misunderstandings about water rights, and install boundary fencing.

When he analyzed the situation in 1966, Broadbent estimated that because of a combination of grazing agreements and water rights, the National Park Service had effective administration over less than half of the legally established monument area.[3] In that same year, he discovered that no special-use permit had ever been recorded to allow ranchers Cooper or Lyall (and now Schulze who bought Lyall's ranch) to use monument water for their cattle. Even the stock troughs had been built at NPS expense and maintained over the years by Tonto staff. Broadbent also noted that there was no special-use permit or other agreement for the fencing of the stock runway in the canyon south of the visitor center, and that no one was responsible for its maintenance. He described the fences as unsightly nuisances and "certainly opposed to the traditional concept of park values."[4] While the area was small, he considered it "an excellent opportunity for a nature trail, picnic area, bird photography, etc." and added that the fences were "incompatible with any such use."[5]

Broadbent discussed the removal of the fences with Dwight Cooper, Chester Cooper's son, who was then actively managing the ranch. An ironic aspect of Tonto's long-standing disputes with area ranchers was illustrated in Park Ranger Ron Ice's recollection that Dwight Cooper served as a laborer for Tonto National Monument during the late 1960s and was thus paid by the Park Service to fix the water lines for his own cows.[6] In response to Broadbent's initiative, Cooper agreed to the Park Service removing the fence and cattle from the canyon. However, in exchange for this loss of access to water and grazing close to the visitor center, Cooper asked for grazing lands elsewhere on the monument.

Broadbent recommended an analysis of Deadman Canyon. He further suggested choosing one of three options. The first was practical: eliminate the runway and cattle from Cave Canyon within the monument. The other two were impractical and improbable: have the U.S. Forest Service provide appropriate land in exchange for excluding cattle from the monument; or build a very costly water trough "sufficiently far up the canyon to eliminate objectionable features."[7] He encouraged the development of written agreements with the ranchers about water, fences, and maintenance. He suggested accommodating the ranchers' use even if he did not approve of it and altering the monument boundary to include only areas over which the Park Service had effective control. But the acting regional director disagreed, concluding that the National Park Service owed nothing to the two grazing permittees. Instead, he felt they "used the monument land by permit and the water from habit."[8] But he warned against stirring up a small-scale war, especially as "we're occupied in Viet Nam at the moment."[9] He cautioned Broadbent to move slowly on these long-standing and contentious issues.

In 1972 the perennial boundary issues surfaced again. At that time, staff was concerned not only with managing conflicting claims to access, but also with ensuring natural revegetation. They argued that "existing fences impeded public access to the site, but allowed permittees' cattle to graze on about 640 of the monument's 1,120 acres," and that "before natural succession can begin to reestablish the natural scene within the monument grazing must be terminated."[10]

In August 1973, after compiling the first natural resources management plan for Tonto National Monument, Superintendent Glen Henderson declared that he was finally going to eliminate domestic livestock grazing on monument lands. Approximately 39,000 cattle grazed in the Tonto National Forest, of which one hundred or more grazed on or trailed through portions of the monument.[11] Henderson cited administrative policies for historical areas of the NPS system in support of his proposal:

> Agricultural uses, including domestic livestock grazing, that do not conform to those in practice in the historic period of the area are permitted where they contribute to the maintenance of a historic scene, are sanctioned by law, or are incidental to visitor use. Where grazing has been permitted and its continuation is not specifically covered by the aforestated conditions, it should be eliminated through orderly and cooperative procedures with the individuals concerned.[12]

Henderson proposed to notify the Forest Service and the permittees that the Park Service would not renew grazing permits that expired on December 31, 1974; that it would allow trespass grazing until the monument boundaries were fully fenced; that the runway fence in Cholla Canyon would be removed; that when the permits expired, the Park Service would fence off access to the runway and eliminate the two stock water troughs; and that Tonto National Monument would be fenced to actual park boundaries when funding was available. He expected opposition by the cattlemen and advised his superiors that the Gila County cattle industry's power was still "second only to mining."[13] The industry often issued its views through the Cattle Growers Association, of which Dwight Cooper was vice president; Henderson expected it to do so again.

But he was wrong. In fact, meetings at Tonto National Monument with National Park Service staff, U.S. Forest Service staff, and the ranchers in April 1974 went smoothly, and the parties agreed that the logical date to terminate the permits would be December 31, 1975, when the then current ten-year permits would expire. All agreed that the runway fence from the water trough up Cholla Canyon would be removed immediately, with a 50–60 foot gap left at the head of the draw to keep the fence from becoming a trap for cattle that might stray into the area south of the monument. It was also agreed that the Forest Service would retain rights for watering livestock (but these rights would extend only between the two agencies, not to the ranchers) and that a memorandum of understanding would be entered into by the two agencies for this purpose. The memorandum of understanding was formalized in September 1974.

In February 1975, the legal boundaries of the monument were surveyed in anticipation of fencing. According to a management consultation report of the same month, Tonto National Monument's construction proposal to fence the entire monument ranked seventy-third on the NPS Southern Arizona Office priority list, which did not bode well for funding in the foreseeable future. The report recommended that the monument administration consider fencing vulnerable areas only in an emergency.[14] In December 1974 the grazing permits expired, but it took several more years for Superintendent James Valder to secure the funds necessary to fence the monument's legal boundaries.

Fencing was installed by the Young Adult Conservation Corps from Globe between 1979 and 1981, a task that required jack-hammering holes for each post. The work was completed in November 1981, the "monumental day" when Tonto was completely encircled with fencing, preserving the grounds from cattle and hunters and—for the first time since the National Park Service took over responsibility in 1934—affording it physical control over the total 1,120 acres.

A CULTURAL RESOURCE MILESTONE: 100 PERCENT ARCHEOLOGICAL SURVEY

The monument's archeological sites were traditionally considered the upper and lower cliff dwellings and the annex, although in 1958 archeologist William Bromberg recorded ten additional sites within the monument. In 1967 NPS archeologist Ronald Ice began an informal survey of the monument at the request of Superintendent Broadbent, who loaned Ice an altimeter so he could record the altitudes of any sites he found. Ice recorded fifty-two (including William Bromberg's ten), forty-nine of which were considered contemporaneous with the upper and lower cliff dwellings and three that were considered Apache or Yavapai sites. Ice later recalled that there was not much evidence of pothunting at the time of his survey, although javelinas would wallow in the rock shelters, and cattle would step on and break pottery sherds.[15]

Collaboration with the Forest Service

As Ice conducted his informal survey, he also wrote an archeological research management plan outlining past research in the park, future research needs, and research in progress. He wrote of the need to excavate sites (in the Tonto

Basin) beyond the monument's boundaries to add to knowledge of the Salado culture, calling it a "now or never" proposition because of rampant pothunting in the vicinity.[16] Upon completing his survey, Ice offered to expand it to include Forest Service lands. A May 1968 memorandum of understanding between Tonto National Monument and Tonto National Forest established that it was mutually advantageous to do this, and the Forest Service permitted sherd collections and minor test-trenching within a 15-mile radius of the monument. Ice's 1972 report on forest service lands referred to the several sites William Bromberg recorded in 1958 and a few additional sites recorded in 1963 by Sallie Harris and Louis Caywood of the Southwest Archeological Center. Ice recorded eighteen new sites, but drew no new conclusions about their origin or significance. "Hopefully," he wrote, "someday archeologists will do some major research in the Tonto Basin and answer some of the many questions on the prehistory of the area."[17]

While conducting the expanded survey on acreage north of Roosevelt Lake in 1969, Ice made reference in correspondence to sites on Forest Service land as "being or having been virtually destroyed by pothunters."[18] He also noted that he was "accosted" by a rancher who mistook him for a pothunter. The rancher said that he and others in the area were very angry about pothunting. Ice then wondered whether there might be some way to have the Cattlemen's Association help curtail vandalism to archeological sites on Forest Service land.[19] In addition to their interest in preventing destruction of archeological resources, ranchers were also concerned that some potholes were large enough for cattle to fall into.[20]

Ice consulted with USFS personnel who had the responsibility for prosecuting pothunting, especially Robert Armstrong, then stationed at the Roosevelt Ranger District as a recreation and land staff assistant. No cases were prosecuted on monument lands, for which the Forest Service had no jurisdiction, but Armstrong and fellow ranger Ron Henderson prosecuted a variety of cases on forest lands. One 1970 case involved six Mesa men who took advantage of low lake levels that exposed archeological sites. They pothunted one Salado site on the north side of Roosevelt Lake near Salome, where Armstrong and Henderson caught them in the act. They were fined $50 each. Twenty-four pots were confiscated and eventually donated to the monument.[21]

Archeologist Karen Lundquist followed Ron Ice at the monument in 1970, and her presence strengthened ties with the U.S. Forest Service in several ways. She married Assistant District Forest Ranger Robert Armstrong in

September 1970, and thereafter examined archeological sites threatened by developments in the Tonto National Forest, including sites at Windy Hill, Burnt Corral, and Hidden Lake.

In the 1970s, life at Tonto was affected by events of a distinctly modern and human-caused nature: organizational changes in the National Park Service. In 1972 regional boundaries changed, and Tonto National Monument was switched from the Southwest Region to the Western Region. Also that year, the source of Tonto's archeological expertise was changed. In the past, the Park Service had employed staff archeologists at each of the national monuments in southern Arizona. Under the new management structure, the National Park Service Western Archaeological and Conservation Center (WACC) in Tucson and the Southern Arizona Region (SOAR) office in Phoenix would provide archeological services.

Also in 1972, Ron Ice, who by then was working at another NPS unit, submitted a report on his archeological investigation of sites near Roosevelt, conducted under the 1968 memorandum of understanding between Tonto National Monument and Tonto National Forest. Ice apologized for the delay in submitting his report and added that, since there was no longer a professional archeologist at the monument and "in view of present personnel policy, there may never be an archeologist at Tonto," it was unlikely that the memorandum of understanding would be extended between the national monument and the national forest.[22]

Ice was almost right. After archeologist Karen Amstrong left the monument in 1972, the monument was without a staff archeologist for thirty-two years until one was appointed in 2004. This had important consequences for ruins preservation and management because, beginning in the early 1970s, many activities took place that required impact studies. The 1966 National Historic Preservation Act and subsequent executive orders of 1973 and 1974 required the development of what have become known as cultural resource management programs. The lack of a staff archeologist at Tonto meant that, to be in compliance and to perform stabilization work, monument staff had to call WACC or SOAR for help.

The U.S. Forest Service took the opposite approach. Prior to the 1970s, the Forest Service had only regional archeologists on staff. However, when the National Historic Preservation Act of 1966 took effect, all national historical landmarks were automatically put on the National Register of Historic Places; Section 106 required that the Advisory Council on Historic Preservation be given the opportunity to comment on any federally funded or licensed undertaking that would adversely affect sites on the National Register. As a result, the Forest Service began staffing archeologists at each forest unit and in each district. Tonto National Forest was the first to hire an archeologist, and by the end of the 1970s, all national forests in Arizona employed them.[23]

Cultural Resource Threats and Responses

Pothunters were not the only threats to archeological sites. Even in Arizona, rain was a threat. Heavy rains in 1972 and 1973 caused mudstone slides of several hundred pounds each. A 1975 Management Consultation Report by WACC noted that,

> The continual sloughing of mudstone from two outcroppings adjacent to the trail immediately below the Lower Ruin and the unknown structural stability of cave roofs and walls surrounding both ruins pose an immediate threat to both the safety of visitors and the possible destruction of both ruins—the park's primary resource.
>
> Erosion and danger to human safety becomes most acute during rainy seasons which normally coincide with heaviest visitation. Since the same mudstone formations surround both ruins, a threat exists, including the erosion of the retaining wall for the Lower Ruins. Proper stabilization to eliminate these threats depends on a competent geological structural research study.[24]

The National Park Service set aside $15,000 in fiscal year 1975 to finance the study; consultants recommended that the monument pursue the study and all efforts to stabilize and preserve its cultural resources.

The effects of wind, rain, insects, rodents, and human forces on southwestern archeological resources were well known by the 1970s. In 1974 the Park Service published guidelines for addressing those impacts in *Ruins Stabilization in the Southwestern United States*. The authors, Roland Richert and Gordon Vivian, were both acquainted with Tonto's particular situation, having done stabilization work there in 1952 and 1957. In the section on poisons and rodent repellents, they noted the particularly destructive impact of rodents in Tonto National Monument's cliff dwellings. Richert and Vivian also analyzed the use of materials such as soil cement mortars, nontoxic insecticides, and bonding agents; provided instructions for repairing adobe structures; detailed recording procedures, including stabilization and maintenance records; and had a special section on cliff dwelling stabilization.[25]

In June 1976, WACC archeologists conducted a List of Classified Structures (LCS) Survey of the Monument. The survey team found five structures that met the LCS requirements. Four of them, including the upper ruin, lower ruin, lower ruin annex, and another site, were considered of Salado cultural affiliation dating from AD 1100 to 1450. One additional site, a small rock circle similar to a hogan base of Yavapai or Tonto Apache affiliation, was considered to date from after 1500. The surveyors outlined previous attempts to stabilize the structures as well as persistent problems and threats, including rainwater that undermined stability, cracks due to original construction techniques, and insect and rodent infestation. In the statement of significance, the surveyors outlined several ways in which structures at the monument were unique and worthy of preservation. Concerning future research potential, they noted that previous assumptions that the Salado's cultural traits set them apart from their neighbors had given way to the view that the Salado differed from the Hohokam and Sinagua only in their environmental adaptations. Concerning interpretive merit, they thought the monument offered two excellent trails that provided access to the prehistoric dwellings, and an unusual amount of direct contact with the natural and cultural environment. However, they warned,

> The potential for research and interpretation will remain only so long as the monument is afforded scrupulous protection. Routine stabilization and maintenance of standing ruins will result, paradoxically, in some information loss unless measures are taken to record and collect data as an integral part of maintenance activities.[26]

The team deemed the ruins worthy of preservation and recommended that preservation funds of $23,500 and data-recovery funds of $8,776 be made available.

Throughout the 1970s, WACC and SOAR directed stabilization, clearance, and emergency maintenance projects at Tonto, many of which required review, comment, and approval by the State Historic Preservation Office and the Arizona State Parks Board. In 1973 monument staff proposed rehabilitation that would affect most of the rooms in the lower ruin. Federal regulations were to be followed, including Section 106 of the relatively new National Historic Preservation Act. Loose stones were to be set, missing wall plaster replaced, raveled roof edges tightened, and beaten-down dirt floors refilled to original levels. Room 14 was to receive repairs to wall plaster, modification of steel roof supports, replacement of steel door bars with transparent barriers, and installation of a transparent barrier over the roof vent. The damaged and eroded materials were to be replaced with new materials colored to blend in with the original; the overall effect of the stabilization would be to strengthen and preserve the remaining original portions of the ruin. In requesting comments from the Arizona State Parks Board on this proposal, staff claimed the changes would "bring it up to standard for use as an in-place exhibit of prehistoric household furnishings and equipment."[27]

In the mid-1970s, Tonto National Monument secured clearances to improve trails to the lower ruin and to stabilize mudstone deposits above the lower ruin trail. Abnormally heavy rains in March of 1978 prompted emergency maintenance of the upper ruins, for which WACC archeologist Martin Mayer estimated repairs were needed in six locations and desirable in eight others.[28] These emergency actions were understood to be temporary measures meant to last until systematized actions could be taken to solve the cliff moisture problems. In addition to securing clearances for the trails and ruins, the monument also won approval to construct a new utility building and demonstration garden, to fence the entire 6-mile boundary, to install a wheelchair ramp around the visitor center, and to bury telephone cables.

In May 1977, a visitor to Navajo National Monument died and two were injured by rock falls from the canyon rim. As a consequence, NPS parks and monuments conducted rock motion and structural monitoring projects.[29] Tonto National Monument's monitoring began in 1979 and was carried out through 1985. A honeybee eradiation project was requested in 1984 at the urging of Superintendent James Troutwine, who estimated the honeybee population to have increased by 50 percent over the prior seven years. Two professional rock climbers were hired to rappel the cliff, remove nests, and insert benzaldehyde into the holes.

The 100 Percent Archeological Survey

The 1985 Natural and Cultural Resource Management Plan for Tonto National Monument recognized the need for a systematic archeological survey of the entire monument. In 1985 archeologist Martyn Tagg of WACC conducted what is known as a 100 percent survey. The object was to locate, record, and evaluate all archeologically significant remains within monument boundaries. The survey verified previous work to ensure nothing had been overlooked, gathered new data, analyzed and synthesized what was known, assessed significance, and produced a report that included an archeological resource base map.

Figure 41: Archeological survey at Site 85A–29, 1985.

Tagg led three other archeologists in fieldwork during March 1985. They conducted a 100 percent survey of the flat bajadas in the northeast half of the monument and a "non-random, judgmental survey" of those areas thought to have archeological potential in the mountainous southwestern half of the monument.[30] "Sites" were defined as features with fifteen associated arti-facts. "Artifacts" were defined as up to fifteen things not in association with a site or feature. Collectively, the archeologists recorded a total of sixty-five archeological sites, including forty-six of the fifty previously recorded by Ice and Bromberg; three of the fifty were not located, while one was judged to be not a site, but rather a natural concentration of cobblestones. The net result was the identification of fifteen new sites.

The total of sixty-five sites included sixteen rock shelters, which were subtyped as multiroom rock shelters, natural chambers with two to five masonry-walled rooms, natural chambers with six or more masonry-walled rooms, single-room caves, and dry-laid walls. Three "probable" Apache or Yavapai sites were surveyed, including wickiup rings (bases for shelters) and associated artifacts and features. The team also inventoried and analyzed

Figure 42: Three views of schoolhouse
mound site

Figure 43: Tonto polychrome jar, circa 1300

865 artifacts, including those collected previously by Bromberg and Ice. The survey documented use of the area for the past 6,000–7,000 years, and provided a fuller picture than before of the prehistoric and historic use of the upper bajada and lower mountain zone within the Tonto Basin.

For example, projectile points suggested pre-ceramic people used land on the monument; ceramics and other artifacts were evidence of people from 1200–1450; open-air and cave sites were evidence of Apache or Yavapai habitation; and one historic site with a dense concentration of tin cans and glass bore witness to Euro-American use.

Tagg confirmed that javelinas inhabited almost all of the caves and rock shelters on the monument, and, more important, underscored that vandalism was rampant in the Tonto Basin in general. His survey reported that eleven sites showed evidence of vandalism, with some displaying undated evidence of potholes, trenching, and complete excavation.[31] The Tagg report provided Tonto National Monument with a full picture of its archeological resources for the first time, as well as indications of which sites needed to be monitored for evidence of future disturbance and vandalism. The inventory also gave rise to new questions about the relationship of the open-air sites, the field houses, and the five- to fifteen-room pueblos to the cliff dwellings.

The archeological services from WACC and SOAR kept the monument in compliance with federal regulations, and periodically provided survey, data recovery, and stabilization work. Nonetheless, the monument suffered from the lack of an archeologist on staff from 1972 to 2004. Unfortunately for Tonto National Monument, these years were also extremely important in the evolution of understanding of the term *Salado* and the archeological remains in the Tonto Basin. Without an archeologist on staff, it was difficult for staff to keep abreast of changing archeological theory and to interpret the changes for the public.

The longstanding concept of the Salado, as defined in the 1930s by the Gladwins and Haury,

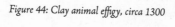

Figure 44: Clay animal effigy, circa 1300

was challenged by archeological finds in the 1960s and 1970s, and seen to be more complex. The neat lines that archeologists once drew around cultural areas, geographically binding the groups they named the Anasazi, Mogollon, Hohokam, and Salado and defining distinct traditions, were no longer considered so clear-cut. Al Schroeder and others had argued in the 1950s that Gladwin's definition of Salado was incomplete and recognized only one part of a much more complex pattern. By the mid-1960s and 1970s, researchers were increasingly contesting the issue of the Salado as a distinct culture or as a manifestation of influence by Hohokam, Mogollon, Sinagua, or Anasazi (now called ancestral Puebloan). Rather than looking primarily at the material culture of prehistoric people, archeologists in the Southwest were pursuing ideas and technologies of the "new archeology." This meant approaching these questions with the aid of systems theory and developing a new understanding of the behaviors shared by many prehistoric southwestern inhabitants, based on new evidence about subsistence and settlement patterns.

The new archeology created both excitement and rivalry between the University of Arizona/Arizona State Museum and Arizona State University. The annual Pecos Conference became occasions for these to play out; in addition, conferences on the significance and meaning of *Salado* were held in 1976, 1992, and 1995.

Tonto National Forest archeologists played a prominent role in these lively debates because they were responsible for three million acres of national forest that included all four major prehistoric cultural areas. By contrast, Tonto National Monument had no archeologist on staff during this period, and consequently could not participate in developing the radical new understandings that the professionals were pursuing at conferences and in print. As a result, the interpretation of Salado remained static and new questions, theories, and understandings in archeology did not make their way into Tonto National Monument interpretation.[32]

GENERAL MANAGEMENT ISSUES

During the 1970s, several other NPS changes began that exerted impacts on Tonto National Monument management. For instance, the National Environmental Education Development program increased the Park Service's commitment to environmental education. A law enforcement office opened in Washington, D.C., in 1971, followed by a law enforcement training program that focused on visitor protection and safety. Fire management policies changed after 1978 when the Park Service declared fires to be natural phenomena that should be permitted to burn. Finally, the "State of the Parks" report in the 1980s called for a comprehensive inventory of natural resources, for programs to monitor changes in parks' ecology, and for an increase in staffing and training.[33]

The 1975 management consultation report characterized Tonto National Monument as well managed and a credit to the NPS system, but raised concerns that no one on staff had a strong interpretive background. Training for NPS employees became available when the Interpretive Planning and Design Center opened in 1970 at Harpers Ferry, West Virginia, but Superintendent Valder's applications to attend were repeatedly turned down. He persevered, and was finally able attend a training session in 1979. Unfortunately, he retired a year later.[34]

The 1975 consultation report also noted that resource management and visitor protection skills were lacking at the monument. Two years later, when James Troutwine joined the staff in 1977, he became the first Tonto National Monument law enforcement-commissioned employee, having completed the three-month law enforcement program in Washington, D.C. Violations noted during this period included stealing trail markers, hunting, killing rattlesnakes, defecating in the lower ruins, jojoba picking, and collecting pot sherds. Serious burglaries also occurred. In December 1969, a revolver, binoculars, camera, and cash were stolen; another burglary occurred in 1970. The most serious break-in—with decidedly more serious consequences for the monument—happened in 1979, shortly after the Archaeological Resources Protection Act came into law. Someone removed a window to gain entry to the visitor center, then made off with an exhibit case containing two Salado bowls. The exhibit case was discovered by staff the next day; the bowls were never found.[35]

Fires continued to threaten both natural and cultural resources at Tonto National Monument. The 1970 Cottonwood Fire began on Forest Service land, then spread to monument land and threatened both the visitor center and housing complex. Fire crews worked to save the park's scenic values; the maintenance staff later reclaimed the scar by replanting plants and trees. Other smaller fires resulting from lightning strikes occurred throughout the period, including the Ruin and Tonto Fire in 1973, the Trough Fire in 1974, the Monument and Deadman Fire in 1976, the Dead Fire in 1979, the Monument Fire in 1980, the Honey Fire in 1983, and the Monument Fire in 1984.

In 1976 Superintendent Valder's Statement for Management reflected a fairly static period at Tonto. Although visitation had increased from 27,000 in 1966 to 68,000 in 1976, Valder characterized the facilities and staff as adequate to meet the increase. He cited the housing situation as adequate, the visitor center as adequate except for the challenge of getting wheelchairs to the upper deck, and the restrooms in need of remodeling to accommodate visitors with disabilities. The one problem Valder noted was the lack of adequate storage and workshop facilities for maintenance operations. Accordingly, the existing 16 x 16 foot tin shed was replaced with a new utility building.[36] His five-year plan included a request to determine visitor impact on the cliff dwellings, identify stabilization needs, conduct an archeological survey, and synthesize the Salado cultural sequencing. At that time, the monument was experimenting with reintroducing native grass species and piñon pine, and its first natural and cultural resource management plans were in rough draft.

The "Scope of Collections" report of 1976 identified only one area of continuing concern: the longstanding need to gain the return of the "Tonto shirt" from the Arizona State Museum. Superintendent Valder discussed the situation with Emil Haury, who agreed that the shirt would return to Tonto when he retired from the museum. Valder himself retired shortly after these informal discussions, and it remains unclear whether Haury had had the authority to make such a promise. In any event, the Tonto shirt stayed put.[37] In 1985 Tonto National Monument Superintendent Troutwine again asked the Arizona State Museum staff to clarify the provenance of the Salado lace shirt, and Curator of Collections Jane Bell agreed that "the importance of the piece certainly warrants better documentation, and I will see if I can find a student who can undertake some research on it this fall. If that should work out I will certainly let you know the outcome."[38] The shirt was featured in the Arizona State Museum's long-term exhibit on dry cave preservation of archeological materials and was rotated off exhibit every few months for a rest period. A poster for the exhibit featured a 1984 Helga Teiwes photograph of the upper ruin with a Tonto polychrome vessel and the lace shirt. Bell offered to send a copy of the poster to Troutwine if he didn't already have one.[39] The shirt itself remains in Tucson. Two other collection issues from this period bear noting: in the early 1980s, the last human remains were removed from exhibit; and in 1985, the last of the collections were removed from the basement and transferred to WACC.

After Superintendent Valder's retirement, the Park Service experimented with a new management structure. Rather than hiring a superintendent for each park, site managers were hired to manage day-to-day operations. The site managers reported to SOAR, which was responsible for planning. James Troutwine became the site manager of Tonto National Monument in 1980.

The management structure changed again in 1983 and Troutwine became superintendent.

For its national "State of the Parks" reports in 1980, the National Park Service evaluated the natural and cultural resources of each unit in the NPS system and found none immune to threat. The report listed seventy-three types of threats, highlighting those with special impact in the West because of mining.[40] The follow-up report in 1981 noted that 154 natural resource specialists were then working in 62 of the 333 park units, but it would take until 1999 for one to be hired at Tonto National Monument.

In 1982 the Tonto National Forest had many day-trip visitors for hiking, horseback riding, vehicle touring, camping, picnicking, wildlife viewing, boating, swimming and fishing.[41] Nearby Roosevelt Lake had no campgrounds for overnight stays, and lake visitors rarely visited the monument. The typical monument visitor was a retired Phoenix resident or snowbird who drove up the Apache Trail in the morning, toured the monument, had a picnic lunch, and drove back down to the valley via Globe the same day.

By the mid-1980s, however, the Bureau of Reclamation was planning the renovation of Roosevelt Dam, and the Forest Service was planning overnight facilities—both of which were thought to eventually increase the number of monument visitors. By 1985, parking at Tonto was already inadequate at certain times of the year, especially during heavy winter visitation, when the lot would fill and a staff member would have to open and close the gate at the main road as parking spaces opened up. The expected increase in visitation led to consideration of placing a parking area between the highway and the lake and bringing visitors up by shuttle bus. Such casual conversations became more serious as the monument staff became more aware of, and involved in, the major changes about to take place around them.

1. Runte (1997, 173).

2. Sellars (1997, 189).

3. Memo from superintendent, Tonto, to regional director, Southwest Region, September 26, 1966, NA/WACC, Grazing 1941–1971, p. 3.

4. Ibid., p. 2.

5. Ibid.

6. Telephone interview with Ron Ice by author, September 26, 2005.

7. Ibid.

8. Memo from Acting Assistant Regional Director to TNM Superintendent, 1966, Subject: Grazing and Water Use, NA/WACC.

9. Ibid.

10. Cited in Barbour (1999, 30).

11. Ibid., p. 31.

12. Cited in Memo from superintendent, Tonto, to general superintendent, SOAR, September 28, 1973, Subject: Grazing, p. 2. NA/WACC, Grazing 1941–1975. The Natural Resources Management Plan, Tonto National Monument, August 10, 1973 is cited in Barbour (1999, 32).

13. Ibid., p. 3.

14. Tonto National Monument, Arizona, Management Consultation Report, February 1975, NPS Western Region, NA/WACC.

15. Telephone interview with Ron Ice by author, September 29, 2005.

16. Ice (n.d., 4).

17. Ice (1972, 3).

18. Memo from Archeologist Ice to Archeologist Schroeder, March 26, 1969, NA/WACC.

19. Ibid.

20. Telephone interview with Ron Ice by author, September 29, 2005. The results of Ice's survey of USFS lands surrounding Tonto National Monument were published in 1972.

21. Telephone interview with Robert Armstrong by author, September 29, 2005; TNM Log of Significant Events and Important Contacts, July 2 and 30, 1970. Arizona Record June 25, 1970. *Arizona Republic* July 15, 1970. On one two-day period in 1977, six pothunters were arrested at three different locations on the Cave Creek District of TNM. One ton of artifacts was recovered. Gillio (2005, 29)

22. Memo from superintendent at Sanford Recreation Area to Al Schroeder, Southwest Regional Office April 4, 1972 re: Tonto National Forest Site Survey. Ice assumed that since the staffing situation changed there was no need to update the memo of understanding since TNM did not have an archeologist on staff.

23. See Gillio (2005) on the hiring of the first archeologists in the Southwest Region as well as the development of the cultural resource management programs in Arizona. In a telephone conversation with the author, Martin McAllister, the first TNF archeologist, characterized the 1970s hiring of archeologists as essential in staying in compliance with all the surface disturbance programs going on in the forests at that time.

24. Management Consultation Report, Tonto National Monument, Arizona, February 1975, p. 5.

25. Richert and Vivian (1975).

26. List of Classified Structures Survey: Tonto National Monument, June 1976, p. 26.

27. Letter from Douglas H. Scovill, acting chief, Arizona Archeological Center to Dennis McCarthy, director, Arizona State Parks Board, December 5, 1973, p. 1. NA/WACC.

28. Memo from Western Archeological Center supervisor, Ruins Stabilization to chief, Division of Cultural Properties Conservation, May 3, 1978, NA/WACC.

29. Memo from chief, Western Archeological Center, to regional director, Western Region, Subject: Rock Motion Hazard Report (Wachter), December 8, 1978, p. 1, NA/Denver TIC.

30. Memo from Martyn Tagg, Western Archeological and Conservation Center to chief, Division of Archeology, April 9, 1985, p. 2, NA/WACC.

31. Tagg (1985, 165).

32. Lange and Germick (1992) and Dean (2000) provide conference proceedings that document the evolution in the understanding of the Salado.

33. Sellars (1997) provides an overview of changes in preserving nature in the parks during this period.

34. "Management Consultation Report," Tonto National Monument, Arizona, February 1975, p. 5.

35. Telephone interview with Philip Young by author, September 27, 2005. The Archeological Resources Protection Act was enacted October 31, 1979.

36. Statement for Management, Tonto National Monument, 1976, pp. 7–10.

37. Telephone interview with James Valder by author, October 5, 2005.

38. Letter from Jan Bell, Arizona State Museum curator of collections to James W. Troutwine, Superintendent, TNM, August 8, 1985, p. 1. TNM history file.

39. Ibid., p. 2

40. Everhart (1983, 78).

41. Marcus (1983, 91).

chapter seven

RECLAMATION, CONSERVATION, AND PRESERVATION REVISITED: A MISSION REBORN, 1986-2006

Nothing is left to tell the story of their existence save the few earthen vessels which have been found in the ruins, the stone implements occasionally met with, and the fragments of pottery which lie scattered about their former abode. Time has nearly destroyed evidences of their existence. In the lapse of ages their history has grown almost a mythology.

HAMILTON, 1884

As times change, so do values. When Roosevelt Dam was constructed at the beginning of the twentieth century and the Tonto National Forest was reserved to protect it, only two Tonto Basin cliff dwellings were viewed as worthy of national monument status. Nearby platform mounds and other archeological sites in the Salt River and Tonto Creek beds were considered expendable. There was no process in place to analyze the archeological resources affected by the construction of the dam and creation of the lake; as a result, hundreds of prehistoric sites were flooded. Things were quite different eighty years later. Before the dam was raised an additional 77 feet in 1989, a formal federal process required analysis of the potential loss of archeological resources. From the mid-1980s through the mid-1990s, the Bureau of Reclamation spent millions on Plan 6—a plan developed in response to the Central Arizona Water Control Study and the Reclamation Safety of Dams Act, both in 1978, and the pressing need for safe water storage and diversion in the Tonto Basin. In order to mitigate for

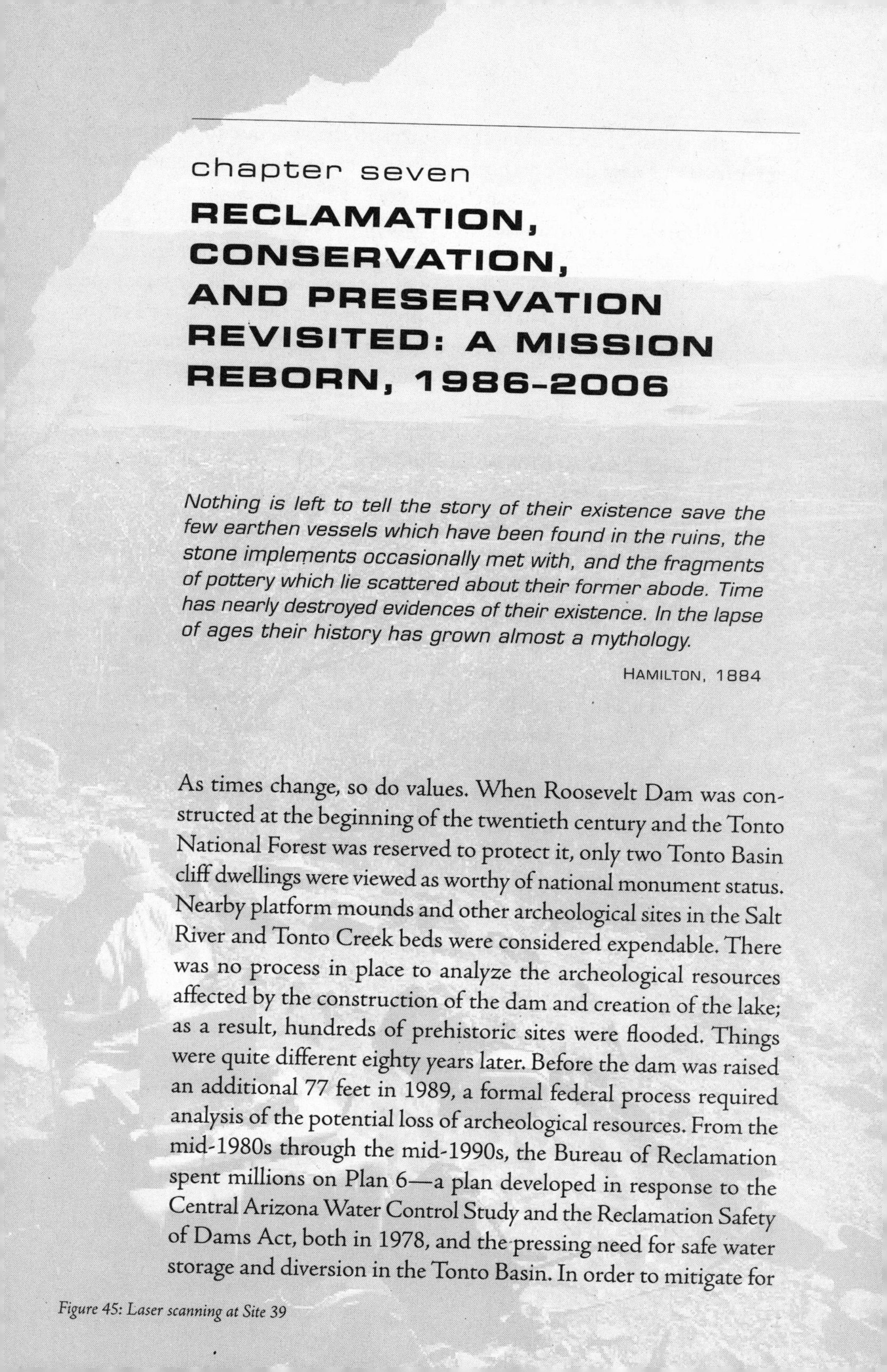

Figure 45: Laser scanning at Site 39

the potential loss of archeological resources in the area due to the planned construction of new dams and other infrastructure, this plan included one of the largest archeological research projects in U.S. history.

Plan 6 brought opportunities and challenges to Tonto National Monument. This chapter opens with an analysis of how Tonto National Monument reacted to Plan 6, then examines the monument's response to the deterioration of the cliff dwellings and to federal requirements to comply with the Native American Graves Protection and Repatriation Act (NAGPRA); it concludes with an account of the creation of a General Management Plan for Tonto National Monument's vision for the twenty-first century.

FEDERAL RECLAMATION AND RECREATION PLANNING FOR THE SALT RIVER AND TONTO CREEK

In the 1970s, the Bureau of Reclamation began making plans to provide increased flood control, water storage, and water distribution for central and southern Arizona. To comply with federal requirements, each plan required an analysis of any possible loss of natural and cultural resources and of the possible need for mitigation funds to offset those losses. An early plan called for the creation of Orme Dam and Reservoir at the confluence of the Salt and Verde rivers. This suggestion, along with several others, was rejected, partly because of the loss of archeological sites. At the time, archeological research in the Tonto Basin and Verde Valley was meager compared to that in many other southwestern areas. Over the next twenty years, however, it would catch up fast and become one of the most studied areas. [1]

In 1984, under the National Dam Safety Program, it became necessary to modify Roosevelt Dam so that it could withstand a "probable maximum flood." Plan 6 was adopted to address this safety need and initially also included construction of the New Waddell Dam on the Agua Fria River, the Cliff Dam on the Verde River (which was not built), and the reconstruction of the Stewart Mountain and Theodore Roosevelt dams on the Salt River.[2] This was a massive undertaking: the modifications for Roosevelt Dam alone cost $424 million. The plan also called for considerable mitigation efforts to reduce the environmental impacts of dam modifications on the area's natural resources, including the creation of the Arizona Bald Eagle Nest Watch Program, a Tonto Creek Riparian Unit, and the acquisition of habitat for the endangered southwestern willow flycatcher.

To mitigate the loss of cultural resources, the Bureau of Reclamation awarded contracts in excess of $15 million to research more than 250 archeological sites. Arizona State University conducted the Roosevelt Platform Mound Study, which investigated several platform mounds and their relationship to Hohokam platform mounds. The Center for Desert Archaeology conducted the Roosevelt Community Development Study, focusing on the origins and development of platform mounds in the Tonto Basin over the 1,000-year period between AD 300 and 1325. Statistical Research, Inc. conducted the Roosevelt Rural Sites Study, which examined six small site complexes and associated farming practices. The Bureau of Reclamation added a fourth project, the Roosevelt Bajada Study, in which SWCA Environmental Consultants conducted a sample survey of upland sites.[3] As none of the sites studied were located on the monument, Superintendent Kruse could only note that, "Information retrieval related to Hohokam and Salado occupation will be significant, and should enhance base data for the monument as well."[4]

TONTO NATIONAL MONUMENT DURING THE EARLY STAGES OF PLAN 6

Tonto National Monument was not positioned well to capitalize on the impending changes and massive amounts of federal dollars on their doorstep. Superintendent Troutwine was transferred to Tumacácori in October of 1986, and two staff members served jointly as acting superintendent until Carol Kruse took the post full time in March 1987.

Kruse immediately began responding to the impacts of Plan 6. Her 1988 Superintendent's Annual Report contains the first reference to Plan 6 developments. She noted three major impending issues: (1) raising the Roosevelt Dam 77 feet, which would enlarge the lake and bring the lakeshore almost to the monument's northern boundary; (2) constructing a new bridge to span the lake near the dam, which would increase traffic in the area; and (3) upgrading Forest Service visitor facilities, including campgrounds, boat launches, marinas, a resort, and a visitor information station, which was projected to double the number of lake visitors within five years. Clearly, monument staff also expected dramatic increases in visitors—accompanied by increases in demands on monument facilities and staff. For the most part, monument staff viewed the coming changes as positive. But they regretted the loss of the unobstructed view of the lake from the monument, which they expected to be marred by the construction of campgrounds and a resort complex along the shore.[5]

During the 1970s and early 1980s, visitor numbers at Tonto National Monument remained fairly constant at approximately 70,000 per year; for

1986–88, however, they increased to more than 80,000 annually. Economic and demographic projections indicated this upward trend would continue, and the major recreational developments taking place in the immediate vicinity of the monument caused Superintendent Kruse concern over the consequences of rising visitation at the monument. In 1988 she wrote that the twenty- and thirty-year-old facilities were insufficient for the current staff and visitors, to say nothing of those expected in the near future. She declared the entrance road unsafe, the parking lot inadequate, the visitor center poorly designed and only partially accessible to people with disabilities, and the audiovisual program inaccessible.[6] Kruse tried to maintain good communications with the other federal agencies involved in Plan 6, but was hampered by what she termed the "total lack" of planning documents for the monument. The superintendent believed that a general management plan and interpretive prospectus were "urgently needed."[7]

Tonto National Monument was certainly suffering from a lack of funding for both staff and programming. For instance, funding for fiscal year 1988 totaled a mere $172,475, and 95 percent was for personnel costs.[8] With limited resources to help staff with mounting informational, interpretive, clerical, and maintenance duties, staff began the monument's first volunteer program to help with patrol work, site bulletin preparation, and slide file and library maintenance. The Youth Conservation Corps also helped ease the staff's workload, and the monument's first computers offered some increased efficiency. For the most part, however, the budget severely restricted programming, maintenance, and natural and cultural resource management. Kruse championed professional development for staff and sent them to numerous training sessions, such as safety training, personal liability for federal managers, fee collection for supervisors, microcomputer training, law enforcement, and Red Cross first aid instructors' certification courses.

The lack of sufficient funds also meant that no ruins preservation work was performed for several years. In 1988 deterioration was noticeable in both the upper and lower cliff dwellings. In that same year, one preventative measure was taken at the upper cliff dwellings: a 4-foot-high, 12-gauge field fence was installed with one strand of barbed wire on top and one on the bottom to prevent damage from javelinas. Meanwhile, termites continued to undermine the visitor center foundation from below and rainwater leaked into the museum from above. In 1989 the center's aged foam roof was replaced with a metal one.

Figure 46: Construction of new entrance kiosk, 1988

An entrance fee collection station was installed for motorists, also in 1989, which helped on the several days each year with serious traffic congestion.[9] Beginning in March of the same year, however, visitor volume declined dramatically when, for the next four years, road building forced repeated closures along the Apache Trail and State Route 88. During the Columbus Day weekend of October 6–9, 1990, all monument visitors were turned away when most federal employees throughout the country were put on furlough due to the temporary lack of a national budget.

On a more positive note, Ranger Eddie Colyott made two new discoveries in the late 1980s. In 1987 Colyott determined that a fire hearth in the lower cliff dwellings might yield information about when they were occupied. The hearth was being eroded by a drip line in a room excavated in the 1950s, so Colyott requested that an archeomagnetic dating process be conducted immediately, before water compromised the integrity of the hearth. The Western Archaeological and Conservation Center of the National Park Service agreed, and two archeologists from the Arizona State Museum were contracted to do the work. Archeomagnetism enabled the archeologists to determine the location of magnetic north at points in time by examining burned clay, in this case, from the hearth. Test samples showed that people might have occupied the ruins as late as 1450, later than archeologists had previously thought. Colyott made another discovery when he identified an unmapped terrace near Rooms 18 and 19 at the lower ruin. For the first time in nearly half a century, a new feature at the lower cliff dwelling was exposed, recorded, and stabilized.

A different sort of "first" came in 1989 when the monument began an environmental education outreach program called Project Desert with the Miami School District. The program targeted six fourth-grade classrooms in four separate Miami schools. Bill Crozier, a retired superintendent of schools from Oakland, California, was a seasonal employee at Tonto National Monument, and developed a curriculum-based program for the Miami School District.

Accessibility to the monument was addressed in 1991 when a disabled access survey was conducted and recommended several modifications. The goal was to provide access to the three levels of the visitor center, convert living quarters number 12 to a fully accessible unit, and provide "friendly access" for three other residences.[10]

THE THREATS AND OPPORTUNITIES OF PLAN 6

In September 1992, the U.S. General Accounting Office gathered information about "external threats" to National Park Service units. The Subcommittee on National Parks and Public Lands of the House Committee on Interior and Insular Affairs required all park administrators to identify these threats, and Lee Baiza, Tonto National Monument superintendent since March 1992, identified Plan 6 as the most severe specific external threat to the monument. His report proposed projects to assess the impacts of Plan 6 on cultural resources, wildlife, and habitat; to coordinate with adjacent land users to protect monument resources; to continue air-quality and visibility monitoring; and to monitor aircraft overflights and assess their impacts on prehistoric structures, visitor experience, and wildlife. The report anticipated that Plan 6's immediate effects—increased large vehicle traffic, noise, dust, vibrations, and other construction impacts—would be followed by long-term impacts, including

1. Visual intrusions caused by large campgrounds and resort complexes;
2. Increased visitation by more diverse populations;
3. Changes in peak visitation seasons and hours;

4. Increased after-hours and trespass visitation to archeological sites;

5. Increased interactions between visitors, vehicles, domestic animals, and wildlife;

6. Loss of native habitat due to construction or increased public use;

7. Increased use of visitor facilities, i.e. trails, parking, water and sewer systems, picnic area, *etc.*;

8. Increased incidental use of "Lower 40," a 136-acre parcel located between Roosevelt Lake and Highway 88. This part of the monument already receives unknown amounts of unauthorized use, including camping, hunting, and trespass cattle, and is difficult to patrol on a regular basis. A large campground, marina, and resort complex will be located between this property and the lake, and proposed access routes skirt the monument boundary.[11]

Baiza reiterated what Superintendent Kruse had previously reported, that the monument was

unprepared for the changes and impacts of Plan 6 development. Staffing, funding, and facilities are inadequate for present conditions. Resource-oriented patrols are accomplished irregularly, and continuity is lacking due to small staff and frequent turnover. Cultural resource inspections and preservation are dependent on special funding each year. Baseline data is lacking for both natural and cultural resources, making future (post-Plan 6) comparisons questionable.[12]

Baiza saw threats, but he also saw opportunities for Tonto to benefit from the massive infusion of federal dollars occurring all around the monument. He knew that the monument had already lost opportunities to tie in to Plan 6, "because of limitations of the NPS priority, planning, and budget process." So Baiza made a point of attending monthly planning meetings with the U.S. Forest Service, Bureau of Reclamation, Arizona Department of Transportation, and others, and partnered on projects with the other federal agencies whenever possible.[13]

The first opportunity Baiza pursued was to tie the monument's needs to the transportation changes taking place at its entrance. For the several years of dam raising and bridge construction, road closures restricted the monument's visiting hours. Anticipating an increase in visitors when the new roads were completed, Baiza set out to acquire a new entrance to the monument. The entrance was not only uninviting, with its cattle guard and ineffective signage, but also was too steep at the main highway to meet safety requirements. The Arizona Department of Transportation (ADOT) was improving the road in a westerly direction from the new dam; it was important to the monument and to the cities of Globe and Miami that the road running east from the dam—portions of which were still not paved—also be upgraded, so that visitors could come up from Phoenix via the Apache Trail and then return through Globe and Miami. Baiza and others lobbied for the improvements.

The picture was complicated by the mix of funding sources feeding the work around the monument: ADOT provided state funds and the National Park Service used federal funds. Further complications arose from regulations based on whether a project was for rehabilitation of existing conditions or for new construction. The monument needed to relocate the 1-mile entrance road and turning lanes, for which it required both federal and state funding. One-eighth of a mile was considered new construction, and the rest was considered rehabilitation.

Additional complications came from the fact that the highway was being constructed in five geographical phases, and the monument needed to hook into the process at the right phase. Baiza somehow managed to make it work. He coordinated both funding sources and the construction schedule so that the monument was able to relocate and improve the entrance road and get the necessary turning lanes during phase two of the schedule. A scenic pullout was added to the road from the dam to Globe and Miami, thanks to a collaborative effort among the U.S. Forest Service, ADOT, and the chambers of commerce of the cities of Globe, Miami, and Apache Junction. ADOT installed it on Forest Service land, providing travelers a safe place to see the monument cliff dwellings from a distance. As the upper dwellings are closed to visitors during the summer, this is the only way to see them during those months.

Baiza also used Plan 6 as an opportunity to rethink the option of combining Tonto National Monument operations with those of the Forest Service. He studied how land swaps might be of mutual benefit and discussed collaboration on a new visitor center. His efforts, however, produced few tangible results.

The anticipated increase in visitors to the monument meant more water would be needed, and in 1993 the staff developed a new "water protection strategy." The idea was in keeping with the National Parks and Conservation Association "Parks in Peril" report that called for "expanding park boundaries where feasible to include important park watershed lands."[14] The strategy suggested shifting monument boundaries to include the entire Canyon Creek water drainage. Once staff secured the Cave Canyon drainage area from the Forest Service, the strategy proposed was to remove the dam from the upper reach of Cave Creek, reshape the terrain to allow a natural flow, and prevent sediment from accumulating in the stream channel. By securing the entire drainage area, the monument would remove the threat posed by potential Forest Service prescribed burns upstream, which could result in ash, silt, erosion, and negative effects on the water table and on the well. The only disadvantage cited in the strategy was that the monument would need to supplement its supply system by purchasing potable water from the forest service, and that 1.5 miles of pipeline would be needed to pump water 650 feet up to monument headquarters.[15] Due to the unavailability of Land and Water Conservation funds, however, the plan went no further.

The water strategy document also proposed establishing a new visitor center on the south side of State Route 88 for both the U.S. Forest Service and the National Park Service. It described the benefits of a site with a view of the upper cliff dwelling, citing the Grand Canyon, where only a few wished to walk to Phantom Ranch, "but everyone wants to see the canyon."[16] With the addition of telescopes, the document argued, the vantage point at the new monument headquarters would offer visitors an excellent view and also reduce traffic.

Full of hope for collaboration, monument staff drew up a visitor center demolition plan in 1994. The plan also reflected staff's frustration with their thirty-year-old Mission 66 visitor center facilities, especially the exhibit area. The light, temperature, and humidity controls were insufficient; only 129 items were on display, out of an inventory of 2,966; and among these, some textiles were laid directly on the painted surface of the exhibit cases. Despite such clear deficiencies, however, it was doubtful that the plan would be adopted because the Park Service was urging staff to treat Mission 66 structures as if they were eligible for the National Register, and there was a moratorium on demolishing them.[17]

The U.S. Forest Service rejected the monument's proposed entrance site for a new joint visitor center in favor of its current location, 4 miles west on the north side of the highway. Again, the Bureau of Reclamation, U.S. Forest Service, and National Park Service discussed collaborating on a visitor center at this location. The new center would feature museum exhibits and serve as the central point from which people would be directed out to the monument's cliff dwellings, as well as to a series of other interpretive sites on

Forest Service land, including Cline Terrace, Rye Creek, and Indian Point.[18] In this scenario, NPS expertise and resources would combine with those of the Forest Service to create a major heritage access point—a heritage hub—that would interpret not only the cliff dwellings at the monument, but also the archeological history of the surrounding area, including the latest research. Visitors might even be allowed to view current archeological work at one of the large platform mound sites. However tantalizing, these plans also went nowhere, largely because their window of opportunity closed when the national mood swung against federal spending.

In response to termination of the "camp anywhere" policy and the loss of the Forest Service ranger station, the Bureau of Reclamation funded extensive Forest Service lakeside construction, which provided 1,515 individual campsites, 80 picnic sites, 9 group campgrounds, 9 boat launch areas, and 6 fish-cleaning stations—all in anticipation of a massive increase in recreational tourism. Plan 6 provided a large increase in USFS recreational facilities as part of its mitigation package, but made relatively little investment in interpretation and exhibition at the new visitor center—an imbalance reminiscent of the NPS Mission 66 era. In the end, the discussions about the U.S. Forest Service and the National Park Service collaborating amounted to little: even Tonto National Monument's request that the Forest Service install green roofs at the campground was denied. Instead, blue roofs—now visible from the monument—were chosen to match the blue bridge spanning Roosevelt Lake.

Some infrastructure upgrades were successful. During the latter phases of Plan 6 and beyond, for example, Tonto National Monument installed a new picnic area, complete with a comfort station; extended the visitor center parking lot; removed the transformers from the visitor center basement and renovated it as offices; made the visitor center bathrooms fully accessible; connected the park's two wastewater systems by installing a new sewer line, septic tank, and leach field; and buried power and telephone lines in the new sewer pipe trench.

In addition to these significant local changes, the mid-1990s also brought extensive reorganizations within the Park Service. In 1994, Tonto National Monument was shifted from the Western Region to the Southwest Region; shortly thereafter, the Southwest Region was joined with the Rocky Mountain Region to form the Intermountain Region. In addition, since 1937, the monument had reported to a regional office, Southwest Monuments, which in turn reported to Washington. In 1995 the Southern Arizona Office (SOAR) became an advisory office for Tonto, rather than a supervisory office, leaving

Figure 47: Parking lot and picnic tables, 1985

the monument without a regional supervisory office for the first time since 1937. These organizational changes meant that monument staff needed to establish new contacts in Washington, D.C., set new priorities, and compete for attention and funding with much larger parks and monuments.

VANISHING TREASURES INITIATIVE RESPONDS TO CRISIS OF CARE

Patrick Hamilton chronicled the resources of Arizona in 1884, including accounts of its counties and towns, rail and stage lines, mines and mining, flocks and herds, and Indian tribes. In his chapter on prehistoric Arizona, he posed the same questions that intrigue us today:

Who were those people who built imposing structures, dug immense canals, and redeemed from the desert such vast stretches of land? From whence did they come, and what has been the cause of their extinction. Did war, pestilence, famine, or some mighty convulsion of nature destroy them? Nothing is left to tell the story of their existence save the few earthen vessels which have been found in the ruins, the stone implements occasionally met with, and the fragments of pottery which lie scattered about their former abode. Time has nearly destroyed evidences of their existence. In the lapse of ages their history has grown almost a mythology. As to their customs and religious beliefs all is conjecture, but from the few hieroglyphics which they have left behind, it has been supposed they were sun-worshippers.[19]

One hundred years later, the archeological ruins in the Southwest were deteriorating at a rate that far exceeded NPS abilities and resources to respond. Managers from several NPS parks and monuments pooled information and identified three major common deficits: not enough parks and monuments with management plans based on good scientific evidence, preservation specialists aging out of the workforce without a program to replace them, and inadequate and inconsistent funding. The managers produced a video to dramatize the deficiencies and set four goals for a program they called Vanishing Treasures: (1) develop a computerized management system with a comprehensive database for ruins preservation, (2) develop a career development program for preservation specialists, (3) ensure adequate funding, and (4) define a ruins preservation program. Former NPS Director Roger Kennedy supported the park managers, declaring an "undeniable crisis of care" and seeking support for "buildings made of the stuff of earth itself . . . as old as time and human labor, the containers of the experience of community, ours in trust."[20] Vanishing Treasures became an NPS program in 1998 with an appropriation of $1 million—$497,000 for emergency preservation projects, $493,000 for recruiting and training craftspeople, and $10,000 for program management. Tonto National Monument was among the first to secure Vanishing Treasures funds for personnel and projects.[21] It came not a moment too soon.

CLIFF CWELLING DETERIORATION

By the early 1990s at Tonto, the consequences of decades of limiting work to emergency response could no longer be ignored. The cliff dwellings were replete with bulging and cracking walls, collapsing walls and roofs, loose wall cobbles, and melting of the adobe used to face the cobble walls and cover the wood roofs. For years, repeated cycles of rain saturation and drying had weakened ruin walls. Saturation, coupled with rodent infestations, weakened one section of the upper cliff dwelling so much that Seasonal Ranger Faye Morrison stepped on what she thought was solid ground and fell through a hole in Room 15.

These appalling conditions required Superintendent Baiza to develop a preservation plan as soon as he arrived in 1992. He convened natural and

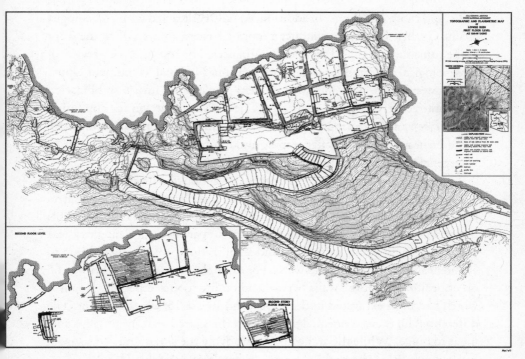

Figure 48: Topographic map of lower cliff dwelling, 2006

cultural resource specialists to create a long-term plan to assess and treat extensive pest damage to the upper cliff dwelling. Staff from SOAR (especially Jim Rancier for cultural resources and Kathy Davis for natural resources), WACC, and the chief of cultural resources for the Western Region collaborated on a strategy. The work began with Natural Resource Park Protection funds to inventory and monitor water and pest damage, but conditions became even more acute with above-average rainfalls in 1992 and 1993.

A two-year infrared photography study revealed extensive damage from burrowing rodents, especially rock squirrels. This reflected a particular dilemma for the monument: the key to managing pests is to usually remove what attracts them. In this case, however, the attraction was the ruins themselves, whose deep soils provided ideal sites for den construction and whose cliffs provided shelter and lookouts.

In 1994 WACC contracted with Collins-Pina Consulting Engineers, Inc. to produce the first computer-assisted design of the upper cliff dwellings. For the first time, the monument possessed a single source map of Tonto National Monument that included all doors, rooms, vigas, viga holes, latillas, posts, walls, and room elevations. In addition WACC contracted with archeologist Elaine Guthrie in 1994 to conduct a room-by-room analysis of all the work at the ruins that produced ground disturbances. The result, "An Overview of Archeological and Stabilization Work at Tonto National Monument Upper and Lower Ruins," was intended to help in planning future stabilization and data-recovery projects, and to provide a research design for any future subsurface work at the monument.[22] Before Guthrie's work was completed, however, heavy rains sent water seeping into Rooms 15 and 16, which required emergency salvage at the upper dwelling.

In 1995 WACC archeologist Gregory Fox conducted limited test excavations at the upper cliff dwelling prior to the installation of a water-control feature and wall buttresses. The excavation revealed an array of perishable materials and artifacts. Fox found that the upper dwelling's integrity was threatened by previous excavation and stabilization projects, in addition to erosion caused by rodents and water. For example, prior work left uneven fill on opposite sides of the walls between adjoining rooms, especially Room 7, which had been excavated in the 1950s, and Room 15, which had not. The differential fill exerted unequal pressure on the shared wall, eventually causing it to bulge. While the archeologists studying the situation tried to avoid further excavation themselves, it was ultimately unavoidable.[23]

In 1997 WACC contracted with archeologist Mark Elson to develop a research design to direct recovery of archaeological deposits, "whether in terms of emergency salvage, research, or routine maintenance of the Upper and Lower Ruins."[24] Elson proposed a set of research questions; some were practical, with the expectation that data collection would yield direct answers, while others were more theoretical efforts to shape future research on Tonto Basin's prehistoric economy, regional networks, and regional movement.

In 1998 Fox excavated Rooms 15 and 16, supported by $125,000 in Vanishing Treasures funds dedicated to address major structural problems at the upper cliff dwellings caused by continuing rodent and rain damage. Fox was assisted by a University of Arizona employee and ten monument and WACC volunteers. Vanishing Treasures funding was also used to train Chief of Maintenance Ruben Avalos, who was responsible for ruins preservation, to assist in the upper cliff dwelling excavation and stabilization. Fox wrote that it was difficult to convey how severely compromised Rooms 15 and 16 were, but that the damage was confined to only those rooms along the northern shelter wall.[25] All cultural remains were removed, including 5,011 pot sherds from Room 15 and 11,723 from Room 16. The rooms also yielded more than 6,600 fish, reptile, and bird bones, as well as cotton, yucca, and agave fabrics and botanical remains.[26] But even the presence of people working in the ruins for more than two months failed to decrease the rodent activity. Fox warned that the rodents would continue to undermine walls and wall intersections.[27]

Vanishing Treasures then financed a one-year project to complete the excavation report and implement the prescribed stabilization treatment.[28] Vanishing Treasures also funded archeologists and exhibit specialist positions as part of its mission to help parks create databases for ruins preservation and to provide ruins preservation specialists to parks and monuments in the Southwest. Baiza elected to hire an exhibit specialist; Miguel Estrada, trained in ruins preservation, joined the staff in 1998. Over the next several years, the staff was able to conduct long-overdue stabilization and maintenance work.

In the mid-twentieth century, Americans noted the deteriorating physical conditions of national parks and monuments and worried that we were "loving the parks to death." At the century's end, however, they were more likely to ask whether we were "preserving the ruins to death." Was the National Park Service, the lead preservation agency, sometimes going too far by encapsulating ruins, thereby destroying the archeological resources it was charged with preserving? Underlying such concerns was the deeper question of whether each generation must inevitably settle for experiencing less of the real thing—in other words, how to find the proper balance between preservation and access.[29] At Tonto National Monument, the cliff dwellings began receiving crack-filling treatments in the 1930s; Steen developed a comprehensive plan in the 1940s, and the preservation process was continued by Richert in 1957, Mayer in 1965, and Lorrain in 1990. Throughout the 1990s, NPS staff did likewise.

In Arizona, the State Historic Preservation Office (SHPO) had a programmatic agreement with the National Park Service to ensure that acceptable procedures were followed in striking this balance. In 1996, however, SHPO learned that preservation work at Montezuma Castle had been conducted beyond the scope of the agreement. SHPO contended that the mortar color of the newly plastered walls did not match the original construction, that repair work was done to an area larger than necessary, and that the work modified the appearance of the structure too much.[30]

For Tonto National Monument these issues hit home in 2004 when the monument notified SHPO that, in addition to the excessive crack-filling treatments applied since the 1930s, a 2003 treatment at the upper dwelling had caused significant modification to its appearance. Laborers with little ruins preservation experience had carried out a project begun by the monument's exhibit specialist, who unfortunately was not on staff to monitor the work. The result was physically and visually incompatible with the upper cliff dwelling and was also improperly documented. NPS staff is currently faced with the task of monitoring the effects of natural erosion on this inappropriate treatment and exploring other techniques for its removal.

NATURAL RESOURCE DOCUMENTATION

In 1988 the national parks were characterized as our "ecological canaries," and it was declared that "our canaries are in trouble."[31] At Tonto National Monument, however, conditions were improving following the elimination of grazing, with one study even concluding that saguaros on the monument were in better shape than those at the Saguaro National Monument.[32] Funding for natural resource studies became available, and several were conducted at Tonto in the early 1990s by the Cooperative National Park Resources Studies Unit/University of Arizona. In 1992 Barbara Phillips completed a nonnative plant species technical report that recorded thirteen species, three for the first time.[33] In 1997 she completed a history of fire and fire impacts at the monument.[34] Kathy Hiett, Michael Kunzman, and Bill Halborson updated and verified bird records, produced a new checklist, and made recommendations for monitoring.[35] Don Swann conducted research projects on mammals, reptiles, and amphibians.[36]

The National Park Service, as a result of its profound "lack of information about park plants, animals, ecosystems, and their interrelationship," made a commitment to research in 1999 through "The Natural Resource Challenge: The National Park Service's Action Plan for Preserving Natural Resources."[37] The plan divided NPS parks and monuments into thirty-two networks. Tonto National Monument and ten other parks became part of the Sonoran Desert Network.[38] Program funds became available in the late 1990s to assist parks and monuments in collecting data on natural resources, enabling the monument by 2005 to finalize the most complete inventory of plants and animals to date. Tonto was also able to secure Natural Resource Challenge funds for a new position: the monument's first natural resource specialist, Shirley Hoh, joined the staff in 1999.

NAGPRA: SHARING INFORMATION ON PREHISTORIC AND PRESENT-DAY GROUP IDENTITIES

The Vanishing Treasures and Natural Resource Challenge programs were the results of "bottom up" efforts by Park Service staff. However, they were

Figure 49: Tonto National Monument staff and tribal members at a consultation meeting, 1995

the exceptions; most changes occurred "top down" through new federal requirements. One notable example was the 1990 NAGPRA law, which required federal agencies holding Native American human remains and funerary objects to compile an inventory and determine which present-day Indian tribe or Native Hawaiian group had a "cultural affiliation" with them. "Cultural affiliation" was defined as having a relationship of shared group identity that could reasonably be traced historically or prehistorically to the remains of the earlier group. To comply with NAGPRA regulations, Tonto National Monument staff was required to consult with the six tribes that claimed cultural affiliation with the site.

Staff from seven NPS parks and WACC took part in a two-day tribal consultation meeting on July 18–19, 1995, in Tucson to discuss human remains and funerary objects identified as Hohokam, Salado, or Sinagua. Two staff from Tonto attended, along with representatives from the Gila River Indian Community, the Hopi Tribe, the Pueblo of Zuni, the Salt River Pima-Maricopa Indian Community, and the Tohono O'odham Nation.[39] The Park Service's goals were to explain how NPS units in southern Arizona were preparing their inventories, to begin the consultation process by seeking information from tribes about their affiliation with items in the inventories, and to discuss concerns about repatriation and reburial.[40]

Other than the opening and closing prayers that bracketed the meeting, the agenda was routine. Throughout the first day, nontribal attendees gave an overview of meeting goals and consultation procedures, as well as of Hohokam, Salado, and Sinagua prehistory and other matters. Tribal representatives were invited to respond only on the second day, and transcripts reveal a deep cultural divide that needed bridging before repatriation and reburial could even begin to be discussed.

In response to the first-day presentation mapping Hohokam, Salado, and Sinagua prehistory, Joseph Joaquin of the Tohono O'odham Nation expressed the need to understand the fundamental differences in beliefs that would shape the discussions. To begin with, he said, the terms *Hohokam*, *Salado*, and *Sinagua*, used regularly by archeologists to describe prehistory, were not meaningful for him:

> Yesterday we sat here and discussed this issue but we never talked about what they're telling us on the map up there. You are here, you are there, you are that. We are all one, and we know that amongst our people. Our Native American people. That we are one. We believe in one spiritual being that got us to here, that put us here. And that is how we came to be.[41]

Leigh Jenkins, cultural preservation officer for the Hopi, said he was aware of the mistakes and misrepresentations of early ethnographic work. These, he said, suggested that the early work was missing the "essence," because the essence of clan traditions and ceremonial knowledge were what most needed to be protected:

> When you get initiated into these societies you make a vow to uphold the integrity of your ceremonial information. It is an oath you take when you get initiated. So to divulge and talk about it publicly is very hard for Hopis.[42]

Another Hopi representative, Emory Sekaquaptewa, who had twenty-six years of experience in the Department of Anthropology at the University of Arizona, talked of the Hopi concept of *navoti*, or traditional knowledge, and the attempt to document it in each word that was being included in a Hopi dictionary.[43] Ronald Chiago of the Salt River Pima-Maricopa Indian

Community, remarked what a "hard, long process" it was to come up with resolutions regarding repatriation and reburials.[44] Joseph Dishta of Zuni Pueblo echoed these sentiments and noted how sensitive an issue burial was for the Zuni:

> For the Zuni culture, burial is something that is done once, it is final, and should remain like that. It is unfortunate that it happens, it is a sad time, but we look at these things once. When an individual has reached the end of its existence, there is ritual and prayer that we use to return them back to the Mother Earth, they are returned back to the Mother Earth, they are returned to the spirit world, where the journey begins. As far as returning them back to the Zuni homeland we feel that we should not do this, we feel that it causes a cultural conflict, to bring back remains would be taboo, and they might bring harm to the current populations.[45]

Finally, Wilton Niiha of Zuni Pueblo said that, although she listened to the presentation about Arizona native peoples—the Hohokam, Salado, and Sinagua—she didn't agree with the designations because she saw the ancestors as one. However she did agree on the importance of the remains:

> For me those remains are special. They're our ancestral remains which were wrongfully taken from their homelands. Wrongfully taken, put in boxes, sent to museums. Those spiritual things of our ancestors selected us to get those remains back and place them where they once were. That is special to me, to be the one to get our ancestors back to that area where they continue on their journey.[46]

The 1995 NAGPRA meeting was the first time monument staff took part in formal discussions with culturally affiliated tribes. Over the next ten years, follow-up was minimal. In 1997 most NAGPRA items were removed, put in storage for future decisions about ownership, and replaced with other artifacts or replicas.[47] Tonto National Monument staff, in collaboration with the tribes, developed a plan to handle inadvertent discoveries. These attempts to consult were tentative, at best. The tribes held simultaneous discussions with the Tonto National Forest, which resulted in repatriations to the southern Arizona tribes but not to the Hopi and Zuni. The impact of this parallel consultation process remains unclear. TNM staff filed a Notice of Inventory Completion in 2006 for six burials and twenty-nine associated funerary objects, as well as two additional burials and twenty-three associated funerary objects recorded on the NAGPRA inventory of the Western Archaeological and Conservation Center (WACC) that were excavated from the upper cliff dwelling but remained in WACC's possession. Following the inventory, the culturally affiliated tribes will have an opportunity to state their claims, view the materials, and proceed with repatriation and reburial.

And what of the Tonto shirt? As noted in previous chapters, monument staff corresponded with Arizona State Museum staff about the provenance of the shirt during the construction of the Mission 66 visitor center and again in 1985. The issue takes on added meaning in light of NAGPRA regulations: if the shirt was a funerary item, the culturally affiliated tribes must be brought into the discussions. Like the exquisitely crafted Tonto shirt itself, progress on this matter will require the delicate interplay of knowledge, understanding, and communication skills.

THE GENERAL MANAGEMENT PLAN

TNM staff collaborated with representatives from the Intermountain Region, the Southern Arizona Office, and WACC to develop a general management plan (GMP) in three phases between 1996 and 2002 (to replace the 1962 management plan). The bulk of the work came in the last phase, between 2000 and 2002. At that point the monument had the biggest staff in its history, including the three new full-time positions of natural resource specialist, exhibit specialist, and a law enforcement officer. The plan again assumed increased tourism within the Tonto Basin as a result of the expanded recreational facilities at Roosevelt Lake, improved highway access from Globe and Payson, and the continuing rapid growth of the Phoenix metropolitan area. The planning considered cultural resources, natural resources, natural quiet, visitor use/experience and accessibility, scenic view sheds, adjacent land/partnerships, facilities, staffing, and boundaries.[48] Finalized in 2002, the GMP presented and analyzed four alternatives to guide management of Tonto National Monument for the next ten to fifteen years.

The preferred alternative contained two major recommendations. The first was to move the administrative operation out of the visitor center to a new facility constructed near the maintenance facility, in order to accommodate staff work-space needs. The second was to remodel the visitor center building to provide slightly increased visitor educational experiences.[49] Several other recommendations are also noteworth, two of them involving monument boundaries. The planners called for revising the boundary to include the entire Cave Canyon watershed, as it was not entirely contained within the existing fence line; this echoed the 1993 findings that grazing, hunting, and other activities upstream from the monument negatively impacted its natural and cultural resources. The planners also noted that the fence did not always follow the legal boundary, and recommended a new fence line to prevent trespass and incompatible use and to allow for safe wildlife crossings.[50]

One suggestion addressed the monument's name. In an effort to more accurately reflect the monument's heritage values, the GMP recommended changing its name from Tonto National Monument to Salado Cliff Dwellings National Monument. This was thought to be a more descriptive phrase, as it includes references to both the culture and the feature that visitors could expect to encounter at the monument.[51]

A TIME FOR SYNTHESIS

The GMP was approved in 2003. In less than a year, a new superintendent inherited the plan and became responsible for its implementation. In 2004, Bradley S. Traver took over Tonto National Monument. With the GMP in place, Traver began the process of determining eligibility of the visitor center for the National Register, planning for its expansion and new exhibits in 2011, and building a new 2,500-square-foot administration building with seven offices and a conference room. When completed, the administration building will be the first in the NPS system to be constructed of rammed earth. In addition to making green building principles a priority, the monument is making it a priority to keep up with the revolution in information technology. This effort includes electronic reporting, televised training, digital scans of the ruins, GIS information, new technology in the new exhibits, and virtual tours of the monument on its web site.

Traver raised the question of the name change with officials and business-people in Globe and Payson and with the Gila County Board of Supervisors, all of whom supported the change. He also consulted with the four affiliated southern tribes and the Hopi; the tribes did not find the term *Salado* any more appropriate than *Tonto*, given that both were chosen by outsiders to refer to the tribal ancestors. As a result, monument staff dropped the name-change idea. On the matter of bringing the entire Cave Canyon watershed under monument control, Traver determined that there was no indication that the Forest Service was managing the land in such a way that the effects were detrimental to the monument. He chose to pursue good working relations with the Forest Service to keep it that way.

Figure 50: Digital relief map of Tonto National Monument

Traver converted the position held by Duane Hubbard from exhibit specialist to archeologist, and in 2004 Tonto National Monument officially had an archeologist on staff for the first time in thirty-two years. Hubbard began several projects to create a database on the ruins, including photographs, dendrochronology, highly accurate computer models, and maps of the dwellings. One project, a collaboration with the Northern Arizona University Anthropology Department, builds on Guthrie's earlier stabilization history report and will result in a wall-by-wall searchable database containing photographs and descriptive material pertaining to past stabilization and preservation activities. Staff is also conducting condition assessments of backcountry sites to identify threats and disturbances. The goal was 100 percent correction of deficiencies by 2006 and the achievement of national goals regarding updating site-condition information.

Figure 51: Superintendent Bradley Traver in lower cliff dwelling for laser scanning, 2007

The appointment of an archeologist is also important for Tonto because it corresponds to the completion of the research conducted by the four contractors for Plan 6. Archeologist Jeffrey Dean concluded that the research was scientifically sound: each project had a well-conceived research design, the field implementation was inventive and flexible, the data analysis was both sophisticated and comprehensive, the results were carefully evaluated, and well-reasoned conclusions and hypotheses were drawn from the totality of the research. In summary, he characterized the results of Plan 6 archeology by stating, "The Roosevelt Archeology Project has elevated a scientific platform from which to launch future, more advanced investigations of Salado and all its

Figure 52: Highly accurate mesh model of lower cliff dwelling created by digital scanning. Used to track changes in the dwelling over time as well as for interpretation at the monument

Figure 53: Archeologist Duane Hubbard stabilizing a lower cliff dwelling wall, 2006

Figure 54: Archeologists Duane Hubbard and Matt Guebard stabilize a wall at Site 89A–39, 2007

ramifications."[52] While Tonto National Monument sites were not examined by the Plan 6 contractors, Hubbard can now benefit from the synthesis of this professional work and begin addressing some of the research questions identified specifically for Tonto by Elson in 1997.[53] It is time, in other words, to stitch the story of the cliff dwellings back in to the ongoing investigations of Salado. That work has already begun.

Tonto National Monument is partnering with the Center for Desert Archaeology to improve knowledge of Salado polychrome production and of obsidian exchange. Archeologist Jeffrey Clark of the center defined four aspects of migration to be investigated: the archeological record, the motivation, the organization and logistical requirements, and the socioeconomic impact on the destination area. According to Clark, Salado polychrome pottery is the ideal research context in which to study migration, because it was distributed over 50,000 square miles in Arizona, New Mexico, and northern Mexico, and was used by the ancestral Puebloan, Hohokam,

Mogollon, and Sinagua. Clark identifies Salado polychrome as the only consistent marker in the Salado horizon, and especially Gila polychrome, which had the widest distribution of any decorated ceramic type in the prehistoric Southwest.[54] Grants from the National Science Foundation and Western National Parks Association are supporting a fresh look at migration and analysis of artifacts—including artifacts recovered in the 1998 excavation—which are being examined at Arizona State University's Archaeological Research Institute to determine what clues they can yield about the temporal and spatial variability of population decline, and the cultural and biological factors that contributed to decline.

The diverse textiles collected at Tonto are of critical importance in understanding the Tonto Basin's connection to southwestern prehistory. Lynn Teague estimates that the upper cliff dwelling has produced, "the second largest assemblage of woven fabrics recovered from any site in the greater Southwest; only Antelope House in Canyon de Chelly has produced a greater number."[55] Tonto National Forest Archeologist Scott Wood also argues that the most important data set of the cliff dwellings at Tonto National Monument is their textile collection, which he sees as a key to understanding the economic production of the textile industry. Wood considers the intricate weaving technology to be evidence of a sophisticated cotton production and trade system, and argues that the macrobotanicals available from Tonto National Monument will yield important contributions to our understanding of plant species availability in the Tonto Basin. Hubbard will be an important link in the study of this textile collection and in interpreting its significance.

---

1. Fuller, Rogge, Gregonis (1976, 21). This publication cited the Orme Reservoir archeological mitigation costs to be $22 million. The Orme Alternative Study called for raising Roosevelt Dam 30 feet and Horseshoe Dam 140 feet and estimated the monetary significance of the resources potentially to be affected at a range from $53,772,700 to $118,044,200, p. 212.

According to Rogge, 65 miles were surveyed, resulting in the recording of 178 sites. In response to the $22 million mitigation costs, Rogge said, "It is an understatement to say that the draft report sent shock waves through the agency. Reclamation personnel became deeply involved in reviewing the report and a number of meetings were held over the next 2 years before a final version was printed." The controversy led to an $11 million 4-year search for alternatives to Orme. Rogge (1983, 134).

The Fort McDowell Indian Reservation fought construction of the Orme Dam, which would have flooded 15,000 acres of tribal land. In 1976 the Yavapai Tribe rejected the sale of the land for the dam and in 1981 the federal government scrapped the Orme Dam concept. The tribe honors the victory that prevented the dam annually with Orme Dam Victory Days Celebration.

2. Construction of the Cliff Dam would have affected 559 known sites. Environmentalists fought the construction of the Cliff Dam, and when it was dropped from Plan 6, all attention was focused on Roosevelt. Originally it was thought that 539 sites would be impacted by expanding the size of the Roosevelt Lake, but that number increased to more than 700 when BOR expanded the construction staging areas and access routes. Rice (1998, 2).

3. Rice (1998) provides a synthesis of the BOR archeology projects in the Tonto Basin 1989–1998. Dean's (2000) preface gives an overview of the studies, which resulted in 17 massive descriptive reports in 29 volumes. Clark's (2000) preface notes that as a result of all the cultural resource management projects in the Tonto Basin conducted by the Bureau of Reclamation for dam construction and by the Arizona Department of Transportation for road construction, the Tonto Basin became one of the most thoroughly investigated areas in the Southwest. In addition to the archeological research, the contractors hosted events where the public was invited to excavation sites. Contractors created newsletters, exhibits, and events. "Mystery beneath the Lake: Who Were the Salado" was at the Pueblo Grande Museum in Phoenix for a year, followed by three years at the Arizona State University Anthropology Museum.

4. Superintendent's Annual Report, March 1, 1990, p. 1.

5. Superintendent's Annual Report, March 25, 1988, p. 1 and Statement for Management (1989, 5).

6. Superintendent's Annual Report, March 25, 1988, p. 2.

7. Superintendent's Annual Report, March 15, 1989, p.2.

8. Superintendent's Annual Report, March 15, 1989, p. 4.

9. Between December 26, 1986, and March 31, 1987, there were 25 days (approximately 26 percent of the time) when the parking lot was completely full and visitors had to be detained from coming into the area until a parking space was vacated. A larger parking lot was needed, and the monument road entrance station helped alleviate this problem. (Superintendent's Annual Report, March 25, 1988, p. 6).

10. Tonto National Monument Accessibility Survey, 1991. The survey team assessed the visitor center, including the observation deck, men's and women's toilet rooms; the administrative offices; and residence number 12.

11. "External Threats to National Parks." U.S. General Accounting Office report, 1992, pp. 45–46.

12. Ibid., p. 46.

13. Statement for Management, Tonto National Monument, revised September 1996, p. 15.

14. Quoted in attachment to July 29, 1993, memorandum from William Werrell, Hydrologist, Water Operations Branch, to chief, Water Operations Branch (Water Resources Division, WASO, NPS), subject: Trip Report for Travel to Tonto NM and Chiricahua NM, March 20–25, 1993, p. 2.

15. Ibid., pp. 2–3.

16. Ibid., p. 4.

17. Scope of Collections Statement, November 1992, NA/WACC. This statement had appended to it a set of recommendations from July 1989 for an ongoing museum environment monitoring program and corrective action requiring a complete redesign, including installation of temperature and humidity monitoring equipment.

18. There was precedent for this collaboration between the FS and NPS. In 1969, the Gila Cliff Dwelling Visitor Center was built on Forest Service land and jointly operated with NPS. Information about the potential collaboration between the FS and TNM came from telephone interviews by the author with Tom Lincoln on November 4, 2005, and Scott Wood, USFS TNF on November 5, 2005.

19. Ibid., pp. 354–355.

20. NPS (1998, 1); also see NPS (1995) on Vanishing Treasures strategic planning.

21. NPS (1998, pp. 4, 7–8.

22. Guthrie (1994).

23. Elson (1997, 7).

24. Ibid.

25. Fox (2000, 57).

26. Ibid., pp. 61, 139, 193, 197.

27. Ibid., p. 242.

28. The final report is Fox (2000). NPS (2000), section 6, page 6–12, gives the details of the stabilization measures as consisting of redistributing the excess fill/soils from the excavated rooms in the Upper Ruin to other rooms to minimize the differential fill problem in adjacent rooms. Walls exposed during excavation were subsequently stabilized. A trench two feet from the walls of Room 16 was dug and filled with sand to minimize rodent activity and hardware cloth between the trench and the base of the wall was added and covered with mud.

29. Frome (1992, 4). Frome and Sellars provide overviews of the efforts to preserve nature in the national parks.

30. Protas (2002, 230).

31. Hartzog (1988, 255).

32. Superintendent's Annual Report, March 15, 1989, p. 6

33. Phillips (1992).

34. Phillips (1997).

35. Hiett, Kunxman, and Halborson (1996, 1999).

36. Swann (1996, 1997, 1998).

37. NPS (1999, 4).

38. The eleven Sonoran Desert Network parks are: Montezuma Castle, Tuzigoot, Organ Pipe Cactus, Casa Grande, Saguaro, Tumacácori, Coronado, Chiricahua, Fort Bowie, Gila Cliff Dwellings, and Tonto.

39. The Gila River Indian Reservation represented the Ak-Chin Indian Community at that meeting. The NPS parks included the Casa Grade Ruins National Monument, Montezuma Castle National Monument, Organ Pipe Cactus National Monument, Saguaro National Park, Tonto National Monument, Tumacacori National Monument, and Tuzigoot National Monument.

40. Zedeño and Stoffle (1995, 3).

TNM's inventory summary listed:

• six burials and seven groups of fragmentary remains. Three burials were from the lower ruin and annex and two burials and six groups of fragmentary remains from the upper ruin, Tonto National Monument. One burial was found along State Highway 188, two miles north of Punkin Center. Provenience of the remaining group of fragmentary remains is unknown.

• approximately 30 associated funerary objects including bowls, a gourd container, textiles/matting, a spindle, awls, a cradleboard, a rattle, a ring, a staff, a crystal, a tessera, and a soil sample.

The remains and funerary objects from Tonto National Monument are attributed to the Salado of the Gila Phase (A.D. 1300–1450). The burial along State Highway 188 is Salado and probably dates from A.D. 1100–1400. Physical anthropological examination could not confirm that the remaining fragmentary human remains are Native American. (Ibid., pp. 60–61).

41. Ibid., p. 72.

42. Ibid., p. 76.

43. Ibid., p. 81.

44. Ibid., p. 89.

45. Ibid., p. 95.

46. Ibid., p. 97.

47. Superintendent's Annual Report 1997, p. 8. The following year two twill baskets were removed from exhibition.

48. NPS (2003, 1–3).

49. Ibid., p. 47.

50. Ibid., pp. 113–114.

51. Ibid., p. 13.

52. Dean (2000, 16).

53. Elson (1997, 38–54) identified the need for baseline information on the integrity of the deposits and the site formation process; a chronology, including how the settlement ties into the larger picture of Tonto Basin history; the function of the cliff dwellings; the economy of the Salado, including subsistence, raw-material procurement, artifact production, exchange, interaction; the migration and ethnicity of the population; and the social and political organization, including ideological beliefs, kinship practices, social stratification, community/communication boundaries, group integration, and regional alliance formation.

54. Clark (2001, preface and p. 23).

55. Teague (2000, 136).

epilogue

Where is Tonto National Monument now and what can it learn from its hundred-year history? For one thing, its relationship to national policies in reclamation, conservation, and preservation was formative and remains so. For despite its isolation and modest size, almost every significant event in the history of the monument reflected its connection to contemporary national policies, values, and controversies. Much has been gained by having the acreage set aside as a national monument. Much has been fought for and preserved. Much has also been lost because the monument was left with insufficient resources during critical periods of its history. The one constant at Tonto has been the dedication of the staff. Sometimes in isolation, often in difficult circumstances, persistently under-resourced, and not always equipped with the knowledge, skills, and connections to do what was needed, the monument staff consistently performed with unquestioned dedication. Perhaps most important, they persisted through the generations in seeking answers to, and sharing knowledge about, the overriding questions of who the Salado were, how they lived, and what happened to them.

appendix a

American Antiquities Act of 1906

16 USC 431-433

Be it enacted by the Senate and House of Representatives of the United States of America in Congress assembled, That any person who shall appropriate, excavate, injure, or destroy any historic or prehistoric ruin or monument, or any object of antiquity, situated on lands owned or controlled by the Government of the United States, without the permission of the Secretary of the Department of the Government having jurisdiction over the lands on which said antiquities are situated, shall, upon conviction, be fined in a sum of not more than five hundred dollars or be imprisoned for a period of not more than ninety days, or shall suffer both fine and imprisonment, in the discretion of the court.

Sec. 2. That the President of the United States is hereby authorized, in his discretion, to declare by public proclamation historic landmarks, historic and prehistoric structures, and other objects of historic or scientific interest that are situated upon the lands owned or controlled by the Government of the United States to be national monuments, and may reserve as a part thereof parcels of land, the limits of which in all cases shall be confined to the smallest area compatible with proper care and management of the objects to be protected: Provided, That when such objects are situated upon a tract covered by a bona fide unperfected claim or held in private ownership, the tract, or so much thereof as may be necessary for the proper care and management of the object, may be relinquished to the Government, and the Secretary of the Interior is hereby authorized to accept the relinquishment of such tracts in behalf of the Government of the United States.

Sec. 3. That permits for the examination of ruins, the excavation of archaeological sites, and the gathering of objects of antiquity upon the lands under their respective jurisdictions may be granted by the Secretaries of the Interior, Agriculture, and War to institutions which they may deem properly qualified to conduct such examination, excavation, or gathering, subject to such rules and regulation as they may prescribe: Provided, That the examinations, excavations, and gatherings are undertaken for the benefit of reputable museums, universities, colleges, or other recognized scientific or educational institutions, with a view to increasing the knowledge of such objects, and that the gatherings shall be made for permanent preservation in public museums.

Sec. 4. That the Secretaries of the Departments aforesaid shall make and publish from time to time uniform rules and regulations for the purpose of carrying out the provisions of this Act.

Approved, June 8, 1906

appendix b

Tonto National Monument Proclamations

Establishment: Proclamation (No. 787) of December 19, 1907
BY THE PRESIDENT OF THE UNITED STATES OF AMERICA
A PROCLAMATION
(No. 787–Dec. 19, 1907–35 Stat. 2168)

WHEREAS, two prehistoric ruins of ancient cliff dwellings situated upon public lands of the United States, and located in the region commonly known as the Tonto Drainage Basin, about two miles south of the Salt River Reservoir, Gila County, Arizona, are of great ethnologic, scientific and educational interest and it appears that the public interests would be promoted by reserving these relics of a vanished people as a National Monument with as much land as may be necessary for the proper protection thereof;

NOW, THEREFORE, I, Theodore Roosevelt, President of the United States of America, by virtue of the power in me vested by section two of the Act of Congress approved June 8, 1906, National Monument, subject to any valid interest or rights, the prehistoric cliff dwelling ruins and one section of land upon which same are located, situated in Gila County, Arizona, more particularly described as follows, to wit:

Section thirty-four, unsurveyed, in township four north, range twelve east of the Gila and Salt River Meridian, Arizona, as shown upon the diagram hereto attached and made a part of this Proclamation.

Warning is hereby expressly given to all unauthorized persons not to appropriate, excavate, injure or destroy any of the prehistoric ruins or remains thereof declared to be a National Monument, or to locate or settle upon any of the lands reserved and made a part of said Monument by this Proclamation.

IN WITNESS WHEREOF, I have hereunto set my hand and caused the seal of the United States to be affixed.

DONE at the City of Washington this 19th day of December in the year of our Lord one thousand nine hundred and seven, and of the Independence of the United States the one hundred and thirty-second.

Theodore Roosevelt

BY THE PRESIDENT OF THE UNITED STATES OF AMERICA
A PROCLAMATION
(No. 2230–Apr. 1, 1937–50 Stat. 1825)

WHEREAS, the area in the State of Arizona established as the Tonto National Monument by Proclamation of December 19, 1907, has situated thereon prehistoric ruins and ancient cliff dwellings which are of great ethnologic, scientific and educational interest to the public; and

WHEREAS, it appears that there are certain government-owned lands reserved by proclamation of January 13, 1908, as a part of the Tonto National Forest, adjacent to the boundaries of the said Monument, which are required for the proper care, management and protection of the said historic ruins and ancient cliff dwellings:

NOW, THEREFORE, I Franklin D. Roosevelt, President of the Untied States of America, under and by virtue of the authority vested in me by Section 1 of the act of June 4, 1897, ch. 2, 30 Stat. 11 (U.S.C., title 16, sec. 473), and section 2 of the act of June 8, 1906, ch. 3060, 34 Stat. 225 (U.S.C., title 16, sec. 431), do proclaim that, subject to all valid existing rights, the following-described lands in Arizona are hereby excluded from the Tonto National Forest and reserved from all forms of appropriation under the public-land laws and added to and made a part of the Tonto National Monument:

T.4N., R.12E., sec. 26, SW1/4; sec. 27, SE1/4; sec. 35, NW1/4 (unsurveyed), containing approximately 480 acres.

Warning is hereby expressly given to all unauthorized persons not to appropriate, injure, destroy, or remove any features of this monument and not to locate or settle upon any of the lands thereof.

The Director of the National Park Service, under the direction of the Secretary of the Interior, shall have the supervision, management, and control of this monument as provided in the act of Congress entitled "An Act to Establish a National Park Service, and for other purposes," approved August 25, 1916 (ch. 408, 39 Stat. 535, U.S.C., title 16, secs. 1 and 2), and acts supplementary thereto or amendatory thereof; Provided, that the administration of the monument shall be subject to the withdrawal for the Salt River Irrigation project, Arizona.

IN WITNESS WHEREOF, I have hereunto set my hand and caused the seal of the United States to be affixed.

Done at the City of Washington this first day of April in the year of our Lord nineteen hundred and thirty-seven and of the Independence of the United States the one hundred and sixty-first.

Franklin D. Roosevelt

appendix c

Tonto National Monument Custodians and Superintendents

(Established 12/19/1907; transferred from U.S. Department of Agriculture 8/10/1933)

Charles R. Steen, Cust. July 1934–July 1935
Woodrow Spires, Cust. August 1935–1936
Tom Onstott, Cust. 1937
Ira John Peavy, Cust. October 1939–July 1942
Elmer C. Gipe, Cust. October 1942–August 1947
Charles C. Sharp, Supt. August 1947–February 1956
Theodore R. Thompson, Supt. June 1956–May 1957
Wiffler R. Oakes, Supt. June 1957–December 1965
John M. Broadbent, Supt. February 1966–January 1969
Harold F. Schaafsma, Supt.[1] March 1969–January 1971
Zeb V. McKinney, Supt. January 1971–December 1972
John O. Cook, Acting Supt. December 1972–March 1973
Glen E. Henderson, Supt. April 1973–August 1974
James B. Valder, Supt. September 1974–March 1980
James W. Troutwine, Ranger in Charge April 1980–July 1983
James W. Troutwine, Supt. July 1983–September 1986
Carol Kruse, Supt. March 1987–December 1991
Lee Baiza, Supt. March 1992–May 2003
Bradley S. Traver, Supt. September 2003–present

[1] Administration supervised by Gen. Supt., Southern Arizona Group from 1/10/1971.

appendix d

Tonto National Monument Visitors Per Year

Year	Visitors	Year	Visitors	Year	Visitors
1934	7,005	1959	38,000	1984	72,000
1935	5,350	1960	45,000	1985	74,000
1936	5,908	1961	53,000	1986	82,784
1937	5,368	1962	55,000	1987	80,906
1938	4,985	1963	67,000	1988	79, 387
1939	4,432	1964	70,000	1989	61,106
1940	5,250	1965	53,000	1990	45,636
1941	10,200	1966	42,000	1991	62,639
1942	4,800	1967	38,000	1992	60,375
1943	2,650	1968	68,000	1993	70,161
1944	3,450	1969	56,000	1994	69,083
1945	5,000	1970	53,000	1995	70,936
1946	13,000	1971	54,000	1996	71,970
1947	12,800	1972	52,000	1997	79,402
1948	17,000	1973	62,000	1998	78,622
1949	17,800	1974	48,000	1999	72,766
1950	18,000	1975	55,000	2000	76,059
1951	20,000	1976	71,000	2001	80,006
1952	27,000	1977	68,000	2002	57,328
1953	37,000	1978	71,000	2003	59,216
1954	30,000	1979	68,000	2004	63,217
1955	30,000	1980	60,000	2005	75,540
1956	37,000	1981	74,000	2006	63,733
1957	46,000	1982	78,000		
1958	42,000	1983	78,500		

Source: U.S. National Park Service, Public use tabulations of visitors to areas administered by the National Park Service 1904–1940. U.S. Dept. of the Interior, Washington, D.C., Nov. 1956

Month/Source	Total Visitors	Visitors to Lower Ruin	Visitors to Upper Ruin
September 1934	305	N/A	N/A
October 1934	259	165	5
November 1934	421	248	13
December 1934	266	169	16
January 1935	425	206	0
February 1935	599	383	25
March 1935	749	515	11
April 1935	812	511	58
May 1935	398	234	6
June 1935	447	282	19
July 1935	324	220	1
August 1935	360	211	5
September 1935	338	226	22
October 1935	332	227	4
November 1935	396	243	N/A
December 1935	362	N/A	N/A

Source: From a June 1, 1956 letter from Albert H. Schroeder, archeologists to acting superintendent of Tonto regarding an area history that was being compiled at the time. The figures for September 1934–July 1935 were reported by custodian Charles Steen; those for August 1935–December 1935 were reported by custodian Woodrow Spires.

references

Allaback, S. 2000. *Mission 66 Visitor Centers: The History of a Building Type.* Washington, D.C.: National Park Service.

Allin, C. W. 1982. *The Politics of Wilderness Preservation.* Westport, Conn.: Greenwood Press.

Antle, J. J. 1992. "Grazing on Arizona's National Forests, 1891–1960: An Environmental History." Master's thesis, Arizona State University, Tempe.

Ashton, H. D. 1929. "The Roosevelt Road: Motoring through the Salt River Valley. America's Finest Hundred Miles of Highway." *Sunset* 29: 407–14.

Bandelier, A. F. 1892. *Final Report of Investigations among the Indians of the Southwestern United States, Carried on Mainly in the Years from 1880–1885.* Part II. Papers of the Archaeological Institute of America, American Series 4. Cambridge, Mass.: J. Wilson and Son.

Barbour, B. 1999. "Tonto National Monument Grazing History." Final draft. Tonto National Monument.

Barnes, W. C. 1941. *Apaches & Longhorn: The Reminiscences of Will C. Barnes.* Los Angeles, Calif.: Ward Ritchie Press.

Basso, K. H., ed. 1971. *Western Apache Raiding and Warfare: From the Notes of Grenville Goodwin.* Tucson: University of Arizona Press.

———. 1983. "Western Apache." In *Handbook of North American Indians,* vol. 10.: *Southwest,* ed. A. Ortiz, 462–88. Washington, D.C.: Smithsonian Institution.

———. 1996. *Wisdom Sits in Places: Landscape and Language among the Western Apache.* Albuquerque: University of New Mexico Press.

Bohrer, V. L. 1962. "Nature and Interpretation of Ethnobotanical Materials from Tonto National Monument, 1957." In *Archeological Studies at Tonto National Monument*, ed. L. R. Caywood, 79–114. Globe, Ariz.: Southwest Archeological Center.

Bostwick, T. W. 2003. "Revisiting the Dean: Byron Cumming and Southwestern Archaeology, 1893–1954." Ph.D. diss., History Department, Tempe, Arizona State University.

Brown, A. 1880. "The Diary of Angeline Brown." On file at Sharlot Hall Museum, Flagstaff.

Burgess, R. 1965. "A Checklist of the Vascular Flora of Tonto National Monument, Arizona." *Journal of the Arizona Academy of Science* 3(4: 213–223.

Campbell, L. 1926. "The Apache Trail." *Sunset* 56: 36–37.

Carriker, R. 1998. "Grazing and Environmental Change within Tonto National Monument: A Review of Source Material." Report for the National Park Service, Southwest Region, Phoenix.

Caywood, L. R. 1946. *Tonto Cliff Dwellings: A Brief Resume of the History, Ecology, Geology, and Archeology of Tonto National Monument in Southern Arizona.* Guidebook. Globe Ariz.: Tonto National Monument.

_____., ed. 1962. *Archeological Studies at Tonto National Monument, Arizona.* Southwestern Monuments Association Technical Series. Globe, Ariz.: Southwestern Monuments Association.

Ciolek-Torello, R. and J. R. Welch., eds. 1994. *The Roosevelt Rural Sites Study.* Vol. 3, *Changing Land Use in the Tonto Basin.* Tucson, Ariz.: Statistical Research.

Clark, J. J. 2001. *Tracking Prehistoric Migrations: Pueblo Settlers among the Tonto Basin Hohokam.* Tucson: University of Arizona Press.

Clum, J. P. 1931. *The Truth about Apaches: Told in Annual Reports by John P. Clum, United States Indian Agent for the Apache Indians at San Carlos, Arizona; Submitted to the Commissioner of Indian Affairs for 1874–1875–1876–1877.* Los Angeles, Calif.: Adcraft.

Coder, C., V. Randall, E. Smith-Rocha, and R. Hines. 1995. "CHI CH'IL (Acorns): Dissolution of Traditional Dilzhe'e Gathering Practice(s) due to Federal Control of the Landscape." *USDA Forest Service Proceedings* document RMRS-P-3, 277–81. Available online: www.fs.fed.us/rm/pubs/rmrs_p036/rmrs_p036_277_281.pdf.

Cohoon, A. E. 1904. "Proposed Addition to the Black Mesa Forest Reserve Arizona (A Part of the Verde Withdrawal)." Tonto National Forest. NA/RG 115, General File 1902–1919.

Cohoon, A. E., and S. J. Holsinger. 1905. "The Proposed Tonto Forest Reserve Arizona: Examination by A. E. Cohoon and S. J. Holsinger." Summary of Report and Recommendations. Washington, D.C.: USDA, Bureau of Forestry. NA/RG 115, General File 1902–1919.

Cosner, A. J. 1956. "Area History, Tonto National Monument, Roosevelt, Arizona." Tonto National Monument.

Crown, P. L. 1994. *Ceramics and Ideology: Salado Polychrome Pottery*. Albuquerque: University of New Mexico Press.

————. 1995. The Production of the Salado Polychromes in the American Southwest. In *Ceramic Production in the American Southwest*, ed. B. J. Mills and P. L. Crown, 142–66. Tucson: University of Arizona Press.

Croxen, F. W. 1926. "History of Grazing on Tonto." Paper presented at the Tonto Grazing Conference, Phoenix, Ariz.

Davis, A. P. 1903. "Water Storage on the Salt River, Arizona." Washington, D.C.: GPO.

Dean, J. S., ed. 2000. *Salado*. Albuquerque: University of New Mexico Press.

DeVoto, B. 1953. "Let's Close the National Parks." *Harper's* 207 (October): 49–52.

Dodd, D. W. 2004. Lands above the Ordinary: The U.S. Forest Service and the National Recreation Area Concept." Paper presented to the Western History Association. Las Vegas, Nev.

Downum, C. E. 1993. "Southwestern Archaeology: Past, Present, and Future." *Expedition. The University Museum Magazine of Archaeology and Anthropology* [Philadelphia, University of Pennsylvania] 35: 4–13.

Elliott, M. 1995. *Great Excavations: Tales of Early Southwestern Archaeology, 1888–1939*. Santa Fe, N.M.: School of American Research Press.

Elson, M. D. 1997. *A Research Design for the Upper and Lower Ruins, Tonto National Monument*. Publications in Anthropology No. 71. Tucson: Western Archeological Conservation Center, National Park Service.

Elson, M. D., M. T. Stark, and D. A. Gregory. 1995. "The Roosevelt Community Development Study, New Perspectives on Tonto Basin Prehistory." Center for Desert Archaeology Anthropological Papers, Tucson.

Eubank, V. 1912. "Log of an Auto Prairie Schooner: Motor Pioneers on the 'Trail to Sunset.'" *Sunset* 28: 188–96.

Everhart, W. C. 1983. *The National Park Service.* Boulder, Colo.: Westview Press.

Ferg, A., ed. 1987. *Western Apache Material Culture: The Goodwin and Guenther Collections.* Tucson: University of Arizona Press.

Fewkes, J. W. 1898. *Archeological Expedition to Arizona in 1895.* Glorieta, N.M.: Rio Grande Press.

Fixico, D. L. 2003. *The American Indian Mind in a Linear World: American Indian Studies and Traditional Knowledge.* New York: Routledge.

————., ed. 1997. *Rethinking American Indian History.* Albuquerque: University of New Mexico Press.

Fowler, D. D. 2000. *A Laboratory for Anthropology: Science and Romanticism in the American Southwest, 1946–1930.* Albuquerque: University of New Mexico Press.

Fox, G. L. 2000. "Archeological Investigation of Rooms 15 and 16 at the Upper Cliff Dwelling (AZ U:8:48 [ASM], Tonto National Monument." Publications in Anthropology 73. Tucson: Western Archaeological and Conservation Center, National Park Service.

Fox, G. L. 2000. Archeological Investigation of Rooms 15 and 16 at the Upper Cliff Dwelling (AZ U:8:48 [ASM], Tonto National Monument." Tucson, Ariz. Western Archaeological and Conservation Center, National Park Service.

Frome, M. 1992. *Regreening the National Parks.* Tucson: University of Arizona Press.

Frothingham, R. 1932. *Trails through the Golden West.* New York: McBride.

Fuller, S. L., A. E. Rogge, and L. M. Gregonis 1976. *Orme Alternatives: The Archaeological Resources of Roosevelt Lake and Horseshoe Reservoir,* vol. 1. Archaeological Series No. 98. Tucson: Arizona State Museum.

Gila Centennials, Inc. 1976. *Honor the Past . . . Mold the Future.* Globe, Ariz.: Gila Centennials, Inc.

Gillio, D. 2005. "Flagging the Trail: One Hundred Years of Managing Cultural Resources." Report No. 17. Albuquerque: U.S. Forest Service, Southwestern Region.

Goodwin, G. 1969. *The Social Organization of the Western Apache.* Tucson: University of Arizona Press.

Guthrie, E. A. 1994. "Archeology and Stabilization: Tonto National Monument Upper and Lower Ruins." Tucson, Ariz.: Western Archeological and Conservation Center, National Park Service.

Hall, S. M. 1905. "The Great Tonto Storage Reservoir." *Out West. A Magazine of the Old Pacific and the New* 25: 385–414.

Hamilton, P. 1884. *The Resources of Arizona.* San Francisco, Calif.: A. L. Bancroft & Co.

Hargrave, L. L. 1959–63. "Revised Checklist of Birds, Tonto National Monument." Albuquerque: National Park Service, Southwest Region.

_____. 1964. "Some Comments on Archeological Feather Identification, Tonto National Monument." Albuquerque: National Park Service, Southwest Region.

Hartzog, G. B. Jr. 1988. *Battling for the National Parks.* Mt. Kisco, N.Y.: Moyer Bell.

Hays, S. P. 1959. *Conservation and the Gospel of Efficiency: The Progressive Conservation Movement, 1890–1920.* Cambridge, Mass.: Harvard University Press.

Hewett, E. L. 1906a. "Preservation of American Antiquities: Progress During the Last Year, Needed Legislation." *American Anthropologist* 8(1): 109–14.

_____. 1906b. "Recent Progress in American Anthropology: A Review of the Activities of Institutions and Individuals from 1902 to 1906." *American Anthropologist* 8(3): 441–554.

_____. 1924. "Report on Illegal Excavations in Southwestern Ruins." *American Anthropologist* 26(3): 428–32.

_____. 1930. *Ancient Life in the American Southwest.* Indianapolis: Bobbs-Merrill.

Hiett, K. L., M. R. Kunzman, and W. L. Halborson 1996. "A Checklist of Birds of Tonto National Monument, Gila County, Arizona." Cooperative Park Studies Unit, University of Arizona, Tucson.

_____. 1999. "Inventory and Assessment of Avifauna and a Monitoring Protocol Proposal for Tonto National Monument, Arizona." Technical Report No. 62. Cooperative National Park Resources Studies Unit, University of Arizona, Tucson.

Hirt, P. W. 1994. *A Conspiracy of Optimism: Management of the National Forests since World War II.* Lincoln: University of Nebraska Press.

Holsinger, S. J. 1902. "The Boundary Line between the Desert and the Forest." *Forestry and Irrigation* 8: 21–27.

_____. 1904. "Report on the Proposed Verde River Forest Reserve, Arizona, Not Comprising Portions of the Prescott, Tonto and Crook National Forests." Washington, D.C.: Department of Agriculture, Bureau of Forestry.

Houk, R. 1992. *Salado*. Tucson, Ariz.: Southwest Parks and Monuments Association.

Ice, R. J. (n.d.). "Archeological Research Management Plan." National Park Service, Tonto National Monument.

Ice, R. J. 1972. "A Report on Archeological Sites near Roosevelt, Arizona." National Park Service, Tonto National Monument.

Ise, J. 1961. *Our National Park Policy; A Critical History*. Baltimore, Maryland, John Hopkins Press.

Iverson, P. 1994. *When Indians Became Cowboys: Native Peoples and Cattle Ranching in the American West*. Norman: University of Oklahoma Press.

Jaehn, T. 1998. "The Southern Pacific Launches a New Vehicle to Develop Its Market. In *Sunset Magazine: A Century of Western Living, 1898–1998*, 77–82. Stanford, Calif.: Stanford University Libraries. Available online: http://sunset-magazine.stanford.edu/html/body_eras_2.html.

John, E. A. H., ed. 1989. *Views from the Apache Frontier: Report on the Northern Provinces of New Spain by Jose Cortes, Lieutenant in the Royal Corps of Engineers, 1799*. Norman: University of Oklahoma Press.

Jones, H. L. 1963. "Saguaro Study, Tonto National Monument." Tonto National Monument.

Kibbey, J. H. 1907. "Report of the Governor of the Territory of Arizona." Phoenix: General Land Office.

Kidder, A. V. 1924. *An Introduction to the Study of Southwestern Archaeology*. New Haven: Yale University Press.

Koppes, S. 1990. "Prehistoric Melting Pot." *Arizona State University Research* 5: 16–21.

Kroeber, C. B. 1964. "The Route of James O. Pattie on the Colorado in 1826, A Reappraisal by A. L. Kroeber." *Arizona and the West* 6(2): 119–36.

Lange, C. H. and C. L. Riley, eds. 1970. *The Southwestern Journals of Adolph F. Bandelier 1883–1884*. Albuquerque: University of New Mexico Press.

Lange, R. C. and S. Germick. 1992. *Proceedings of the Second Salado Conference*. Second Salado Conference. Occasional Papers of the Arizona Archaeological Society. Phoenix: Arizona Archaeological Society.

Lauver, M. E. 1938. "History of the Use and Management of the Forested Lands of Arizona, 1862–1936." Master's thesis, Department of History, University of Arizona, Tucson.

LeCount, A., ed. 2003. *The History of Tonto: A Bicentennial Project by the Punkin Center Homemakers*. Tonto Basin, Ariz.: Kiwanis Club of Tonto Basin.

Lee, R. F. 1970. *The Antiquities Act of 1906*. Washington, D.C.: Department of the Interior, National Park Service.

Limerick, P. N. and C. Puska. 2003. "Making the Most of Science in the American West: An Experiment." Report from the Center #5. Boulder: Center of the American West, University of Colorado. Available online: www.centerwest.org/publications/pdf/science.pdf

Lindauer, O., ed. 1995. *Where the Rivers Converge. Roosevelt Platform Mound Study*. Roosevelt Monograph Series. Tempe: Arizona State University.

Lister, R. H. 1994. *Those Who Came Before, Southwestern Archeology in the National Park System*. Tucson, Ariz.: Southwest Parks and Monuments Association.

Marcus, L. 1983. "The Spatial and Temporal Evolution of Tonto National Forest, Arizona." Master's thesis, Department of Geography. Tempe: Arizona State University.

Martin, P. S. and F. Plog. 1973. *The Archaeology of Arizona: A Study of the Southwest Region*. Garden City, N.Y.: Natural History Press for the American Museum of Natural History.

McChristian, D. 1999. Notes for Tonto Historic Resource Study, Tonto National Monument, March 23.

McClintock, J. H. 1916. *Arizona, Prehistoric—Aboriginal—Pioneer—Modern: The Nation's Youngest Commonwealth within a Land of Ancient Culture*. Chicago: S. J. Clarke.

Mead, E. 1929. *Dams and Control Works. A Description of Representative Storage and Diversion Dams and High-Pressure Reservoir Outlet Works Constructed by the Bureau of Reclamation*. Washington, D.C.: GPO.

Miles, D. C. and P. R. Machula. 1997. *History of the San Carlos Apache*. San Carlos, Ariz.: San Carlos Apache Historic and Cultural Preservation Office.

Miller, C. and H. Rothman, eds. 1997. *Out of the Woods. Essays in Environmental History*. Pittsburgh, Pa.: University of Pittsburgh Press.

Mills, B. J. and P. L. Crown, eds. 1995. *Ceramic Production in the American Southwest*. Tucson: University of Arizona Press.

Monroe, J. S. 1986. "Architecture in the National Parks: Cecil Doty and Mission 66." Master's thesis, College of Architecture, University of Washington, Seattle.

Myrick, D. F. 1980. *Railroads of Arizona*. Volume 2, *Phoenix and the Central Roads*. San Diego, Calif.: Howell North Books.

Nash, R. 1982. *Wilderness and the American Mind*. New Haven, Conn.: Yale University Press.

Northern Gila County Historical Society. 1984. *Rim Country History*. Payson, Ariz.: Rim Country Printery.

NPS. 2003. Final Environmental Impact Statement, General Management Plan, Tonto National Monument, Arizona, National Park Service, U.S. Department of the Interior: 171.

_____. 1940. "Southwestern National Monuments, A Bibliography.: Washington, D.C.: Department of the Interior, National Park Service.

_____. 1954. "Conducted Trips. Training Bulletin for Field Employees of the National Park Service." Washington, D.C.: Department of the Interior, National Park Service.

_____. 1962. *Handbook for Ruins Stabilization*. Part 2, *Field Methods*. Department of the Interior, National Park Service. Washington, D.C.: GPO.

_____. 1991. Tonto National Monument Accessibility Survey Report, National Park Service, Tonto National Monument.

_____. 1995. "Vanishing Treasures: A Legacy in Ruins. Ruins Preservation in the American Southwest. Strategic Plan." July. Washington, D.C.: Department of the Interior, National Park Service.

_____. 1998. "Vanishing Treasures: A Legacy in Ruins. Ruins Preservation in the American Southwest. Year-End Report Fiscal Year 1998." December. Washington, D.C.: Department of the Interior, National Park Service.

_____. 1999. "The Natural Resource Challenge: The NPS's Action Plan for Preserving Natural Resources." Washington, D.C.: Department of the Interior, National Park Service.

_____. 2000. "Vanishing Treasures: Year-End Report, Fiscal Year 1999." Washington, D.C.: Department of the Interior, National Park Service.

_____. 2001. "Vanishing Treasures: Year-End Report Fiscal Year 2000 and Proposed Activities in FY 2001." Washington, D.C.: Department of the Interior, National Park Service.

_____. 2002. Vanishing Treasures: Year-End Report Fiscal Year 2001 and Proposed Activities for FY 2002." Washington, D.C.: Department of the Interior, National Park Service.

Olson, G. C. 1986. "A History of Natural Resource Management within the National Park Service." PhD diss., Slippery Rock, Ark, Slippery Rock University.

Orsi, R. J. 2005. *Sunset Limited: The Southern Pacific Railroad and the Development of the American West 1850–1930.* Berkeley: University of California Press.

Ortiz, A., ed. 1983. *Handbook of North American Indians.* Vol. 10: *Southwest.* Washington, D.C.: Smithsonian Institution.

Phillips, B. 1992. "Status of Non-native Plant Species, Tonto National Monument, Arizona." University of Arizona Cooperative National Park Resources Studies Unit, Tucson, Ariz.

————. 1997. *History of Fire and Fire Impacts at Tonto National Monument, Arizona.* Technical Report. Tucson: U.S. Geological Survey, Cooperative Park Studies Unit, School of Renewable Natural Resources.

Pinchot, G. 1907. *The Use of the National Forests.* Guidebook. Washington, D.C.: USDA, Bureau of Forestry.

Potter, A. F. 1902. "Grazing and Water Storage in the Black Mesa Forest Reserve." *Forestry and Irrigation* 8: 236–41.

Protas, J. 2002. *A Past Preserved in Stone: A History of Montezuma Castle National Monument.* Tucson, Ariz.: Western National Parks Association.

Pyne, S. J. 1982. *Fire in America: A Cultural History of Wildland and Rural Fire.* Princeton: Princeton University Press.

Raup, R. B. Jr. 1959. "Some Geologic Features of the Tonto National Monument, Gila County, Arizona." Roosevelt, Ariz.: Tonto National Monument.

Redman, C. L. 1993. *People of the Tonto Rim.* Washington, D.C.: Smithsonian Institution Press.

Reid, J. and S. Whittlesey. 1997. *The Archaeology of Ancient Arizona.* Tucson: University of Arizona Press.

Reidy, W. 1905. "How Living Waters Have Been Brought unto the Thirsty Land." *Arizona Republican* [Phoenix].

Rice, G. E., ed. 1998. *A Synthesis of Tonto Basin Prehistory: The Roosevelt Archaeology Studies, 1989–1998.* Anthropological Field Studies, Roosevelt Monograph Series. Tempe, Ariz.: Office of Cultural Resource Management, Department of Anthropology, Arizona State University.

Rice, G. E., and C. Redman. 1993. "Platform Mounds of the Arizona Desert: An Experiment in Organizational Complexity." *Expedition* [University of Pennsylvania] 35: 53–63.

Richert, R. 1957. "Stabilization Report, Upper and Lower Ruins, Tonto National Monument, 1957." Globe, Ariz. Southwestern National Monuments.

Richert, R. V. S. and G. Vivian. 1975. *Ruins Stabilization in the Southwestern United States*. Publications in Archeology 10. Washington, D.C.: Department of the Interior, National Park Service.

Rogge, A. E., D. L. McWatters, M. Keane, and R. P. Emanuel 1995. *Raising Arizona's Dams: Daily Life, Danger, and Discrimination in the Dam Construction Camps of Central Arizona 1890s–1940s*. Tucson: University of Arizona Press.

Rogge, G. 1983. "Little Archeology, Big Archeology: The Changing Context of Archaeological Research." PhD diss., Department of Archeology, University of Arizona, Tucson.

Rothman, H. K. 1985. "Protected by a Gold Fence with Diamond Tips: A Cultural History of the American National Monuments." PhD diss., Department of History, University of Texas at Austin. 2 vols.

_____. 1986a. "Forged by One Man's Will: Frank Pinkley and the Administration of the Southwestern National Monuments, 1923–1932." *The Public Historian* 8(2): 83–100.

_____. 1986b. "Second-Class Sites: National Monuments and the Growth of the National Park System." *Environmental Review* 10(1): 44–56.

_____. 1989a. *America's National Monuments: The Politics of Preservation*. Lawrence: University Press of Kansas.

_____. 1989b. "A Regular Ding-Dong Fight: Agency Culture and Evolution in the NPS-USFS Dispute, 1916–1937." *Western Historical Quarterly* 20(2): 141–61.

Rowley, W. M. 1985. *U.S. Forest Service Grazing and Rangelands*. College Station: Texas A&M University Press.

Runte, A. 1990. *Trains of Discovery: Western Railroads and the National Parks*. Niwot, Colo.: Roberts Rinehard Publishers.

_____. 1991. *Public Lands, Public Heritage: The National Forest Idea*. Niwot, Colo.: Roberts Rinehard Publishers.

_____. 1997. *National Parks: The American Experience*. 3rd ed. Lincoln: University of Nebraska Press.

Rusho, W. L. 1983. *Everett Ruess: A Vagabond for Beauty*. Salt Lake City, Utah: Peregrine Smith Books.

Saunders, C. F. 1918. "Lodging with Montezuma: A One-Night's Camp in the Dust of the Prehistoric." *Sunset* 40: 41–43.

Schreier, J. 1992. *Camp Reno: Outpost in Apacheria, 1867–1870.* Tucson: Arizona Historical Society.

Sellars, R. W. 1997. *Preserving Nature in the National Parks: A History.* New Haven, Conn.: Yale University Press.

Shaffer, M. S. 2001. *See America First: Tourism and National Identity, 1880–1940.* Washington, D.C.: Smithsonian Institution Press.

Sheridan, T. E. 1995. *Arizona: A History.* Tucson: University of Arizona Press.

Simmons, J. W. 1930. "Catalogue of Manuscripts. Bureau of American Ethnography." NA, Laguna Niguel.

Smith, K. L. 1982. "The Magnificent Experiment: Building the Salt River Reclamation Project, 1890–1917." PhD diss., Department of History, University of California at Santa Barbara.

————. 1986. *Th e Magnificent Experiment: Building the Salt River Reclamation Project 1890–1917.* Tucson: University of Arizona Press.

Snead, J. E. 2001. *Ruins and Rivals: The Making of Southwest Archaeology.* Tucson: University of Arizona Press.

Sowards, A. M. 1997. Range Rivalries: An Environmental and Cultural History of Arizona's Tonto National Forest Region. Master's thesis, Department of History, Arizona State University, Tempe.

————. 2000. "Administrative Trials, Environmental Consequences, and the Use of History in Arizona's Tonto National Forest, 1926–1996." *Western Historical Quarterly* 31 (Summer): 189–214.

Spence, M. D. 1999. *Dispossessing the Wilderness: Indian Removal and the Making of the National Parks.* New York: Oxford University Press.

Starr, K. 1998. "Sunset and the Phenomenon of the Far West." In *Sunset Magazine: A Century of Western Living, 1989–1998,* 31–77. Stanford, Calif.: Stanford University Libraries.

Steele, R. 1918. "On the Warpath for Fun: Joy-Riding along the Historic Trail of the Apaches Where Today Meets Yesterday." *Sunset.* 40: 49–52, 68.

Steen, C. R. 1962. "Excavations at the Upper Ruin, Tonto National Monument, 1940." In *Archeological Studies at Tonto National Monument, Arizona,* ed. L. R. Caywood, 1–30. Globe, Ariz.: Southwest Archeological Center.

Steen, H. K. 1976. *The U.S. Forest Service: A History*. Seattle: University of Washington Press.

_____. ed. 1992. *The Origins of the National Forests*. Durham, N.C.: Forest History Society.

Stephenson, A. 1992."Artifacts as Art." *Arizona Highways* 68: 20–26.

Sunset Magazine: A Century of Western Living, 1898–1998: Historical Portraits and a Chronological Bibliography of Selected Topics. 1998. Stanford, Calif.: Stanford University Libraries.

Swann, D. E. 1998. *Reptiles, Amphibians, and Mammals Handbook of Tonto National Monument*. Roosevelt, Ariz.: Tonto National Monument.

Swann, D. E., R. C. Murray, C. R. Schwalbe, and W. W. Shaw 1997."Long-term Monitoring of the Amphibians, Reptiles, and Mammals of Tonto National Monument." Southern Arizona Group, Phoenix, Arizona.

Swann, D. E., C. R. Schwalbe, R. C. Murray, and W. W. Shaw. 1996."An Inventory of the Terrestrial Vertebrates at Tonto National Monument, Arizona." University of Arizona, Cooperative Park Studies Unit, Tucson.

Swarth, H. S. 1920. *Birds of the Papago Saguaro National Monument and the Neighboring Regions, Arizona*. Washington, D.C.: GPO.

Tagg, M. D. 1985. *Tonto National Monument: An Archeological Survey*. Publications in Anthropology No. 31. Tucson: Western Archeological and Conservation Center, National Park Service.

Teague, Lynne S., "Revealing Clothes: Textiles of the Upper Ruin, Tonto National Monument," in *Beyond Cloth and Cordage: Archeological Textile Research in the Americas*, ed. Penelope Drooker and Laurie Webster, Salt Lake City: University of Utah Press, 2000.

Thompson, R. H., ed. 2000."Special Issue on the Antiquities Act of 1906." *Journal of the Southwest* 42(2): 197–269.

TNM [Tonto National Monument]. 1989. "Statement for Management, Tonto National Monument, Arizona." Washington, D.C.: Department of the Interior, National Park Service.

_____. 1992."External Threats to National Parks." Washington, D.C.: U.S. General Accounting Office.

_____. 1996. "Statement for Management, Tonto National Monument." Revised September 1996. Washington, D.C.: U.S. General Accounting Office.

Toll, R. W. 1932. 5. Letter to the director of the National Park Service, March 23, 1932. National Park Service: Western Archeological Conservation Center.

Twight, B. W. 1983. *Organizational Values and Political Power: The Forest Service Versus the Olympic National Park*. University Park: Pennsylvania State University Press.

U.S. Congress. 1882. *Congressional Record*, 47th Cong., 1st sess. 1882, p. 3777.

U.S. Forest Service, Southwest Region. "Timeless Heritage: A History of the Forest Service in the Southwest." Available online: www.fs.fed.us/r3/about/history/timeless/th_index.html.

Vivian, G., and R. Richert. 1952. *Stabilization Report, Lower Ruin, 1952*. Globe, Ariz.: Southwestern National Monuments.

Welles, P. 1955. "Preliminary Report on the Mammals of Tonto National Monument." Tonto National Monument.

Wilkinson, C. F., and H. M. Anderson. 1987. *Land and Resource Planning in the National Forests*. Washington, D.C.: Island Press.

Winter, K. E. 1999. More Than 100 Years of Digging: A History of the Arizona State Museum. Master's thesis, Department of History, Arizona State University, Tempe.

Wirth, C. L. 1980. *Parks, Politics, and the People*. Norman: University of Oklahoma Press.

Woehlke, W. 1916. Through Apache Land: Riding on Rubber tires over Geronimo's Trail. *Sunset* 37: 13–16, 18, 82.

Wood, J. S., M. E. McAllister, and M. A. Sullivan 1990. *11,000 Years on Tonto National Forest*. Albuquerque: Southwest Natural and Cultural Heritage Association.

Wright, N. K. 1912. *Sharlot Herself: Selected Writings of Sharlot Hall*. Prescott, Ariz.: Sharlot Hall Museum Press.

Zedeño, M. N. and R. W. Stoffle. 1995. *Hohokam, Salado, and Sinagua Consultation Meeting, Tucson, July 18–19, 1995: Meeting Summary, Final Report*. Tucson: Bureau of Applied Research in Anthropology, University of Arizona.

Zenzen, J. M. 1997. "Promoting the National Parks: Images of the West in the American Imagination, 1864–1972." PhD diss., Department of American Studies, University of Maryland, College Park.

index

about the author

Nancy Dallett is a public historian and academic associate in the Public History Program of the History Department at Arizona State University in Tempe. In her consulting business, Projects in the Public Interest, she collaborates on public history and public art master plans, cultural inventories, radio documentaries, exhibits, trail signage, oral history projects, and historic preservation, to engage the imagination of audiences and to facilitate understanding of the twentieth-century American West. For the National Park Service, she conducted the Ellis Island Oral History Project, contributed to the Governor's Island Historic Resource Study, and is currently writing administrative histories and resource studies for other national monuments, including Tuzigoot, Walnut Canyon, Sunset Crater Volcano, and Wupatki.